At a time of profound unrest o
can educational scene, of which
ley crisis" is disturbingly
Beyond Alienation wi

understand alienation in history and contemporary life. We must explore the means of liberating man's inherent goodness and creative powers by furthering his self-understanding and his cosmic vision. If alienation is the negative pole of human experience, the positive is found in a moral view of man and his world. Here Becker brings into play a vast knowledge of modern science to forge a world-view within which the full range of human potentialities may find expression.

In his final section, the author applies this broad philosophical perspective to the concrete problems of the core curriculum. He demonstrates the possibility that what hitherto appeared merely as isolated courses may be oriented within the study of human alienation and the search, beyond alienation, for a new moral view of the universe.

Beyond Alienation is a utopian book in the best sense of the word. It invites reflective reading, discussion and healthy controversy by raising the vital issues of education to a level at which alone controversy can prove fruitful.

ERNEST BECKER has been Lecturer in Sociology and, currently, in Anthropology at the University of California, Berkeley. Dr. Becker received his Ph.D. in Social Anthropology at Syracuse University (1960). In addition to many articles in the fields of sociology, psychology and psychiatry, he is the author of *Zen: A Rational Critique; The Birth and Death of Meaning: A Perspective in Psychiatry and Anthropology;* and *The Revolution in Psychiatry: The New Understanding of Man.* Of his recent books one critic wrote: "These are exciting contributions. They deserve to be widely read, carefully studied and intelligently debated."

Beyond Alienation

Beyond Alienation

A Philosophy of Education for the Crisis of Democracy

by ERNEST BECKER

George Braziller, New York

For information address the publisher:
George Braziller, Inc.
One Park Avenue, New York, N.Y. 10016

First Printing, April, 1967
Second Printing, May, 1967
Third Printing, April, 1969

Library of Congress Catalog Card Number: 67–12951
Designed by Jennie R. Bush
Printed in the United States

Acknowledgments

My friend Harvey Bates read the work in manuscript, and I want to thank him for his extensive critical comments. My wife Marie, as usual, put in a lion's share of work on the manuscript in its preparatory stages, a labor which I have come to rely on and take for granted, and thus usually fail to mention. Let me express my gratitude for it now, and for what is even more important: the continuing provision of an atmosphere and incentive without which this book would not have been written.

For permission to quote in this book, I wish to thank the respective publishers and authors of the following works:

Bernard Iddings Bell, *Crisis in Education,* McGraw-Hill, 1949; John Dewey, *The Problems of Men,* Philosophical Library, 1946; John Dewey, *The Way Out of Educational Confusion,* Harvard University Press, 1931; José Ortega y Gasset, *Mission of the University,* trans. by Howard Lee Nostrand, Princeton University Press, 1944; Peyton Jacob, "A Reorientation of the Arts College: A Way of Quickening the Intellectual Life of Our Students," *Journal of Higher Education IV:* 407–412, 1933; M. L. Jacks, *Total Education: A Plea for Synthesis,* Routledge & Keagan Paul, Ltd., 1946; Horace Kallen, *The Education of Free Men,* Farrar, Straus & Giroux, Inc., 1949; Everett Dean Martin, *The Meaning of a Liberal Education,* copyright 1926, by W. W. Norton & Company, Inc., copyright renewed, 1954, by Mrs. Daphne Mason; Gorham Munson, *The Dilemma of the Liberated,* Putnam's & Coward-McCann, 1930; Harold Rosenberg, "It Can Happen to Anyone," © 1964 by *The New York Times Company*. Reprinted by permission; Max Scheler, *On the Eternal in Man,* SCM Press, Ltd., 1921, Harper & Row, 1960; Mark Van Doren, *Liberal Education,* © 1943 by Mark Van Doren, reprinted by permission of Nannine Joseph, agent for Mark Van Doren; H. G. Wells, *World Brain,* by permission of the Executors of H. G. Wells; Hans Zinsser, "What is Liberal Education?" *School and Society 45,* 1937.

To those many eager college students
who have wondered with great bafflement
how so much effort and activity
could produce so little result

A Note on References

References to bibliography are put in a form which is becoming widely adopted, and which spares the reader distracting footnoting: works are referred to in parenthesis by year and page, following the author's name; and they are listed alphabetically by author, and chronologically, at the end of this book. Where the same author has written several works in one year, they are referred to and listed as "a," "b," "c," etc.

A tender-hearted man, weakly with systematic undernourishment, worn with persistent seeking of stable truth, he knew no pleasures in life other than books; and when it seemed to him that he had reconciled the contradictions between some two powerful minds, his soft, dark eyes would glow in a smile of childlike happiness. . . . Mortally ill with tuberculosis, spitting blood, he attempted to reconcile Nietzsche with Marx. Gripping my hands between his clammy palms, he wheezed:

"Life without synthesis—it's impossible!"

He died in a streetcar, on the way to the University.

I have met no few such martyrs in the cause of reason. I hold their memory sacred.

—Maxim Gorky (1923, pp. 60-61)

Preface

Still *another* book on the "problem" of education? Frankly, no. At least I *claim* not. What I do claim is so ambitious and decisive, that it risks appearing pure charlatanry. Yet, I must make my distinctive claim. The noted philosopher E. A. Burtt, in a preface to one of his books, says that an author should claim much for his work, whether he delivers what he claims or not. The reader will soon judge if the work lives up to the author's hope, and if the author does not have a high ambition, there is little point in offering just another book to join the already ponderous stacks. Perhaps nowhere is one tasked to put forth such an ambitious claim as in the field of education. There are already so many books, so much material, so many suggestions and discussions of the problem of education; is it enough merely to budge the volume a bit, to keep the discussion "going"? Or must one really try to advance to some sort of definitive solution? To anyone who has tried to wade through the vast numbers of volumes, erudite and otherwise, the answer is clear: we must try to say something important and substantial, make a big step forward, or else have the decency to be still and not complicate the problem any further by adding to the mere bulk of the discussion.

My distinctive claim, then, is this: that after one hundred and fifty years of groping we are at last in a position to offer what we have always wanted, but could not in modern times achieve: namely, a unified, universal college curriculum, a curriculum that provides modern man with the necessary unitary, critical world view that will give him maximum strength, flexibility, and freedom for solving the basic problems of human adaptation. It is a curriculum that could and should be taught to everyone, in any country that is interested in the fullest possible liberation of creative human energies—in any country, that is to say, that aspires to become a true democracy.

I invite the reader to follow as I unfold the support for this claim: first, through a brief sketch of the historical problem of a unified world view; then, through a discussion of the various attempts to meet the problem—the New Humanist movement of the 1920's and 1930's, the Great Books series, Ortega y Gasset's, H. G. Wells's and others' solutions; and finally, through a presentation of what I consider to be the authentic solution that has taken shape in our time, and can now be offered for discussion to the intelligent public at large.

Let the criticism fall hard and heavy whenever there appears to be good reason for it: on unsupported assumptions, naiveness, distortion, incompleteness—and even possibly fraud, in view of the immensity of what I claim. Only one indulgence I ask: that the reader give me an honest reading, as I have tried honestly to map out what I see as the great historical breakthrough in the problem of education and democracy. My discussion draws from, and extends, a much larger thesis which I developed in a previous book *The New Unified Science of Man: A History and Theory.* It will not always be possible for me to sum up convincingly in the format of the present book arguments that I there elaborated at some length; so perhaps it will be necessary for the reader to grant me the further indulgence of referring to the previous book for a more complete presentation of some of my critical points, whenever he feels this is needed. In fact, the present work should be treated as a companion piece to the previous one, and ideally, read and judged along with it: the unification of the science of man and the unity of the college curriculum are interdependent ideas which form one logical whole. If the science of man has truly been unified in our time, then the problem of education is naturally solved—and this is what I propose to the reader.

The educator will recognize the kinship of my general thesis to the basic Hegelian framework for a self-liberating education—especially as expounded and developed by Hegel's follower J. K. F. Rosenkranz. This is true for the underlying philosophy of history, but especially for my discussions of the classics curriculum and Rousseau's ideal-type, as models that give one a critical perspective on his own society. Hegel and Rosenkranz understood this as a necessary "self-estrangement" from one's own culture, that served to "universalize" the self. The noted W. T. Harris introduced these views to the United States in the nineteenth century (see his edition of Rosenkranz's *The Philosophy of Education,* N.Y., Appleton, 1890, and compare especially pp. 251–52, 277–78, and 282–83). Seen in terms of these precise historical antecedents, it will be clear that the task of the last century has been to fill in the *critical content* for the earlier framework.

Contents

PREFACE ix

PART ONE: THE PROBLEM

I. The Problem Introduced

CHAPTER ONE: The Problem of the Unity of Knowledge in the Modern World 3

II. The Groping of Modern Education

CHAPTER TWO: The Conservatives 9
1. The "New Humanism" Movement 2. The Great Books Program 3. The Counterassault of the Critics

CHAPTER THREE: The Progressives 33
1. The Tragic Paradox: Education and the State 2. Ortega y Gasset's Reminder 3. H.G. Wells's "World Brain"

III. Retrospect

CHAPTER FOUR: The Central Problem Clarified 62
1. The Historical Moral Problem 2. The Need for a Secular Moral Creed 3. Conclusion

PART TWO: THE SOLUTION

I. Introduction

CHAPTER FIVE: Alienation: A Spirit in Search of Substance 87
1. The Ever-Present Eighteenth Century 2. Conclusion

II. The New Moral View of the World

CHAPTER SIX: The Scientific Dimension: The Solution to the Riddle of Human Nature (Psychology and Sociology) 114
1. Psychology 2. Sociology

CHAPTER SEVEN: The Scientific Dimension (Psychiatry) 148
1. Psychiatry 2. Conclusion

CHAPTER EIGHT: Toward the Theological Dimension 165
1. Naturalistic Ontology: How Life Achieves Maximum Meaning and Conviction 2. The Need for a Critical Individual and Social Aesthetics 3. Conclusion

CHAPTER NINE: The Theological Dimension 196
1. The Inadequacy of the Secular Ideal 2. Freedom to Do What? 3. Conclusion

III. Retrospect

CHAPTER TEN: A Theory of Alienation as a Philosophy of Education 226
1. The Natural Solution of the Problem of Liberal Education 2. The Natural Solution of the Problem of Education Versus the State

PART THREE: CONCLUSION: THE SPECIAL PROBLEM OF THE CURRICULUM

CHAPTER ELEVEN: The Orientation 251

CHAPTER TWELVE: The General Body of Knowledge 257
1. The Individual Dimension of Alienation 2. The Social and Historical Dimension of Alienation 3. The Theological Dimension of Alienation 4. Conclusion

CHAPTER THIRTEEN: The Place of the Curriculum in the University 279
1. The Principle of the Economy of Knowledge 2. Conclusion

EPILOGUE 291

REFERENCES 295

INDEX 301

PART ONE

The Problem

". . . we are a sick folk . . . education in these United States is in crisis . . . it is being judged by the relentless impact of reality . . . and found wanting. Once we realize this, we shall soon have both wisdom and bravery to set about a radical and comprehensive reform."

—Bernard Iddings Bell (1949, pp. 229-230)

I. THE PROBLEM INTRODUCED

CHAPTER ONE

The Problem of the Unity of Knowledge in the Modern World

> "The state of society is one in which the members have suffered amputation from the trunk, and strut about so many walking monsters—a good finger, a neck, a stomach, an elbow, but never a man."
>
> —Ralph Waldo Emerson (1837)

Emerson was surely a master of the graphic image: like his friend Carlyle he lashed his contemporaries with the striking phrase. The point is that they had to be lashed. The poetic and critical thinker must dazzle and shock his audience with a new and colorful version of reality precisely because he sees a truth to which they are blind. Carlyle, for example, invented the insidious phrase "the condition-of-England question"—at a time when very few in England imagined that its condition *could* be called into question. Everyone thought that things were simply grand in the booming industrial world.

Why exactly did Emerson picture Americans as parts of a dismembered corpse? Wasn't the original Great Society still a-building? It was—but its energies were charging off in all directions, and it had no clear idea where it was going, or where it should go. Herman Melville seized the problem—again, as the poet does, with picture after striking picture of walking monsters rushing singly to their doom. This was the "American Renaissance," as

F. O. Matthiessen so well named it (1941)—and, like the earlier Renaissance, it was a time of great individual unfolding, of color, power, splendor, personal intensity—a huge fireworks display that thrills and mesmerizes only by means of the unexpected shock of everything coming apart.

This is what Emerson was sensitive to, but which the makers of public policy did not understand. They saw the color, but not the disintegration of the social fabric. Francis Wayland, for example—clergyman, educator, president of Brown University for nearly thirty years—had little idea of the real drama of the nineteenth century. So he encouraged his generation, and the ones that followed, to avoid trying to bite off the world all in one piece. He liberalized the college curriculum, furthered subdivision and specialization. Little could he have realized where his well-intentioned beginnings would end over a century later—or have they ended? The disciplines themselves have become hopelessly specialized, so much so that even anthropologists can hardly talk with one another. Formerly they talked about primitives, now they are separately occupied with feeding kinship charts into computers, and studying blood chemistry. It seems that we no longer have even "a good finger," but simply an array of joints.

Emerson saw the danger, then, and Wayland didn't. But Wayland was not an obtuse thinker—what led him to step so confidently away from the broad synthesis of knowledge, a synthesis without which man loses his grip on the world? Howard Nostrand, who broaches this very contrast between Emerson and Wayland, also gives us the answer: Wayland thought that his generation had common values, a basic ideology which would serve as a binder for the knowledge in all fields, from physics to fine arts. What was the basic ideology? The traditional religion, the belief in God. Unlike today, the idea of God was implicated in all knowledge. As Nostrand says, "The recurrent references to God, in the sciences as in the humanities, indicate the persistent cohesion of the expanding world of knowledge" (1963, pp. 144-145). This was Wayland's faith, that Emerson already saw was a fallacy. The American Renaissance, like the earlier one, pursued its relentless course. Traditional religion, the ever-present idea of God as a common social value, was not a real binding cement in either Renaissance. With social mobility running rampant, with knowledge proceeding under its own momentum, religion as a common value could not maintain its hold. The Enlightenment that began around 1680 shattered the last pretense of social cement, and a new type of man was born out of the Renaissance: harder, sharper, more incisively rational and skeptical, devoted no longer to God and society, but to knowledge and discovery. By an odd coincidence, the same kind of man emerged after the American Renaissance, beginning in the 1880's.

This was the time when synthesis and common values seemed like a constraint on the pursuit of knowledge; it was the time when all the various disciplines broke off from the parent organization that previously held them together: the American Social Science Association weakened and died, as its offspring—Political Science, History, Sociology—thrived in their separatist quests. They wanted freedom and they got it by leaving behind them the lifeless corpse of synthesis. In the short space of fourteen years even the heroes of synthesis fell by the wayside: for example, in 1878 F. B. Sanborn wrote in the *Journal of Social Science* that the fathers of social science were Smith, Vico, and Comte. Writing in the same journal in 1892, Sanborn dropped out Comte, and replaced him with Ben Franklin. Evidently Comte reminded him too strongly of the ambition of a bygone day, the ambition to organize knowledge and contain it within common values, even if knowledge itself had to be restrained. The generation of 1880 had had its say, and the forces that Wayland unleashed in liberalizing the college curriculum followed their own relentless logic: Knowledge is a hydra that hacks at its own heads, only for the pleasure of seeing them fill the world. Emerson's vision of dismemberment was apt in more ways than he perhaps imagined.

The history of American professional thought since that time obeys the old metaphor: It is a history of cycles rather than a history of progression. There are attempts to reestablish some kind of synthesis of knowledge, some kind of control—only to be fought again at other periods by the strain toward freedom and further unbridled specialization. In 1910 there was a reaction and groping for synthesis, and the sensitive sociologist Albion Small, a man of broad vision, cautioned: "We are now swinging into a scientific era in which we shall give ourselves fewer airs about the type of knowledge which becomes impressive by arbitrarily limiting its outlook" (1910, pp. 122-123). World War I of course did its damage to knowledge by interrupting this new groping, and the effort toward synthesis had to be made again in the 1930's and the 1940's. World War II again interrupted the process, and it is only in the 1960's that the problem of synthesis once more becomes urgent. In the 1940's, as Howard Nostrand points out (1963, p. 170), the response to the problem went under the name of General Education, and he cautions us against the fallacy of considering General Education to be a mere fad. It sums up the problem that has been outstanding for over a hundred years—the Emerson-versus-Wayland problem as we might now call it.

But it goes deeper, far deeper, than Emerson and Wayland, and the hundred years of American history they symbolize. It reaches back to the Middle Ages—and further still, even to the very sources of civilization and human society. Perhaps this is the reason Emerson was attuned to it, and Wayland not. I mean that Emerson shared with Carlyle the influence of German thought, and so probably inherited the spirit of German idealism and the great Wissenschaft ideal. This was the great hope of keeping knowledge unified for the liberation of man's best energies; and of using these energies not for the selfish advantage of the individuals themselves, but rather for the good of the whole society—for uplifting all in pursuit of a common ideal. It was a spiritual quest and a humanistic one at the same time: for the spirit was in man, and it unfolded as he unfolded. Men, nature, and society would blossom forth—all the more brilliant because part of one inseparable whole, each part furthering the development of the rest. Who could tell what would be the product of such harmonious creative development? There was even an awesome hope that man could create God . . . in fact, the whole process already *was* God, the unfolding of the Absolute Spirit in the world of time. The important thing was unity and harmony.

Today as we look back on the spirit that stirred Schiller and Goethe, Lessing and Herder, and Fichte at Jena, it seems like a pleasant enough dream. At least the thinkers of the German Enlightenment struck out for the whole man in society, nature, and history. There was none of the worship of the nude goddess Reason that the French Enlightenment showed, with its wholesale destruction of traditional values. Yet which dream proved to be the more "unreal"—the more naively ambitious: the French dream of Reason, or the German dream of Spirit, Nation, and Harmony? Both, no doubt, were equally starry. Yet, we would have been quicker to expect that cocky Reason would quickly be exposed than we could ever have believed that the gas ovens of Buchenwald would be built on Goethe's earthly pedestal—Weimar.

Such is history and the dreams of men, but we know it is not the dreamers who are at fault. Rather, it is all the forces which they could not foresee, and which no man or group of men can easily forestall. German Idealism was not up to the real forces of the time, and the nineteenth century made short work of it. In fact, the thinkers of the nineteenth century—Feuerbach, Kierkegaard, Marx, and the rest—actually exonerated German Idealism even while they dethroned it. They proved that the Idealists were naive because they simply could not *know* better in their day. It was not until the nineteenth century that man really began to find out what social forces were made of, and how they worked. In Germany at the turn of the century, one was justified in believing that there was something natural about social harmony, that things could be held together by effort and good faith, and sincere devotion to duty. Goethe was even shocked by the geological theory which said that the earth had not been formed harmoniously, but rather by cataclysmic eruptions—and he would have none of it. And wasn't Leibnitz the father of German Idealism? And wasn't it this same Leibnitz who approached Bossuet, and repeatedly attempted to heal the rift of the Reformation, and reunify all Christendom? Unity was what he wanted above all, and if his efforts on the social scale seemed absurdly doomed to fail, his philosophic work speaks eloquently and conclusively for the great fertility of the unitary mind.

To heal the rift of the Reformation! This was the real heart of the problem. Leibnitz was tilting in a hopelessly unequal match, but at least he was fighting the real adversary—the adversary of over a century, and indeed of several centuries: the decline of the medieval unity, of the harmonious world view and social accord that held men together in society, subservient to God and the religious ideal. Little did it matter that the seams of this unity had been split at least since Dante, and that they were gapingly sewn even at the height of the medieval feudal harmony. At least there was something unified to work with, something to build on and for. No matter how complicated or complex things became, they fitted within a single vision and ideal. And "we can only rejoice in variety when it is reduced to unity," warned Leibnitz, who knew (Meyer, 1952, p. 94).

The roots of German Idealism, then, were buried deep in the Middle Age hope. And as scholars have shown us, during the Middle Ages man's allegiance began to be devoted frankly to the Earthly City, and not the Heavenly one. There was a clearly humanist, this-worldly idealism in the work of Dante, and the inspired Gioacchino da Fiore. We might say that the Germans of the eighteenth century hoped to fulfill their work. If Leibnitz couldn't heal the jagged wound of the Reformation, then they would make the best of it: They would carry on its frank humanism and its spirituality, make of mankind a splendid panorama on earth and in time. This was Lessing's and Herder's plan for the education of humanity as the unfolding of the spirit. But as we saw, like Leibnitz, they too failed, and the reason was the same: There was no real social unity, and there was no deep spirituality —there was only societal form and a veil of religious camouflage. It was the same form and veil that had fooled Wayland in Providence, across the sea. And this Providence was the name of a merchant city in Rhode Island, and not the Guiding Love that had watched over the medieval community.

II. THE GROPING OF MODERN EDUCATION

CHAPTER TWO

The Conservatives

> "Nations are not truly great solely because the individuals composing them are numerous, free, and active; but they are great when these numbers, this freedom, and this activity are employed in the service of an ideal higher than that of an ordinary man, taken by himself. Our society is probably destined to become much more democratic; who or what will give a high tone to the nation then?"
>
> —Matthew Arnold (in Trilling, 1949, p. 137)

When we take our stand on the heights of history, the problems of man in society seem dizzying in their range and complexity. It is little wonder that when the historical consciousness entered the world with the Hebrew prophets, they could only propose eschatological solutions. The meaningful perspective on the cauldron of historical happenings has to come from beyond. Look once at the problem of bringing about the good life, and you shrink back under the will of God.

It is all the more, then, to the credit of man when he can face the stark problems that Leibnitz and the German Idealists faced, and still propose a human solution. Once we realize this, we will look more kindly upon the hardy thinkers who sprang up in America and offered ambitious, global schemes for solving the crisis of knowledge: the aimless drift of education, the fragmentation of thought resulting from specialization and the ascendancy of narrow science. These schemes are part of a great groping in the educational crisis of the last two centuries, and it is important for us to see clearly what they proposed—and why they failed. Let us then consider what seem to be among the best representative attempts to solve the crisis. The names will be familiar to most of us because, in fact, the dust of controversy has hardly settled around them.

1. The "New Humanism" Movement

One of life's mysteries has always seemed to men most eerie: I mean the awful, anonymous silence that settles over the most heartfelt human cries and controversies. We feel the mysterious injustice of it in the Colosseum at Rome, and in the dead green ruins of the once-flourishing port at Ostia, where Augustine once stopped with his mother. We see it, too, in the shelves of our libraries, with their volumes of books and journals that contain the record of words and feelings that raged out of the conviction of living minds. Gone, all gone but the silent traces. Someone once proposed that the words and sounds of man never die, but lie embedded in their waves in the air; and that someday man will invent a technique for finding a way to "play back" the sounds of the ages. Not all at once, we hope; we should all surely be struck dead by the din, or turned inside-out by the anguish. But our own progress in knowledge would certainly benefit if we could recapture the human heat of some of the controversies.

The New Humanist movement of the early part of this century was one such debate: the libraries contain its record, but we have little idea of the fire of the argument. The movement culminated in the 1930's, and was championed by the notable figures of Paul Elmer More and Irving Babbitt. And how the sparks did fly! Proposals, counterproposals, critique, and countercritique, accusation and counteraccusation. Little wonder: These people were ambitious; they wanted to solve the crisis in knowledge. And to do this they suggested nothing less than a return to Renaissance humanism. Not the Middle Ages, not the Reformation, not the end of the eighteenth century or the nineteenth, and certainly not the twentieth. They wanted the unity of the New Birth of rational man, the New Athenian Celebration of the Renaissance and early Enlightenment—before it gave way to Romanticism, and undisturbed by dogmatic religious disputes. The goal was human happiness and dignity; the ideals were classical; the means were reason and critical intellect; and the enemy was many-headed.

The New Humanists were against mechanistic science, with its denial of the priority of the distinctively human and its worship of the world of things. But they were also against Romanticism as they understood it, even though it championed individual subjectivity and revered the depth and uniqueness of each man's spirit. They saw Romanticism as irresponsible and emotional, uncritical and weak. Babbitt's attack on Rousseau is a classic document in their case. They were also against superstition and supernaturalism and the authoritarianism that supported them. Thus they could never be comfortable with the Classic-Catholic humanists of England—with T. S. Eliot or G. K. Chesterton. Medieval authority cast too great a shadow on this kind of Renaissance: They wanted the Athenian man *pur sang*. Man is not made of mush; he has a will; train it, they said, without fear of irresponsible willfulness. Man also has a deep, inborn conscience; cultivate it, and he will know self-control. Train an elite, cultivate excellence, and you will change the world. They wanted, in sum, a new man who would reintroduce responsible humanity into the mechanical shell of modern living. Mechanism, uncritical drift, childish emotionality, stupidity and blind trust—these were the target. The weapon was to be a new humanistic education; the ammunition was the vast store of literature accumulated by the great and balanced minds of the best ages of history (see Munson, 1930, for a very fair account of the movement).

It was a reasonable and even an inspired program on the face of it, with very much the same appeal as any stirring ideal like French Rationalism and German Idealism. But unlike them, the New Humanism never had to answer for its failure, because (as far as I know) it was never really given much of a chance: instead of being crowned on the throne, the humanities have had to fight for a place at the banquet. And today, some thirty years after the peak intensity of the debate, the humanities are reduced to a weak, rear-guard skirmish—for the most part. The fate of ideals is saddening, and the best that we can perhaps hope for is that they will remain in memory and somehow continue to influence our aspirations; that if they die, they at least leave a visible reminder. But the New Humanist movement did better than that: It left a vigorous offspring. As Leibnitz's great hope fathered German Idealism, so the New Humanism fathered the "Great Books" curriculum. Neither parent would quite recognize the offspring, even though the spirit was carried on: Leibnitz's heirs made a truce with the national State; and the Great Books made a truce with Aquinas and the Middle Ages.

2. The Great Books Program

We have not yet seen what the critics of the New Humanist movement had against it, objections which would at least partly explain why it failed to take broad root. But if we pause first to see what its offspring proposed to accomplish, we can get a better perspective on the whole movement: in this case the sins of the fathers show up with glaring clarity in the child.

One of the things that made the Great Books program vigorous is the testiness of its principal champion, Robert Maynard Hutchins. Here truly is a fearless fighter. Why, when he was young and eager for his ideal, he even dared to josh the greatest philosopher of the age, John Dewey. And since Dewey never dealt with trivial matters, we can see that something very big was at stake.

It is the same big question to which we are directing this entire inquiry; the one that troubled Comenius and Leibnitz: how to keep the unity of knowledge in the face of the growing manifoldness of empirical experience? And beneath the question, the haunting problem of the breakup of the medieval community, of the common life and dependable morality. This is the hidden aspect of the problem— the anguish about a common moral life. And it is this hidden anguish that justifies our repeating again and again what is at stake in modern education, and what has been at stake for five hundred years—no, better twenty-three hundred years, since the decline of the Athenian city-state. The idea of the "unity of knowledge" is not a dry intellectual quest by odd rationalists who want to envisage a "perfect scheme of things," and so solve the highest mental puzzle. It is rather more like the formula $E = mc^2$—that is, a rational shorthand that covers the dark abyss of natural mystery. But the idea of the "unity of knowledge" covers, if anything, an abyss much closer to the natural fears of man because, simply, the problem of the common moral life is basic to human adaptation and well being. If I do not know how my neighbors will act when I step out daily into the world, my very existence is threatened literally with each man I meet, or with each group of lads at the street corner, or with each passage near an outlying neighborhood. We can appreciate the anguish more today than ever, since our individualistic, commercial-industrial society has literally become a struggle of man against man. Carlyle saw very clearly that our commercial-industrial society is not sustained by any "invisible hand"—but rather by the very visible club of the police officer. Today we see the old-fashioned club giving way to sophisticated riot squad techniques, and we realize that the problem that preoccupied Carlyle has hardly been buried by the sands of a mere century. The "unity of knowledge," then, means life and death for growing numbers of citizens in the modern world, just as it has since the breakup of the medieval world, with sect and city and tribe and nation providing living sacrifices to the struggle between world views.

From Plato's *Republic* to Hutchins' Great Books program, then, the sensitive thinker has been aware of the volcano that seethes under the division and fragmentation of knowledge; and if he seems hard on the enemies of his vision, we have only to realize that anguish about his own well-being is at stake—well-being as a man, a citizen, a member of a human community, living in a dependable, meaningful world. Hutchins let fall the entreaty from his own lips, the deeper meaning of the Great Books program: "If any common program is impossible, if there is no such thing as an education that everybody ought to have, then we must admit that any community is impossible" (1954, p. 18). Small wonder, then, that Plato would have condemned all future Socrates' in his *Republic,* that even his former teacher was less to be prized than common morality and social order. But wasn't this exactly Socrates' own message, and the reason he subserviently drank the hemlock? Small wonder, too, that Hutchins snapped at Dewey, when Dewey criticized his plan. Hutchins wanted a Great Community, a community now and in the future. And the way he proposed to get it was by a Great Conversation, a conversation between specialists and generalists, all sharing a common fund of knowledge and ideas. How else talk with anyone, unless you share with him a common fund of knowledge and presuppositions? And in this way, one generation could be in touch with the other, draw from it, and build on it, steadily and surely.

Like all strong ideals, this one was drawn from life experience, specifically from Hutchins' presidency of a large university (Chicago) and from daily involvement in knowledge with all types of intellectuals. Hutchins had literally lived the fallacy of modern fragmented knowledge—the alienation of the intellectual not only from community, but from other intellectuals, even from the colleagues in his own discipline. Specialization and fragmentation not only made a common life impossible, they made the university itself a hoax—a very profitable and busy one, but a hoax nevertheless. Hutchins saw that professors cannot talk to one another, because they lack a common stock of fundamental ideas (1962, p. 59). This is how science becomes scientism, divided against itself, unrelated to intelligible human concerns. And since the unity of knowledge is a bridge over the abyss of social morality, a little learning is a dangerous thing. "We see now that we need more learning, more real learning, for everybody" (1954, p. 103).

A Great Conversation for a Great Community, then. And what makes a conversation great rather than trivial? Simply, that it asks the big questions, the questions of ultimate concern. The reason that our conversations are not great, and that we have no real community, is that we steadfastly refuse to ask the big questions, or to try to seek answers to them in common. Instead we ask the little questions, the questions that keep our daily work going in its prescribed ruts, the questions that look out for tomorrow by automatically following the routine of the day, by accepting uncritically the world as we find it, and by not caring too strongly what we are really doing in it, or are supposed to be doing. The big concerns and the big designs pass us by, as we keep each to his own narrow game. Try posing the big questions at a cocktail party, and see the quality of discussion you can get: What is the good life? What is the good State? What is the nature of the cosmos? What is the nature and destiny of man in the cosmos?

There was a time when these questions were generally discussed among intellectuals of all types; and not only during the Renaissance, or the Enlightenment, or the nineteenth century. In America they were discussed at the Harvard clubs formed by William James, Royce, and others, in this century. People from various disciplines shared a common fund of knowledge and large concerns, as Hutchins says. As one offhand piece of evidence, consider the two books by Nathaniel S. Shaler, written in 1904 and 1905: *The Neighbor: The Natural History of Human Contacts,* and *The Individual: a Study of Life and Death.* My point is that Shaler was Professor of Geology at Harvard, and Dean of the Lawrence Scientific School. What did someone like Dean Shaler have that the scientist of today lacks? Or, if we imagine that Shaler was an exceptional geologist, what did Hugo Münsterberg have that the psychologist of today lacks? Münsterberg was also at Harvard, and he was concerned with unity of knowledge, the narrowness of specialization, and the danger of uncriticized mountains of fact, heaped up almost indiscriminately by the disciplines. Try any psychology journal today, and see if you can find a sample of this kind of concern. Decidedly, the people have changed—and the times. If you went to the World's Fair at St. Louis in 1904, you would have met them all. They were there for scientific meetings, specifically to discuss the most vital questions! James, Münsterberg, Royce, Dewey, James Mark Baldwin, Bergson from Paris, Lipps, Toennies and Troeltsch from Germany. Harald Höffding from Denmark—the list is long and astonishing. People from philosophy, psychology, sociology, history, theology, all meeting together—and at a World's Fair, of all places. Not only do we not have the men today, but our whole commercial-industrial system seems to have dropped its mask. The World's Fair is not a place to seek unity on the big questions; it is an unashamed conglomerate of merchants' booths artfully hawking their national wares. Public relations, artfulness, and technique—this is what the modern world is all about. And it is these same values that have laid hold of the university, now that it has disabled itself for asking the big questions.

The reason these people could hold the Great Conversation, then, is that they had a knowledgeable and vital awareness of the big questions. And the reason they had this awareness is that they had all read and digested the Great Books—this is Mr. Hutchins' basic point, and the foundation of his whole argument and program. What exactly did the Great Books represent, that they could lead to such commonness of conception, and such quality of concern? According to Mark Van Doren (1943), who shared the highest quality of concern, the Great Books fulfilled a truly astonishing ambition. In the first place, they were a record of all man's adventures in the past; they recaptured man's history, and the story of the development of his humanity, the history of the achievements of his mind as well as his soul. They were, in other words, the source books for the pageant of the human spirit, for the story that man must know, and that each generation should aspire to learn and revere. It is the story that Lessing wanted to tell and Kant and Herder and Condorcet and Vico; the one that future generations will also want to tell, until it ends; or, hope beyond hope, until some higher power makes its meaning fully known, once and for all time.

The heart of the story is literature, poetry, history and drama. Literature is nothing less than the autobiography of the human race, the "Life and Remains of the natural man," as Newman called it (Van Doren, 1943, p. 160). And as such, it performs the great function of true autobiography: It educates the reader in how life should be lived. It is not mere antiquarianism, or food for idle curiosity. It is a basis for present judgment; history, poetry, drama, teach us *how* to feel, as well as how to think. By elevating judgment and taste, they afford a basis for criticism of both present and future. They provide the highest standards for the products of life and art. And tragic drama, as Van Doren says, is perhaps the highest education of man: It is man's noblest self-assessment; it lays before him the inevitable limitations of existence, allows him to measure his own true strength, and the chances of the human condition (1943, p. 164). These lessons do not die with any age; Sophocles and Shakespeare are always new because life ever begins again from the same basic terms. Thus literature is the fund for the lasting education of the human race. Only when man sees truth full in the face, the truth of several thousand years of dignity and pathetic struggle—only then can he be free to meet life with his highest energies. The poetic record of his condition will make of him the best kind of fighter: humble, yet hopeful; it rids him of ignorance while instilling temperance—and in this way, and this way alone, confers upon him not mere knowledge, but wisdom. In this record he can read the principles of moral and philosophic truth by which present judgment can be guided! And if only all men could read and know these truths; if all men could scan the record, and draw the breath of its inspiration as well as the weight of its moral; if all men could together take this great nourishment, it might truly be the sanctified feast that would consecrate mankind in its full glory and nobility. If this could only be, the Great Community itself might be born!

In order to bring about this great vision and hope, the university would have to be reorganized. In the first place, it would have to be thrown open to all, and not simply to the privileged minority as in the past. When aristocrats of the past wanted to limit the best knowledge to a minority, they did so largely for good reasons: Only the select few had the necessary leisure and information to make use of the best knowledge. But as Hutchins says, the views of Burke and others on minority education are now also things of the past. We can now all have these prerequisites in modern industrial society. And since history now provides us with this unique situation, that is, with a situation in which elite education can be available for all, Matthew Arnold's fears about democracy are proved to be utterly groundless. We can *all* have a critical perspective on our age; each citizen can, potentially, earn the moral and intellectual perspective that will infuse society with nobler ideals. The revolt of the masses that Ortega recorded, the unprecedented phenomenon of the industrial age, is now an historical fact. The new task is to take these masses of free men and give into their hands the best knowledge available, so that they themselves can realize the great ideals. Here, truly, is the Jeffersonian vision of democracy in its most modern guise, but stripped of its last aristocratic reserve.

The great stumbling block is the modern university itself. It is not a seat of learning. No matter how wide the doors are thrown open, how many new accommodations are built, how much scholarship money is voted by Congress and the states, the terrible fact remains: The American university exists to shape candidates for the jobs of the American commercial-industrial system. It is a professional and vocational institution, not truly an "educative" one. It is a place where one spends four or more years mechanically earning the right to fill the better available jobs. It is education *for* society as it now stands, rather than for the *ideals* of a society as it might better be. It is higher learning conducted as a business, as Veblen saw and satirized already after World War I; and it is conducted according to the best rules of automatically functioning bureaucracy, as Max Weber predicted: It goes on under its own weight, with the daily chores dictating the "great" decisions and the reigning fads of the society laying down the best plans. No matter how many earnest critics raise their agonized voices, the juggernaut grinds on: more funds equal "more" success; more buildings and grounds equal "better" operation; more students equal "more" education; better processing of examinations and grades equals "more efficient" educational operation; more publications equal "better" faculty; three hour-long lectures per week "equal" three hours of knowledge, payable at a fixed rate; one full fifty-minute lecture "equals" educational value received. And so the familiar story goes. Anything which stops or causes this efficient giant to stumble, is automatically "bad" for education: a student demonstration for any cause whatsoever; an article in the campus newspaper that attacks established opinion and practice; a professor who takes it into his head to champion a certain cause, even so harmless a one as teaching according to his vision of the knowledge-process rather than the three-hour ledger account. So many, many things can irk the efficient giant; and the reason is that the great bureaucracy of modern education is not a real brave dragon that confronts reality with a shrug, but a dry-as-dust administrative paper tiger; and if you peel back the papier-mâché, you see ordinary men, huffing and puffing inside. And the great lesson of Weber's thesis, and that of his popularizer, Parkinson, is that ordinary men too have needs for prestige, and for a feeling of satisfaction about themselves; and when their "organization" functions smoothly and flourishes, their success is writ plain on the face of nature: in grounds, buildings, equipment, secretaries, quantified *numbers* of things of all kinds—but especially students. The sad but inevitable fact is one that Weber also taught us: that the aim of the whole process gets lost—namely, the best possible development of the student. Alas, this inner development is not really measurable, quantifiable, or visible. And so, the hard reality loses out to the paper tiger; the symbol becomes the thing; the administration *of* education *becomes* education. Critics who have carried on Veblen's analysis and his warning, Paul Goodman for example, now urge the scholars to "secede" from the administrative locus of the university, and put education back into the process, even if it has to be covered by tents. Alas again: Mr. Goodman has not understood the problem. The professors cannot live or function like independent nomads; and the simple reason is that they know no guiding star. Without such a star, without a higher, unitary ideal that organized all educative efforts, they would still be training for the professions and the vocations. And surely a product is not the more attractive if it is hawked from a drafty tent, rather than from a palatial ivy hall.

There is no way to dodge the issue. The university itself must be reorganized: and this brings us to what I think is Hutchins' final major argument in his Great Books proposal. In order to avoid professionalism and vocationalism, the university must rededicate itself to the pursuit of truth, truth for its own sake and not for the sake of uncritical community service. Truth? How can that be? Didn't Kant revolutionize the development of philosophy once and for all time, with his famous Copernican shift? Didn't he show that man is immersed *in* nature, is part *of* nature, and so can never hope to know the inner secret of things? Every fact is "cosmos examined by a speck of cosmos," as Dewey later restated the Kantian revolution; truth is "two-faced": It is reality as discovered *by* man, and not reality "in itself." Truth depends on human groping and knowing, it is "always on the make,"—to use Dewey's pragmatist criterion.

Now, if all this is so, it means that man judges truth in the only way he can; that is, if the knowledge is meaningful and useful to him, in his voyage through the world, then it is true (until corrected when he stumbles in his passage). Of course there are geometrical, mathematical, and logical truths, which have no necessary connection to man's gropings, but are beautiful and perfect in themselves. But this is no contradiction of the pragmatist's thesis: he simply points out that these logical truths are truths which we arrive at *in suspension* of action; and since it is man's primary business to act, then action itself is still the major criterion of truth. There is no need to get hung up on the fine points of philosophical controversy here; on the whole, the pragmatist thesis is sound enough. But when we accept it, an uncomfortable realization dawns: If truth is that which is meaningful and useful to man in his passage through the world, why, then, the university is perfectly justified in turning itself into a service institution; if what professors know is only makeshift at best, why not use it to help keep society going as best it can? How can we claim that truth should be pursued for its own sake, if we will never know what its own sake is?

A weighty objection indeed—in fact, the whole cyclone that has raged over pragmatism has had its funnel churning on this point. We cannot avoid this problem, and as we shall see in later chapters, this whole book is partly an answer to it. Hutchins, unfortunately, does avoid the problem, and as we shall see right away, his critics plunged their pens full into the exposed nerve. But at least Hutchins was logically consistent in proposing the reorganization of the university. If you are going to avoid professionalism and vocationalism, you have to reorganize the university. And if you reorganize something, you need a principle of organization. If each specialist is pursuing his own truth, each running off in his own direction, the university cannot put up any resistance to opportunistic pragmatism. Such a resistance could only come if we knew that some truths were "higher" than others, if we had some unitary principle or hierarchy of truths which would show us which are fundamental and which subsidiary, which are significant, and which not (1962, p. 95). Thus, when Hutchins calls for the pursuit of truth for its own sake, he is really asking for something else: for a way of judging what is significant, rather than being jerked about by the changing fads of social fashion.

In other words, Hutchins wants what the New Humanists wanted: the university as a bastion of real learning, to stand as a bulwark against the philistinism of modern society. And in order to do this, it must carry within it its own standard of excellence, it must be unified according to a hierarchic principle of higher truth. Since there is no such principle in modern knowledge, and since this knowledge is degenerate in its specialism and triviality, let us go back to those times which had a standard, and use their principles: to the Greeks, and borrow their unitary ordering principle of metaphysics; to the Middle Ages, and borrow their principle of theology. Otherwise, says Hutchins, the university cannot exist, and the quest for excellence in our time is doomed. Let us use the best of the past rather than chafe against the old wisdom simply because it is old; let us use it since we have nothing to put in its place.

To the masses, then, with education—no, not just education, really excellent knowledge; to the past, then, not just for the content and form of that knowledge, but for the very principles of truth, for is it not a fact that they were wise, and that we have grown very efficiently foolish? Such is the Great Books program and its proposals. And now we must turn to its critics, and see what they have to say; we have ignored them only to make a coherent presentation, but all the while they have been launching missiles across the moat.

3. The Counterassault of the Critics

The image is apt: to the critics of New Humanism and the Great Books the whole thing smelled of Hellenistic and even medieval antiquarianism, separated by an abysmal gulf from most of the realities of modern society: a fog-shrouded castle that a few well-intentioned but hopelessly misoriented people were trying to construct smack in the middle of the jet runway of modern life.

So many critics had their say; but fortunately we get at the heart of the matter by examining a handful: they all identified the same salient features of the archaic structure. The New Humanism never really had much of a chance, simply because it was truly antiquarian. The ideas were inspiring, but they had the inspiration of an occult séance: Babbitt and More simply drew the curtains of antiquity, and turned their backs on the modern world. The battle of New Humanism against New Mechanism was a sensible one; but to throw science out of the window to gain a victory was hardly the way to combat mechanism—it was to cure a brain tumor by amputating the head. Doesn't classicism include Aristotelian naturalism, as well as Platonism? Small wonder that after World War I, a brand of humanism called Scientific began belatedly to contend with the classic, literary New Humanism. There was simply no way to turn the clock back on the achievements of science, or on the scientific spirit. Rationalism had to give way to experimental naturalism; the experimental attitude had to take over from the authoritarian one. When we read the debate today, we can understand why the sparks flew so violently. These New Humanist gentlemen, with all their professed dislike of superstition, authoritarianism, emotionalism, and medievalism, seemed to want to forget the Industrial Revolution; they seemed to scorn the one great century in which man built up the necessary foundation for liberating himself from the very things they disliked (*cf.* Grattan, 1930). As a result, with all their daring in questioning "the unconscious assumptions of our age," they forfeited the chance to bring to bear realistic standards for judging these assumptions. This, as we shall shortly see, is where the critics of the New Humanism pounced hard. After all, the humanist revolt against mechanism did not spring full-blown from the heads of classics professors of the early twentieth century: it dates from Diderot, and passes through such other giants as Goethe and Carlyle. In other words, it is rooted in a tradition which *includes* science, as we shall see in the next chapter.

By turning back to the Renaissance, the New Humanists committed the fundamental fallacy of all conservatism. "How much better things were in the past, if only we could get them back! How do we go about it? Let us try, simply, to reinstitute some of the things which made the past better, nobler, pleasanter than the present." On the face of it, it seems logical; but the great fallacy is that change is irrevocable and global: It carries everything with it. Not only the "good" things change, the ones we remember with nostalgic longing; everything else changes as well. As a result, if we want them back, we have to do something about most of the other things that have changed as well.

This is where the "progressive" sees more clearly than the conservative, even though he may want to get back to many of the same past enjoyments. He realizes that the changes are here to stay, and that they are far reaching. So that, in order to get back the "betterness" of the past, he advises making truly extensive changes in the present. To take one stride backward needs two giant strides forward. The analogy holds for one's own life as well: To recapture the flavors of youth one must press forward not backward. Does the man of sixty yearn to reexperience the joy of his first love? He is better advised to step radically ahead into the realm, say, of mystical experience, rather than begin pining for girls of 14. It is in this sense that Goethe, the Enlightenment humanist, was conservative in his own life; and Francis of Assisi, the medieval Catholic, was radical.

The New Humanists, in sum, ran right up against the flood tide of American reality, and tried to shoo it away. Science could not be discounted; education could not be limited to an elite; the heavy weight of mechanism in modern life could not be overcome merely by self-cultivation. No matter what we did to cultivate man's "will" and his "self-control," the external world still clamored for attention and for remedy. Surely man had a conscience, but he did not inherit it from the Athenians; it was shaped by the society he lived in. To change man, then, was not enough: You had to change his world along with him—and perhaps even *first.* At this thought, the New Humanists shrugged so violently that their togas raised a wind. From the authority of their erudition, and with firmly folded arms, they enunciated their principle: Change a few things about education, cultivate man from within, and the external world will transform as easily as stage scenery; the excellence of the past stemmed from excellent men, and that's that.

When the critics came to launch out against the Great Books, they were thus attacking the New Humanist credo at its absolutist and most vulnerable point. True, Hutchins' questioning of our age and its unconscious assumptions was not as rudderless as the New Humanists Babbitt and More. He had opted frankly for hierarchical, organizing principles, for Greek metaphysics and Thomistic medieval theology. But this, as we noted above, only compounded the problem; it was the really exposed nerve of the conservative groping for a new standard for education.

What a time the critics had! Their assault was so accurate and devastating, we may well wonder why they did not succeed in sinking the venture with the first broadside volley. Some of the leading names of our time "got in their licks," and the same weaknesses were exposed again and again. The major weakness was, of course, antiquarianism. Another was the avoidance of social studies and social problems. Another was overambitiousness and monopoly. Jacques Barzun said that the Great Books overreach themselves, and at the same time fail to give us the knowledge we need of contemporary problems. They overreach because they attempt to be a *whole* curriculum. Barzun says that John Erskine's original list of fifty-three books was far better than Hutchins' round figure of one hundred. The original fifty-three had a practical as well as a classical intent, and they were not meant to be a whole curriculum; Erskine wanted to use them to help highlight modern problems. But the Great Books begin with ancient historians and end with Vico and Gibbon! (1945, pp. 156-59.) A fine way to convey an understanding of modern history.

Sidney Hook noted that the Great Books contained not a single book since World War I, nor anything on or about the period at that time, or since. Except for documents from the United States Constitution, the Great Books contained only a single American thinker on its list—William James. And what a burden for the student, said Hook: They have to read books now read only by specialists, and by them only after a lifetime of preparation (1946). Imperialism, then, and antiquarianism, and esotericism; it all amounted to a hopeless gap between ambition and reality.

But the really great criticism of the Great Books is the problem of any and all attempts to use the past as a mine for knowledge: namely, how can you study the past unless you take the present as a locus of reference, a locus for finding out what you want to know? We need to study present problems, and only in this way can we find the connections we need to the past. And as the great

Wilhelm Dilthey taught us, each new present gives us a potentially new past. This is the heart of the matter: What do you want to use the past *for*? If you want the best possible use, you must take your stand on the problems of the present—in fact, this is the only way to put it to intelligent use; the rest is antiquarianism, plain idling, or willful evasion. Nietzsche had already pondered these uses and abuses of history in his famous essay of that name; why were we still pretending that we could uncover the secrets of the past, without asking urgent present questions?

And what are these urgent present questions? What is the great problem of the present—the problem that the New Humanists and the Great Books avoided in their scramble backward in time? Why, it is the problem that this whole business is supposed to be about, but which problem curiously gets lost as soon as we begin elaborating the proper education that would remedy it. It is the problem of the decline of the medieval community, Leibnitz' problem, and Emerson's; it is the problem of social morality, of ordered society, the great gaping wound in the center of modern life. It is the problem of social reconstruction, the world-historical problem of civilized society that has haunted man's thoughtless scramble across twenty-five hundred years of Western history. This was the problem with which we began our discussion; and as we noted then, the question of the unity of knowledge was merely the pointer to it, the bridge over it, the symptom of it. What relationship does the unity of knowledge have to the specific social problems of the age? Here is the core of the matter. The unity of knowledge in each age has to spring from its own unique cultural condition; and when Hutchins reached back to Greek metaphysics and medieval theology, he showed that he was not talking to our time. We noted above that *this* was where the critics scored their most telling point; let us now hear from the most cogent and caustic of all—John Dewey, who was also one of the first to take Hutchins' program to task (1937a, p. 104):

> Escape from present evil contemporary social tendencies [*i.e.*, into medieval learning] may require something more than escape. It may demand study of social needs and social potentialities of enduring time span. President Hutchins' discussion is noteworthy for complete absence of any refer-

> ence to this alternative method of social reconstruction. It is conceivable that educational reconstruction cannot be accomplished without a social reconstruction in which higher education has a part to play.

Dewey is here protesting against what the New Humanists and Hutchins carried over from the Ancients and from the Thomists: namely, the idea that man's inner nature—his conscience, his reason—is somehow fixed and independent of the world he lives in. Hook later repeated the same criticism of the Great Books: that they showed man's nature as essentially unchanged and largely unchangeable. What Dewey is arguing for, then, is the thesis that realistic social reconstruction may have to take place along with any effective reform of higher education. This is the "alternative method" in the search for unity of knowledge and for social morality and community.

And it is here that Dewey the philosopher shows his intimate kinship to his predecessors of the past. He knows what bothers true philosophers, and what has always bothered them (p. 104):

> The constant appeal of President Hutchins to Plato, Aristotle, and St. Thomas urgently calls for a very different interpretation from that which is given it. Their work is significant precisely because it does not represent a withdrawal from the science and social affairs of their own times.

The great ages of man were ages of "present concern"—there can be little doubt about that. The Greeks that we admire so much were hardly antiquarians; and the worship of antiquity during the Renaissance was precisely for purposes of building a new society. Let us imagine a "Great Conversation" between Hutchins, Plato, Aristotle, and St. Thomas, in the flesh; imagine that they were somehow transported together for a seminar, across the abyss of time. What would they think of Mr. Hutchins' breathless interest in their dead societies and times, in the textual exactness of their inadequate knowledge and thoughts, all the while that he was completely oblivious of his own times and its unique works? A strange fellow indeed, this man without a century! Had he no world of his own, no great and urgent task that demanded the best of living man and mind? "What do we, Plato and Aristotle know, whose thought was already unacceptable to the later Hellenistic world—indeed, unrelated to it? The *Republic* in a world without independent city-states? Scientific naturalism, the patient, disinterested accumulation of knowledge, in a world that had lost the old sense of order, without replacing it with a new sense of history? And I, Thomas, what can I say to a world which has eclipsed Luther, when his had already eclipsed mine? *You,* Mr. Hutchins, you must tell us what *you* need to know, else our conversation will be wearisome and without point, like most of the seminars in your great universities."

We hasten to beseech pardon from these great souls of the past for using them so simplistically in support of our present argument. But just as Sallustius humbly asked pardon of the gods for attempting to explain the meaning of the great myths—and so justify paganism to the intellect, every age has to do violence to the integral wisdom of the past. It only goes to support our point. What else can we mean by "Great Conversation" except the calling of the past to the account of the present, the *using* of history, as we said. What is the "problem-frame" that makes sense of the world, of its manifold data, of the fantastic panorama of history, of the incredible mountains of recorded words and ideas? What is the "working theory" which guides our vision, what is the narrow footing upon which we take our stance, without which the world of fact overwhelms us? Hutchins argues against Hook's contention that the Great Books are difficult, that not only experts and scholars can profit by carefully reading them. But doesn't Hutchins know that scholars and experts approach knowledge with some kind of critical frame, some kind of awareness of a present problem, upon which they are seeking to throw some light? How can we expect the student to go to Vico and Bentham for "nuggets of knowledge," unless he knows what to look for, what he "wants" to find?

After all, what do "scholarship" and "expertise" mean, if not the ability to choose and to attribute proper weight? At their best, they mean the ability to economize, to cut out, to lop off, to render the difficult clear. And this invariably means extracting for present purposes. Nowhere is Hutchins' failure to understand this more clear than when he says that no prerequisite reading is necessary, but that the books should be read in order, because, historically, the succeeding thinkers read all the previous ones, and so on up to modern times. The authors, says Hutchins, comment on one another, take issue with the opinions of their predecessors so that reading one book makes reading another easier. Exactly—if read in this way, we discover *their* Great Conversation, not ours. Are we asking the student to partake in a sterile, outmoded, and inverted debate, without examining it from a point of view of higher critical perspective? Of course Dante read Plato, and Montaigne read Dante plus Plato. But this is just the point: these men applied their reading to explicitly framed present problems, about which they were clearly troubled and around which stormy debates were raging. We must repeat this again and again since the champions of the Great Books seem so utterly to have missed this crucial fact. The great thinkers had the critical framework of their own genius by means of which they viewed the preceding thinkers. This is how they kept their interest, and this is also why the student cannot be expected to keep his. If Kant had been a Humian or a Leibnitzian, merely bathing himself in their vast erudition, then he would not have written his *Critique*. How can the modern student be interested in Berkeley, without knowing how the nineteenth century solved the problem of ideal realism, where the problem stands today, and what needs to be done with it, if anything? The elite thinkers of the past used the Great Books just in this way, they had interests, and a position to overthrow or defend. Just look at the way the thinkers of the eighteenth century used philosophy and theology sources in their great debate on the truth of revelation. Look how Marx used obscure thinkers to attack the fallacies of his time; how James and Royce battered each other over the timely questions of idealism and monism. Even the most gigantic thinkers, as well as the earlier political and aristocratic elite, had to attribute weight and significance; they could not use the insights of the past irrespective of the needs of the times. Look how Sorel abjured Socrates for championing individualistic reason; Sorel believed that the times needed a Great Myth, and to him Socrates spoke the Great Lie of reason. Should we read Malthus on population, without knowing that he hated Rousseau and progressivism; that he believed in original sin and thus was against contraception? What I mean is, should we read him without knowing exactly the assumptions of *our* age, what we are for and against, and *should be* for and against?

It is this great lesson and warning that Nietzsche held before us; that what we learn from the past depends on the daring of our judgment of it. In his inspired words (1924, Vol. 5, p. 55):

> *You can only explain the past by what is highest in the present.* Only by straining the noblest qualities you have to their highest power will you find out what is greatest in the past, most worth knowing and preserving. Like by like! otherwise you will draw the past to your own level. Do not believe any history that does not spring from the mind of a rare spirit.

This is the Great Conversation: we want to be judged by the past, and the only way to do this is to judge *it* in the most critical way. Take the most brilliant century of modern times, the eighteenth, and see how they scorned history; to them it was the accumulated folly of the dark ages of man's infancy. And how they used this folly to feed the fire of their own genius! Here is the lesson; give the historical conversation your best, otherwise it will be mere pedantry, dilettantism, babble with extensive quotations: "What this or that philosopher has or has not thought; whether this or that essay or dialogue is to be ascribed to him or not . . ." to use Nietzsche's own words (1924, Vol. 3, p. 125).

And this is what it has been, for the most part, even in the great ages of the past. How did the Greek Sophists use their Great Books; how did the Renaissance humanists use them? To gain praise and position, and worldly fortune—with but a few outstanding exceptions. Of course they lauded the ancient wisdom and vaunted the art of careful study of the original sources. It is this that gives "harmonious development of mind, body, and character"—and who would not want that in any age? When the classics were revived during the Renaissance, this was the ideal (Beesley, 1940, p. 30), and it is still the ideal today. Yet, in each age since the Greeks, the revival of the great wisdom of the past has failed to bring sanity to mankind, has failed to bring social morality, has failed to arrest the disordered scramble of civilization. Hutchins believes that all this will change when the very masses themselves enter the university to partake of the ancient wisdom. But we have no reason to expect this, partly because, as scholars tell us, there was already very widespread education in the ancient wisdom at the time of the Hellenic civilization. No, it is not the times, or the sources, or the sheer numbers who imbibe. The mass circulation of the finest reproductions of old masters has not given us great art, and the mass study of Great Books will not give us great wisdom. The reproduction of old masters may make us adept at recognizing the author of a painting when we see it on the wall of twenty-three different houses; the Great Books may likewise make us adept at dialectic, at mastering the necessary steps of subtle and precise argument. But this will hardly make us wise, any more wise than the Russian masses who play so carefully at the elite sport of chess: It is all a game, a great cultural game, as was that of the Greek Sophists who made a thriving business of teaching rhetoric to the sober Romans. And like all cultural games, the chances are that it is taking our minds off something really important, really vital to the survival of our society, just as it took away the Roman minds, and the medieval ones.

Gordon Chalmers got to the heart of the problem when he criticized the Great Books for precisely this error, for suggesting that dialectic characterizes the thinking mind. The "scholars and teachers responsible for making available to the life of the twentieth century the wisdom of ancient times have largely failed" (1944, p. 91). Why have they failed? Simply because it is not dialectic that liberates man, and allows him to reconstruct and master the rich world of confused experience. It is not technique or argument, but passion and vision that free man. We have failed to profit from the classics because we have failed to illuminate them with a passionate spirit characteristic of our age. And so we draw the full and final circle in our long discussion. Imagination and vision—this is what we have needed to lay hold of history. As Chalmers puts it: "any deed or statement of absolutely first class—may appear contemporary only to the man of imagination. Imagination, rightly understood, affords the key to the New View of the World" (p. 92).

The New View of the World—this is even better, this is what

we were wanting: the imaginative theory that organizes the multitude of facts; the ideal vision that digs its roots deep into the real world, and draws from us the living energy to overcome the biggest problems. This is what we have been looking for over a century and a half, ever since, in fact, the time that our experiment in democracy started—ever since the American Renaissance. And this is precisely why the first criticism of the Great Books came out of the Enlightenment and the French Revolution itself: without the New View of the World the Great Books were a hindrance, a corruption, or a trifling. Condorcet said it when he laid down the first great challenge for a radical reorganization of education in 1792; there was little advantage in following the old Classical education; our knowledge had gone beyond theirs, and if we would rummage among their ruins without harm to ourselves, we had better first be armed with a good critical balance (Williams, 1959, p. 307, footnote 16). Here in the Revolution was the final consummation of the argument that began the Enlightenment, the famous dispute between the Ancients and the Moderns. The spirit of the Moderns carried the day completely, even though Condorcet's *Project for a General Organization of Public Education* came to naught. We will return in more detail to Condorcet's plan in the next chapter; but who was it who gave the Enlightenment its first clear voice after Jefferson, who launched the quest that has not yet been consummated for the passionate new vision? It was bound to be Emerson, and his target was the same as Condorcet's: the ruins of the past; not the Ancients this time, but the Europeans themselves:

> Our books are European. We are born within the fame and sphere of Shakespeare and Milton, of Bacon, Dryden, and Pope. Our college text-books are the writings of Butler, Locke, Paley . . . We are sent to a feudal school to learn democracy (quoted in Matthiessen, 1941, p. 475).

Alas, we have not yet learned democracy. But it is time that we learn that the classics, the Great Books, the accumulated wisdom of all of mankind, will never help us learn it until we supply our own New View of the World—our passionate ideal vision that forges our separate fingers into a steady hand, a hand that lays hold of the real and ideal, and that brings them together like a curtain over a century of blind groping. The ideal has to be grounded in the hard world of present fact, of present social and material problems, and not in the tomes of a bygone time. This was Emerson's point, and the lifelong passion of his great moralist disciple, Dewey. It is this cleavage between the real and the ideal that has caused our thought to be so tenuous, as Matthiessen put it, "so without bearing on the tough materialism of our daily practice" (p. 475).

Is there still a skeptic left, still a stalwart champion of the view that ideal knowledge will somehow have its way into the real world, even without an intimate critical link to contemporary social conditions? If so let us close our discussion with an example of just how tough this materialism of our daily practice is, how soft and airy the Great Books. Look here: See how the illustrious Virgil can be trifled away; how the past can be drawn to our level, as Nietzsche warned; look at the advertisement from a brokerage firm, in a society that has lost a passionate image of man, a society that has no New View of the World (*New Yorker,* Sept. 21, 1963, p. 192):

> "Happy is he," wrote Virgil almost 2,000 years ago, "who has been able to learn the causes of things." Happy, indeed —and there's a good chance that he's rich, too, if he wants to be. If an investor knew exactly why stock prices rise and fall . . .

Mining the Great Books for profit without a doubt. It is time that we turned to more productive fields in the modern educators' quest for a curriculum worthy of man.

CHAPTER THREE

The Progressives

> "Doubtless all studies are one study in the end.
> But we do not know its name . . ."
> —Mark Van Doren (1943, p. 116)

"When God wanted to create the world, the conservative angels, with tears in their eyes, shouted to him, 'Lord, do not destroy chaos!' " So wrote Monsieur de Méré, who thereby showed how well he understood the immensity of the problem: How do we abolish chaos except by moving forward? But when we move forward into form, only the Lord Himself knows how far we should move; and if angels quake at the prospect, what are we to expect of mere man? Does he ask for a model at least, a pattern, something on which to go? Surely we cannot reproach him this much lack of temerity. But this is the conservative quest, the looking backward—the nostalgia that drugs our courage for the really fresh vision. The conservative fails, as we said, because he cannot take the giant step forward in order to take the step back—and it is just this colossal step that we need, if we are to reimpose form on chaos. In his relentless push forward man must imitate the gods; but no! the gods show no model or pattern. Is it then possible that man must show more daring and vision than even they?

It certainly seems so, at least when we look at the attempts of the progressives to come to grips with the problem of education in our time. Here truly is the Promethean quest; men who scorned the comfort of a model, picked over the past with sour discontent, scoffed at the best that the present offered, willing to bet their very lives on the unknown. A new man is what they wanted, nature's energies in a new form; and they were quite willing to be surprised by this new man, quite willing to trust their fate to him so long as his energies be fresh and pure. *This* is the very soul of the progressive: the man who asks to be surprised by life and nature; who looks, not caring what he will see; who wants the new to win and hold what the past has forfeited, even if he himself has to watch the triumph from the ranks of the losers. The conservatives are only angels, but such is a man.

And what would such a man propose as he tried to make his way in the labyrinth of modern education? Well, for one thing, he might start with a precise definition and use it as a springboard into the unknown. The word "liberal education," for instance. A good idea, that—but what does it mean? Well, liberal means free, not restricting, not bound by orthodox tenets or established forms—as Webster has it. A liberal education, then, in the precise sense, is a liberating one; and the idea of liberation is suspended on two poles: liberation *from* something, and liberation *to* another thing. And what should a truly free man be liberated from? Why, anything constricting in either the past or the present. And liberated to? Here is where the progressive plunges into the void: liberated to . . . whatever elevates our society, gives it higher form. We should not be surprised, then, that when the progressives came to examine the problem of education in a free society, they literally pulled out all the stops. Trust man, they urged in chorus, trust in the free development of natural energies; and damn all constraints on those energies—even if these constraints stem from our most comfortable and habitual ways of life.

One of the first voices in this chorus, as we might expect, was Emerson's, with its distinctive and inspired rhetoric:

> Our culture has truckled to the times. It is not manworthy . . . It does not make us brave or free. We teach boys to be such men as we are. We do not teach them to aspire to be all they can. We do not give them a training as if we believed in their noble nature (quoted in Van Doren, 1943, p. 3).

Here you have it: comfort with the unknown, if even it makes men who are not as we are. Would Athenians who had the power of life and death over their offspring have dared as much? Listen to another—Everett Dean Martin (1922, pp. vii-viii):

> . . . education is more than information, or skill, or propaganda. In each age education must take into account the condition of that age. But the educated mind is not a mere creature of its own time. Education is emancipation from herd opinion, self-mastery, capacity for self-criticism, suspended judgment, and urbanity . . . I use the term "liberal" not in the political sense, as if it meant half measures, but in its original sense meaning by a liberal education the kind of education which sets the mind free from the servitude of the crowd and from vulgar self-interests.

And in his fine book, Martin proceeds to set up the ideal types that demand our greatest reverence, the free spirits that liberal education should seek to promote: Socrates, Plato, Aristotle, Erasmus, Montaigne, Huxley, Nietzsche, Arnold. Who were these men, if not those who sat ill with the general tone of their times, men who rose above their times only to better guide the way. Free spirits released by nature, only to surprise man and to delight him. We should not wonder that some of them fared so badly at the hands of their contemporaries, who were, as we said, merely angels.

A. D. Henderson attacks the term "liberal education" in his turn (1944, p. 15):

> The term . . . today needs a new definition. It is an education that tends to produce the liberated individual—the person who, because of his perspective of history, his critical observation of contemporary society, and his understanding of social dynamics, helps to facilitate needed change in the world.

The liberal education, then, if it is to deserve the name, is liberation to the higher critical perspective; and its purpose is precisely that of social criticism.

Theodore M. Greene, in his 1952 Inglis Lecture, wondered what on earth could be said in the plethora of theory on liberal education that would at all be new. Not much, he concluded, except the continued asking of the basic questions, the continued tackling of the basic human problems. This was Dewey's peculiar strength, said Greene, and the one that man needs most of all; it made Dewey great, and it makes any man or age great. And the reason is that the basic questions are the truly liberating ones, and it is liberated men that we seek: "Our ultimate educational objective is a self-starting, self-criticizing, and self-nourishing mind—a mind that can function powerfully, creatively, and wisely under its own steam" (1953, p. 29). A man, in other words, who would freely dispose of his own energies, beholden to no one in any uncritical or slavish way—a man who would inject the continually fresh and new into the world. Democratic man, in the original and now-lost meaning of the term.

Kenneth Burke, critic and most original mind, put it very strongly in his turn. He wanted men to learn the limitations of language and of the symbols into which they are trained by their society. Education would seek to expose the motives of secular ambition, it would be an unmasking of the society in which one grows up. In his words (1955, p. 273):

> Education must be thought of as a *technique of preparatory withdrawal,* the institutionalizing of an attitude that one should be able to *recover at crucial moments,* all along the subsequent way.

This kind of education would be liberal in its fullest meaning: It would train man right out of his society, permit him to see and judge the ground from which he sprang.

The sociologist C. Wright Mills wanted liberal education to produce the kind of mind that was so disciplined and informed that it could not be overwhelmed by events (1959, p. 319). For this kind of Olympian strength, man would need to understand his own experience and gauge his own fate, he would have to be able to locate himself in his own period—and for this he would need the highest critical perspective on his own times.

We need not cite any more to feel the smart of the progressive wind that blows the sails set into the unknown. These men are talking about an education of the kind that we have never seen or planned in any society on this earth. But let us hear, finally, from the philosopher Horace Kallen, one of the hardy early pragmatists; he gives us a homely image (1962, p. 69):

> What is the difference between an archaeologist and a garbage collector? . . . neither would make sense save as imagination sets whatever each collects in perspective of causes and consequences which are the all of understanding. . . . Whatever the level, whatever the area, the task is to take anything or everything in the personal experience . . . that seems inwardly low and mean and dirty, and to set it in the transforming perspectives of the . . . arts and the sciences. A person seeing whatever it be that he is or has . . . spanned by these perspectives, experiences them as passages into growing freedom.*

And these transforming perspectives, these critical vistas of history and biography that permit man to collect his life into a meaningful whole, does education in America give them? Alas, no, says Horace Kallen. This education is precisely the one we do not get. In place of self-informing criticism, we get "indoctrination in a dated grammar of assent" (1949, p. 146). In other words, we are trained more in the role of garbage collectors than of archaeologists, if we may so use Kallen's metaphor.

There is no difficulty making out what these people are telling us about the progressive view of liberal education; the difficulty, if any, is in imagining the implications of these views. But then, this is always the difficulty, because this is the crucial problem, the one that Gordon Chalmers pointed out to us in the last chapter, imagination: the word that takes what is ordinary, lifeless, constricting—illiberal—and turns it into something "first class," alive—liberal. Imagination is the key, as we saw, the key to the solution of the problem of education, the key to a New View of the World. And this is what these gentlemen are proposing: A New View of the World, a view that unmasks for man anything and everything that would constrain his free flight; and these constraints are to be found in his present *social* world. Education, in sum, if it is to be truly the New View worthy of man, must set itself—in some way, somehow—in opposition to the very social world out of which it springs! Is this the awful apodictic logic of the redefinition of "liberal education"? No wonder the angels—who have never left off hovering near the progressives' chorus—

* From Kallen, Horace M., *Philosophical Issues in Adult Education*. Courtesy of Charles C. Thomas, Publisher, Springfield, Illinois.

tremble with apprehension. The progressives are proposing that the true antagonist of liberal education is the State itself. But how can this be?

1. The Tragic Paradox: Education and the State

Let us follow out briefly the logic of the progressive argument, as we sketched it above. A liberal education would, according to Emerson, teach youths to be all they can—even if it meant not being like their elders. It would seek to free them as much as possible, free their distinctive personal energies, even if these energies had *unexpected repercussions* on the habitual social world. It would train youth to exercise their own judgment, seek their own solutions, criticize and master the world on their terms; it would allow them maximum scope for their own creativity, by freeing them from the automatic reactions of the crowd. The purpose of this liberation is not to make self-destructive or social-destructive demons, but just the opposite: to help bring about necessary and continuing social changes by truly strong and responsible people. We would try to liberate maximum individuality only because we know that this is the best way to master the new and unexpected problems that arise in each generation. We free our youth only because we trust that they will not repeat our fatal mistakes.

This is the philosophy of the proposed liberal education—it has, as we know, never been tried. And here is where the logical paradox enters, and shows why it has never been tried. If we free youth in this way, they will be free to criticize anything and everything that they judge needs to be changed. They would, theoretically, be free to change our whole way of life—not only harmless habits, like favorite ways of taking tobacco, or mixing drinks, or art styles and popular music, but the very economic and political style with which we feel so much at ease. In other words, if we truly free our youth, they may deprive us of the only world we know, the only one we have learned to be comfortable in, the only one that responds to the years of training and habit that we ourselves have so painfully learned. If we free them, they may threaten the whole state of our society—which is the State itself. By the inexorable logic of things, then, the State must oppose full freedom of education. The full tragedy of the paradox is that this is the only way that the State, as it now stands, can be saved; but in order for the State, as it now stands, to be saved, it must consent to give itself freely over to be changed. A bitter problem, that is rooted at the very core of the human condition: the very thing that man fears most, is the thing he most needs: the unexpected repercussions of the free creative energies of his fellows.

The tragedy of the paradox is not only in the abstractness of logic: it is in the concrete stuff of flesh and blood. The State does not willingly change, but uses instead the lives of its own youth to perpetuate its form. Perhaps this is truly the great lesson of the twentieth century, and the very one that we will not heed. No State has trained its youth to be the responsible critics of their own society, and so we have revolution and war, and repression and more war. Revolution, war, repression: these are synonyms for the failure to educate youth in the capacity peacefully and freely to remake the world. Its cost, as we know, has been terrible. In World War I, the graduating rolls of the English public (private) schools—the true elite—were almost exactly balanced by the rolls of the war dead. France lost a full million of the cream of her youth; and Germany—and Russia—how many? The numbers of dead from World War II are still too close to us to need counting; and for some years we have been preparing for World War III. No particular ideology is involved: neither capitalism nor communism nor socialism nor Nazism: the State is to blame, the structure that will not submit itself to free and peaceful transformation; the everyday habits institutionalized over the whole society, that bind men like chains and make them fearful as rabbits. The youth of these societies, having been denied a "liberal education," can only serve the State like the true slaves that they are: in the uncritical pursuit of the rewards that their elders taught them to prize; in the foreign wars where they try to show that they are worthy sons; or in violent revolution within the State itself, where they try to show that their elders are unworthy.

Why is it that *all* these ideologies cause the same catastrophe to their youth; why is it that they are not really any different from each other in this respect? Ortega answered this question, when he argued that in the modern industrial world everywhere the masses have "revolted." They are free from the old class structure, but they are not yet trained to rule their world intelligently and critically. As a result, the industrial masses in Fascist countries are swayed by demagogues; the industrial masses in Communist countries are swayed by commissars; the industrial masses in capitalist countries are swayed by the uncritical commercial ideology that controls the mass media. And democracy, after all, is the true government by oratory, as Hobbes warned, where the few sway the uncritical passions of the many. The historical problem is no longer a problem of the "right ideology" for modern man; the problem is to convert the *socially* liberated masses in every modern State into *educationally* "liberated" ones. The problem is to give them the freedom in ideas and criticism that turn them against those who tyrannically control the State, whether it be the commercial mass media, the demagogues, or the commissars. In this sense, no people on earth is today free, no matter what its ideology.

The whole bitter paradox that we are discussing has been known to many thinkers and educators. Horace Kallen showed that education has four different aims, but that three of them are subverted by the fourth. The first aim is to teach people how to labor in order to earn; the second aim is to put before each generation the wisdom accumulated through the experiences of mankind down through the ages; the third aim is "to train such persons as are competent so to evaluate both past and present as to help their less perceptive brethren toward a clearer understanding of the truth . . . *in brief,* to minister to the common need." But the fourth aim is the fatal one, which has usurped the first three; it is, as we might expect, the aim that uncritically serves the State (1949, pp. 178-79):

> This fourth job is to keep the general public quiet and tractable while it is being used for the profit and aggrandizement of whatever dominant class happens to be in control of the State. . . . The pressure brought to bear on administrators and teachers to see to it that as few people as possible oppose, or even seriously examine, the principles or lack

> of principles of the economic-industrial-financial-political powers that happen to be, is serious. . . . It is scarcely an exaggeration to say that education's chief enemy . . . is a conspiracy which demands silence about the competency of the social and political order to secure justice and thus to free men and women to attain their true end.

Bernard Iddings Bell is no less courageous and eloquent: "It is now clearly high time that we realize that academic freedom, freedom to seek after the truth, is threatened by no other source as it is by organized secular government." Only with full freedom can education become the instrument to change the world, to shape it to a new design—as Nicholas Murray Butler urged. And it is the State, says Bell, "which is the enemy of that academic freedom" (1949, pp. 190-91).

Only one correction do we propose to Kallen's indictment; it is the great new truth of the twentieth century: the revolt of the masses into power, but a power without knowledge and hence without real control. As we implied there does not need to be any dominant class in control of the State. In our time, the State reflects the automatic functioning of society, no matter what its guiding myth, no matter how many seekers after personal power. As Max Weber taught us, and Thorstein Veblen and C. Wright Mills, we can no longer look at society in the easy Marxian perspective of the "class struggle." It is too simple to be true to life, and in fact, it is not true for a large part of the world. Instead of classes struggling we have something far more difficult and huge to contend with: the nameless, faceless, silent hum of the great Leviathan of the modern age—functional bureaucracy; it gorges and disgorges efficiently to further its own forms, runs on the fuel of the narrowest questions, takes a thought only for the nearest horizon, aims to meet only the standard of its own performance—and this standard is economy and efficiency. It serves any ideology equally well, and is equally stubborn as the enemy of an ideology. In fact, the Leviathan gorges itself so well that it feeds upon its own master: as it spreads, the sharpness of its directing ideology fades and diminishes in size and importance. The ideology itself comes to subserve the function of its bureaucratic servant, and the old prediction is fulfilled—by becoming completely dependent on his efficient slave, the master is unmanned.

No classes contend in much of the modern world; no elite plays the game of war, as did the nobility at the time of Louis XIV; no individual entrepreneurs play the game of ruthless private profit, as did England and America in the nineteenth century. No one is sitting on the free energies of youth, from atop positions of power and censorship in society, as did the rulers of eighteenth-century Europe, controlling publication and education, in the interests of keeping that power. No, no one is holding back the freeing force of liberal education from above. It is coming from much deeper—from down below: It is the collective anxieties of the masses of men against all serious change in their way of life; it is man everywhere joined in dedication to the habitual way of life, with its promise of continued survival and a modicum of pleasure; it is the rule of the masses who staff the Leviathan bureaucracy. The villain, in sum, is not age-old Power in modern guise; it is Power's age-old sister—Sameness, who, if anything, is the more stubborn and certainly the more cowardly of the two. Flexibility and strength are the gifts of vision and imagination, and it is precisely these that Sameness lacks, and that Power often had. Who is to say which antagonist is the more to be feared—the one that hounded Rousseau, or the one that engulfed C. Wright Mills in carefree oblivion?

A. The Enlightenment solution to the paradox

Education versus the State, then; human energies versus the Sameness of organized society everywhere. Not quite class against class as Marx saw it, but rather man against bureaucracy as Weber showed. Or "culture" against the whole world of commercial-industrial mediocrity—as Nietzsche already preached in the nineteenth century (1924, Vol. 3, p. 95). Or back to the original voice of them all, Carlyle's and Nietzsche's Hero-Liberator of the eighteenth; the first real defier of the organized ways of man everywhere; the first scorner of the shackles in which civilization binds its young; the first preacher for the free, unencumbered, natural, instinctive unfolding of human energies—the same sermon that Nietzsche later thundered at his century, but which is really the still-mounting echo of the eighteenth. Back, that is to say, to the original champion of the revolt of youth against the ways of the elders, no matter under what sun or what government they practice their corrupting ways. Rousseau's is the real thundering revolution in human thought; in fact, we have not accommodated ourselves to it yet. A good part of the world is quite comfortable with the arch-heretic Marx—if only they had been able to embalm him, lay him beside that other world-shaker, Lenin: how neat it would all be. The revolution would be completely fetishized, and everyone could have his peek at the life-sized icons, and continue his new empty-headed life. But no one has ever really been at ease with the radical side of Rousseau, simply because his basic message is indigestible to *any* ideology. Marx and Lenin shook the world of the nineteenth and twentieth centuries because they urged a new ideology against the old class-structure; but Rousseau shakes the world of every century, because he urged the free man against *any* uncritical society.

Rousseau saw the problem with a clarity of vision that we have since lost because he saw it in its broadest possible terms. Now that we have understood what the revolt of the masses really means, we can understand too how contemporary the Enlightenment vision is: The quest is still to be fulfilled; it is a quest of man against the constraints of men, and not simply against any particular form of State. The Enlightenment thinkers were much more clear-headed about this than we, who bandy so thoughtlessly, or at best superficially, with the rivalry of ideologies. That is to say, we take this rivalry seriously. What is best—monarchy, oligarchy, republic? It does not matter much, answered the Enlightenment *philosophe*—each has its strengths and drawbacks. The important thing was not to crush the people under despotic rule; and the way to avoid this was by a balance of power that would restrain tyranny, keep one element from usurping the others. And this was much more of a complex problem than merely championing a "type" of ideology (*cf.* Hazard, 1963, pp. 179 ff.). This is another way of saying that *men* are in power over men; that man finds a way of constraining his fellows, no matter what the forms of things; that fragile form sits precariously perched over the shifting substance of human passions; that man and the State are not in an alliance that can be trusted. Today we must see how right they were, that no matter what the form, the

State works to coerce man. Then man must not oppose the State, but the unexamined beliefs of everyone in his society, said Rousseau; and education of the young must seek to promote this opposition, even if it means taking the young out of society and educating them apart.

Why is it that flexibility and broadness of vision almost invariably lead to the radical proposal? Perhaps because they are by nature intimately allied: when we see many parts of the picture and can take many different routes, we step out more confidently into the unknown. But these Enlightenment thinkers were not a race apart; true, the eighteenth century was brilliant, but the greatest genius is still a "fragile reed," as Pascal said. Rousseau himself admits to us how fallibly human he was; Voltaire can't hide his pettiness, or the limitations of his thought; nor Diderot his anxieties about social morality; Helvetius, Holbach, La Mettrie—they were not great men—Carl Becker, in fact, has cut them all down to human size—too far down to suit some contemporary scholars. What, then, gave them the broadness and radicalness that are so hard for us today to come by? One thing, I think, above all: they had a first-row seat at the beginning of the great drama of the modern age, and they saw all the participants in garish detail: Science, the Church, the State, Education, Theology, Philosophy, Technology—and the chorus: Social Morality and Social Chaos. The same cast is playing today, but the pristine plot has become hopelessly complex, and the masks are almost indistinguishable. How many modern men can even identify the players, much less follow the plot?

It was during the eighteenth century that the problem of education versus the State was most clearly etched; and the reason was that the modern secular State emerged in its full vigor during the European Enlightenment. The living alliance of Church and State was for the most part ended, and education became the orphan that the most powerful parent of the time took into custody. In the Protestant countries the rulers made education a department of the secular government; and when the Jesuits were driven from power in France, education there too became an orphan, too dangerous to allow to develop on its own. After all, when Church and State were allied, religious education was not a threat to the ruling power. What did it matter that some of the best youth were educated to renounce society and enter the monastic orders? True, monasticism was a protest against secular life, a rejection of the values that everyone held dear. But it was what we today would call an "institutionalized protest," a built-in and controlled radicalism. Monasticism served this function all through medieval times—it drained off the truly revolutionary energies of the most fervent believers and passionate men. It was, in a strict sense, the accommodation that made revolutionary Christianity "safe" for the social world; it was the institutionalization of the revolution, and hence the end of it. St. Francis wanted no great monastery built for his order—he knew what it would mean. And it was finally the terrible Münzer who showed the way to continue the Christian revolution: He wanted to make *everyone* a monk. Little wonder that the Anabaptists were ruthlessly crushed, that the State moved quickly into the void of potential anarchy awakened by the Reformation; by the time of the Enlightenment, it had completely consolidated its hold. In France it was La Chalotais who, defying the Jesuits, urged that the first thing to do was to take their schools away from them: Education should not be in the hands of people whose ideology runs counter to that of the nation as a whole (Hazard, 1963, p. 198).

So there it was: For a time education was out of alliance with the State, and had quickly to be brought back under control; the State had to move into the gap left by the Church. And when this happened, as we said, the Enlightenment *philosophes,* seated front-row at the drama, clearly recognized the contestants: education, the great, new, secular, liberating force in the service of man, was being pulled from the grasp of one tyranny and wrapped in the cloak of another. Humanity, mankind—the very star and center of the Enlightenment drama—was in danger of being pushed off into the wings. How to prevent this new despotism? The name of the tyrant was changing, and the name, as they knew, did not matter; the important thing was balance of power, how to keep one element from stifling the others. Now the question was, how to keep the State from crushing education? But there was no script for this new act of liberation; it must be written, and written quickly, plainly, and concisely—like everything else in the eighteenth century: direct and clear so that people could understand and act on the basic problems. And it was the Marquis de Condorcet who dashed off and wrote it.

Condorcet is well known as the man who summed up the whole French Enlightenment, just as Lessing, not quite fifteen years before, summed up the German with his mighty *Progressive Education of the Human Race*. Condorcet crowned the work of the *philosophes* with his great optimistic *History of the Progress of the Human Spirit* (1794); this was the unstinting declaration of faith in progress, the progressive liberation of mankind and of the human spirit, effected by reason, by the organization of science to subserve man's well-being in the new social order. Men of the second half of the twentieth century have been too much rocked by world-catastrophic wars, made timid by fears of another, made petty by narrow habits of acquisition and consumption of consumer goods; to them a faith like Condorcet's seems just that—a faith, and a naive one at that. But all faith is naive; beliefs seem preposterous only to those who do not believe; every ideal is unreal, by definition. The point is that modern man is not more "wise" than men at other times; rather, he is almost wholly without ideals; and it is this that makes men of past ages seem naive in their energetic beliefs.

Furthermore, Condorcet was far from naive: he realized that utopias have to be implemented; and in order to realize his ideals he proposed to *organize* science and education in the service of man. This is another part of the vision that modern man has lost: having abandoned ideals, he also abandons their active realization. Then, when he sees that ideals do not come about, he scoffs at them as idle dreams! Impeccable logic.

Here then, is how Condorcet rushed to the aid of the dream of the Enlightenment: continuing human liberation and progress out of the dark ages of past enslavement must be actively implemented and guaranteed by the proper organization. Let the educational establishment be self-governing; let there be a supreme body for the direction of science and learning; and let them be independent of all institutions of the State, even if the State is an equalitarian political system (Manuel, 1962, p. 84). Let there be a National Society of Arts and Sciences, with 318 members, the most distinguished minds, drawn from the four fields of knowledge taught at the *lycées:* mathematics and physical science; technological science; moral and political science; literature and the fine arts. Let the whole educational program be planned from the lower schools up to the highest; let there be continuing adult education, comprising weekly lectures on civil rights and public duties, on scientific discoveries and new knowledge as they become available. This, and this alone will prevent the citizens from becoming docile instruments in the hands of those who seek power over man. The supreme body for the direction of science and education would thus be the custodian of progress and human liberation, as well as the instruments of such progress. They would control education by preparing and appointing teachers, insure academic freedom, award scholarships to the best minds, prepare textbooks and oversee the quality of instruction—everything, in sum, that would have to be done to save future generations from falling into the prejudices of the past, or from any new prejudices that would deprive them of their freedom and human dignity. The whole thing was designed so that "no public power should have the authority nor even the influence to prevent the development of new truths or the teaching of theories contrary to its particular policies or to its momentary interests" (Condorcet, quoted in Williams, 1959, p. 299).

Here was the answer to the problem of both Church and State, then, an autonomous, self-governing community of scholars, protected from encroachments on all sides. But what about the danger from within, what about human greed and the passion for power of the scientists and educators themselves, what about autocracy from within this autonomous structure? Condorcet proposed several guarantees for this (Manuel, 1962, pp. 88 ff.), but the best guarantee was full publicity of elective lists and scientific work, to an increasingly enlightened public, so that the broadest opinion would always be called into play (Kallen, 1949, pp. 135 ff.).

Regardless of what we today may think about the fine points of Condorcet's proposal, about the unfinished nature of his sketches, about his simple understanding of scientific method, about his faith in scientific honesty, in disciplinary collaboration, in reason winning out over pettiness and meanness—regardless of what we think of these, his main aim of keeping the enterprise of education and knowledge separate from the State, no matter what its form, must still remain a superb vision. Jefferson shared it, and it was his hope to give American higher education just this character of a self-governing community of free men. But this was never to be. Even his proposal for a National University in Washington came to naught; it was against the spirit of the times. If the Enlightenment as a whole was a radical break with the past, Condorcet was even too radical for the Enlightenment. His proposals, as the brilliant historian of the Enlightenment, Frank Manuel points out, "went against the grain of the existing mores" (1962, p. 84). What? A State within a State? The idea went against the grain in the nineteenth century, too, when even those least radical of thinkers, Stuart Mill and Herbert Spencer, feared that education would become a monopoly of the State. They go against the grain in our day, too, while education flounders in the miasma of mass society, and swims with the huge and aimless tide of commercial-industrial mediocrity. The proposals were the dream of guaranteeing democracy, of effecting the full ideal of human liberation; and this seems to go against the grain of the organized State in any epoch of earthly time. No Establishment wants to live with a powerful rival, no matter how benevolent and intelligent. The best hope of the Enlightenment, the basic vision of Jefferson for the American democracy, was allowed to lapse. Little wonder that in our day Horace Kallen, in his courageous and challenging work on *The Education of Free Men,* raised a great lament over the demise of Condorcet's proposal and of Jefferson's hope: "Time, now, has vindicated Condorcet's intention . . ." (1949, p. 136).

And so we rejoin our basic argument. The failure to implement the Enlightenment program for guaranteeing the freedom of education from the State has resulted in the victory of the State. And the Enlightenment thinkers were so right not to be concerned about the particular *kind* of State that might vanquish human freedom by controlling education. Look what has happened in the freest and brightest of democracies, in the greatest experiment in government of them all, in the Constitution that is the envy of almost all other nations. Let Horace Kallen tell us in his words:

Education has become the chief vehicle for inculcation and indoctrination, "excluding the sportsman-like consideration of alternatives, and the techniques of free inquiry. It has degraded freedom into a dogma to profess instead of establishing it as a habit of deliberation and action. And it has done so because the democratic ideal of education for democracy never quite broke away from the authoritarianism which has pertained to education from its beginnings" (1949, p. 144). Having failed to do this, education succumbed to new ecclesiastical, economic, and political pressures. How many schools air really controversial public questions, are aware of the "falsehoods regarding the political economy of their home towns? Honest and fair consideration of alternatives is decried as sedition. Teaching is made the art of wearing intellectual blinkers . . ." How many pupils learn "that school administrations are dictatorships; that student self-government is a sham and a pretense; that teachers . . . are unaware of the problems of the communities . . . that *what* they teach has no relation to . . . their pupils? . . . In sum, education in [even] progressive New York State is indoctrination in a dated grammar of assent" (1949, pp. 145-46 *passim*).

Thus, concludes Kallen, the democratic experiment has been a true experiment: it has given us empirical data, proof, in sum, that the educational establishment must be autonomous, if true and living democracy is to be realized. "Realized," we say, not "guaranteed." Notice well the distinction. It underlies the whole problem of the Enlightenment, its fearless and energetic quest, and Condorcet's crowning and summing-up proposals. It underlies the German Enlightenment too, and Kant's, Herder's and Lessing's proposals on the education of man and the development of the human spirit. Democracy is not a discovery of any one country, still less the achievement of any one age, and certainly not the synonym of any particular type of political constitution. Democracy is not a fact, it is an *ideal*. This is the great message of the *Éclaircissement,* the *Aufklärung,* the Enlightenment of any country or time. Democracy is the ideal of progressive liberation of unknown and unknowable human energies—the mysterious powers of nature which reach their highest pitch and complexity in the creative human spirit. Democracy is the ideal of the progressive ennobling of man, and thereby of man in society and of life in nature. And to ennoble means to render more moral, more fine, more beautiful and worthy. Democracy, in its broadest vision, is the ideal of the progressive elevation of life in the cosmos. This is what the Enlightenment bequeathed to man and sought to assure by the proper organization of education and science. And this is what the American experiment in democracy has taught us: By accepting democracy as a fact of economy and politics, rather than as an ideal of the imagination, the American experiment has proved in its turn that no State on earth has been willing to serve as the vehicle for the education of man.

B. Substitute attempts to solve the problem, after the Enlightenment failure

Now we can understand better the true source of that discontent that plagued Emerson and the critical thinkers that followed him. It runs like a thin red line of lively discontent through all the thinkers who faced the fiasco of an educational establishment that had no autonomy: John Jay Chapman, Everett Dean Martin, A. D. Henderson, Theodore M. Greene, Kenneth Burke, Horace Kallen, Bernard Iddings Bell, and so many more. As so often happens in history, the crux of the issue is lost sight of—I mean the place that the real problem started, and just what it is all about *au fond;* as a result, the thinkers lash out without any identifiable target, and though they fight bravely there is no way of tallying the victory. So far as I know, of all the thinkers mentioned above, only Horace Kallen reported the precise historical roots of the problem. Even Emerson had already lost the thread, when he said that education had "truckled to the times"; actually, it had truckled to the State, as we saw.

It seems that during most of the past century, our American democracy has been caught in this dilemma—the dilemma of high intentions combined with a lack of clear vision. D'Alembert had called Condorcet a snow-capped volcano; inward passion under outward calm. We might borrow the image and apply it to our whole society: it conveys the unsteady blend of two contradictory

2. Ortega y Gasset's Reminder

During the same generation in which Peyton Jacob wrote his appeal, the Spanish philosopher Ortega urged the world to recall the "mission of the university." Perhaps it was poetic justice that the last great country in Europe to feel the impact of the Enlightenment should be one of the latest to remind us of it. Ortega saw that the university had to be restored to its cardinal function of "enlightenment"; that its task was that of imparting the full culture of the time, and revealing to mankind, with clarity and truthfulness, the gigantic world of today. This was a task of historic importance that the universities had failed to fulfill (1944, p. 86). The university had to reassert itself "as a major 'spiritual power,' higher than the press, standing for serenity in the midst of frenzy, for seriousness and the grasp of intellect in the face of frivolity and unashamed stupidity" (p. 99).

And we have seen why: the masses had "revolted," as Ortega himself had shown, and the world was sinking into an unprecedented mediocrity. This was the age not of culture, but of "unculture": "We are passing at present . . . through an age of terrific *un-culture.* Never perhaps has the ordinary man been so far below his times and what they demand of him" (p. 85). The task of leading the world had fallen to the lowest common denominator, for the first time in history; as a result, civilization itself was threatened as perhaps never before. "If the working man should become the governing man tomorrow, the problem remains the same: he must govern in accordance with the height of the times —otherwise his regime will be supplanted" (p. 59).

The height of the times—this is the key to whether knowledge will be worthwhile or not. To be uncultured is to fail to be at the height of the times; to be cultured is to have those "vital ideas" with which one can command his age, and its crucial problems. Behind Ortega we recognize the echo of Nietzsche and Lessing. Man needs "culture," the highest level of self-critical and social-critical knowledge; only this knowledge is truly "vital." Culture "is the system of vital ideas which each age possesses; better yet, it is the system of ideas *by* which the age lives. . . . These ideas which I have called 'vital,' meaning ideas by which an age conducts its life, are no more than the repertory of our *active* convictions as to the nature of the world and our fellow creatures, convictions as to the hierarchy of the values of things—which are more to be esteemed, and which less" (p. 81). Culture is the cultivation of excellence, then, excellence that man once had, and that he has now lost. It is as serious as life itself, because without it man is crippled in the struggle to live a truly human existence —an "authentic" existence, as Ortega would have it. The echo of Nietzsche booms again, still louder behind the urgings of the Spanish philosopher, and behind this echo, the same memory of the Enlightenment. "What we call today 'a cultured man' was called more than a century ago 'an enlightened man,' *i.e.,* a man who sees the paths of life in a clear light. Let us chase away once for all those vague notions of enlightenment and culture, which make them appear as some sort of ornamental accessory for the life of leisure. . . . Culture is an indispensable element of life, a dimension of our existence, as much a part of man as his hands" (p. 85). This, then, would be the basic function of the university. "This is what the university must be, above all else" (p. 59). As the eighteenth-century thinkers wanted to uplift public opinion, and render man more dignified and human, the twentieth century must elevate its equally dispossessed masses. It is not only a question of saving society at large, but it is now a matter of giving life itself to the individuals who compose it. "Never has the civilized world so abounded in falsified, cheated lives. Almost nobody is poised squarely upon his proper and authentic place in life . . ." (p. 85-86).

Ortega's appeal was strong and clear—perhaps the most forceful one of our time. And this was due not only to the forcefulness of his own person, but to the utter default of the university in mass society. Furthermore, we needed the strongest possible reminder that due to this default civilization itself was in danger of death, of failure to adapt to the challenge of world-wide evolutionary change. Evolution, in order to continue, needed the best that man could give; instead, he was giving nearly the worst.

But, in a world in which knowledge had grown so voluminous and complex, how would the university fulfill its mission? How could the university put its students "at the height of the times" —*all* its students, all the masses? How could the university "give everyone his hands," "show everyone the paths of life in a clear light?" How could everyone get hold of the "vital ideas" by which the age could be guided?

By a fundamental reorientation of the university itself, answers Ortega: a change in its organization, and a change in the method of imparting knowledge. Away with the complex, the ponderous, the obscure, the attempt to grasp the niceties of the whole world of knowledge; the desire to please all the professors, to offer a glimpse of everything, to meet the vast accumulations of fact at their own ponderous level. Let us instead give the student what he needs in order to meet life on his own terms; let us expose to him what he wants and can integrate in his own mind; let him be the basis and focus of the organization of knowledge; let him learn the essentials that he can use to find a path through his times; and let the university itself, finally, be controlled, directed, and ordered by the students.

Again, we see the unmistakable spirit of the Enlightenment in Ortega's vision. Knowledge is not knowledge if it "stops" man with its depth and breadth. On the contrary, man himself must stop at what is clear and certain, even if it means limiting his scope. The only thing that is important for him is what he can use for his own *active benefit* in the world. Throw the net wide, but take the measure of all things: man, and man alone, is the center of interest and value. The problem of knowledge is qualitative and pragmatic; it has nothing to do with the *amount* of knowledge available, and still less with what the retired and sequestered professors want to propagate (*cf.* Hazard, 1963, p. 272).

Thus, Ortega saw the university as a revitalized institution serving students and mass society in the encounter with life and the problems of the age. Its new principle of organization would be what he called the "principle of economy" of knowledge. "Scarcity of the capacity to learn is the cardinal principle of education. It is necessary to provide for teaching precisely in proportion as the learner is unable to learn" (p. 68). In this way, and in this way alone, would a cultural synthesis be possible; only thus could the truly vital ideas of the time be imparted; and only thus would everyone be able to pose himself "squarely upon his proper and authentic" place. The principle of the economy of knowledge, then, would have the following three indispensable components:

First, universal educational opportunity, so that the masses themselves would come into critical power. Second, individualized education; the guided self-development of students, which is the life of any good university; and in order to effect this, the students would naturally and logically direct the internal ordering of the university, determine its usages and decorum, impose discipline, and be responsible for morale (pp. 70-71).

The third and last component would be crucially important. In a university run by students, for students, where they themselves would be the measure of what was to be learned—in such a university, how would one avoid mediocrity, vocationalism, narrow professionalism? By providing a *critical body* of knowledge that would give a rational standard of social awareness. This would be the basis of culture, of the fund of vital ideas. The autonomy of this knowledge would be guaranteed by making a "Faculty of Culture" the very nucleus of the university, and of the whole higher learning (p. 86).

The synthesis of culture, in a student-run university, would be based on the principle of the economy of knowledge. A splendid vision. We can see exactly what Ortega hoped to accomplish: nothing less than the enfranchisement of the university along full Enlightenment lines. It would realize Lessing's great vision of the progressive education of humanity through the gradual unfolding of the human spirit. The university would be an independent locus of cultural criticism, guiding social change, autonomous from the mediocrity of society at large as well as from the heavy hand of parental and traditional authority. The university would be freed "from within," from within the pragmatic core of knowledge; from within the responsible energies of each generation of students; from within the central Faculty of Culture, which would formulate the guiding ideal.

3. H. G. Wells's "World Brain"

Let us consider one final substitute attempt to solve the problem of education versus the State, after the Enlightenment failure. In a strict sense, it should not be called a substitute attempt, but a real restatement of the Enlightenment vision of the organization of scientific knowledge in the service of man. It is H. G. Wells's project for a "World Brain" or World Encyclopedia. Through Wells we hear the echo of Condorcet and behind him, Diderot; the same voice of progress through science and through the organization of knowledge. The only difference is a biographical one: Condorcet, in the shadow of the guillotine, did not lose his faith in the progress of knowledge; but the aged Wells, in the rumble of war and the shadow of death, did.

"As the centuries pass the mass of books will constantly increase, and one can foresee a time when it will be almost as difficult to learn anything in a library as it would be in going directly to the universe itself." So wrote the prophetic Diderot in his article "Encyclopedia" for the great Encyclopedia of the Enlightenment. We who are today mired in the bog of disciplinary journals, books, intellectual periodicals of all kinds, monographs, notes, brief communications, minutes, special publications, abstracts, anthologies—not to mention encyclopedias—perhaps we *ought* to turn the universities and the academies back into the forests to gather and classify mushrooms and herbs. Diderot proposed to remedy the already ponderous problem in his time by publishing the Encyclopedia, reducing and arranging knowledge in a systematic way. In our time, Wells proposed an equally daring project. The new World Encyclopedia, like its prototype, would form the "mental background of every intelligent man in the world. It would be alive and growing and changing continually under revision, extension and replacement from the original thinkers in the world everywhere. Every university and research institution should be feeding it. . . . It would not be a miscellany, but a concentration, a clarification, and a synthesis. . . . Such an Encyclopedia would play the role of an undogmatic Bible to a world culture. It would do just what our scattered and disoriented intellectual organizations of today fall short of doing. It would hold the world together mentally" (1938).

But no, said Wells, the original Encyclopedia is not its prototype, nor are all the others since then that call themselves encyclopedias, but that are merely brief accounts of fragmented knowledge, hurriedly thrown together. These are not true syntheses. A truly synthetic World Brain would do something unprecedented—it would hold men's minds together in a common interpretation of reality; it would, in a word, provide the very critical standard we need in order to combat conflicting ideology. "A World Encyclopedia as I conceive it would bring together in close juxtaposition and under close critical scrutiny many apparently conflicting systems of statement. It might act not merely as an assembly of fact and statement, but as an organ of adjustment and adjudication, a clearing house of misunderstandings; it would be deliberately a synthesis, and so act as a flux and a filter for a very great quantity of human misapprehension. It would *compel* men to come to terms with one another" (p. 16). It would compel with the force of shared scientific truth, as the microscope compels the skeptical viewer.

The original Encyclopedia of Diderot and d'Alembert did have a synthetic principle. It was based firmly on man, and organized on the basis of the three faculties of the mind—Memory, Imagination, and Reason. Most encyclopedias since have had some kind of organizing principle, usually the most pragmatic one of all: the publishers' desire to make money. Wells overlooks the synthetic principle of Diderot and d'Alembert, probably because it is not adequate to the modern world, split as it is among rival ideologies and even more bloated with undigested fact. The point is that we do not enjoy the background that the eighteenth century enjoyed —the more-or-less unanimous belief in progress and reason, in science and technique, in government by balance of powers, in the possibility of the good life in a harmonious society based on reason and knowledge, in a world getting better and better, more organized, especially more peaceful and prosperous. The only ghost that troubled the serene faith of the eighteenth century was the Gothic ghost of organized religion and antiquated beliefs, of otherworldly fears and hopes. Our closet has new ghosts, and too many of them, for us to support a synthetic principle that is merely a belief in man's reason and goodness. We need a principle that actually forces man to improve, that compels him with the force of science, as Wells saw.

The World Brain, consequently, is really a modern descendant not of Diderot, but of Condorcet's world organization of science, an over-all plan for the collection and integration of data by a growing army of cooperative scientists. In this great vision, science was not limited to the promotion of technique alone; no, it would actually save mankind by putting order in the moral realm itself. There would be no separation between scientific facts and moral facts. The cool reason of the expert, the infallibility of mathematical method, the unshakable domain of reason would extend into the most difficult areas of social confusion. No more need for endless public debate; no need for the State to be run by angry parliamentarians, by unruly passions, grasping self-interest, half-baked knowledge. The scientific expert would decide everything, coolly and quickly and correctly for the benefit of all citizens. Science, armed with the hard data computed with precision by the calculus of probabilities, would decide the issues of the day, would direct political and moral decisions (Manuel, 1962, pp. 92-96).

Writing almost a century and a half later, Wells could not believe with Condorcet's uncomplicated faith in "social mathematics," in the reduction of moral data to mathematical terms. Today we realize that even if it were possible, we should not want such a reduction: when man is reduced to a quantified thing, he becomes the controlled, and not the controller. But there is no doubt that the main burden of Wells's World Brain was the same problem that plagued Condorcet's time: the problem of narrow passions and limited world views, of grasping self-interest and social confusion; the problem of men who want happiness, but who have no clear and rational idea of how to get it in the world of confused and complex reality. Science will somehow have to find a way to attack and solve the moral problem, the problem of social order in each society, and of world social order. As Wells so powerfully put it ". . . what I am saying—and saying with the utmost conviction—is this, that without a World Encyclopaedia to hold men's minds together in something like a common interpretation of reality, there is no hope whatever of anything but an accidental and transitory alleviation of any of our world troubles. As mankind is, so it will remain, until it pulls its mind together. And if it does not pull its mind together then I do not see how it can help but decline. . . . Our species may yet end its strange eventful history as just the last, the cleverest of the great apes. The great ape was clever—but not clever enough. It could escape from most things but not from its own mental confusion" (1938, pp. 24-25). With the World Brain, the common life could be directed by a real world intelligence, and misunderstandings would be readily overcome, once people could see the truth from the same compelling scientific interpretation of their problems. This would be a better investment of time and money, says Wells, than any "definite revolutionary movement, Socialism, Communism, Fascism . . . or any other of the current *isms* into which we pour ourselves and our resources so freely. None of these movements have anything like the intellectual comprehensiveness needed to construct the world anew" (p. 24).

There we have it: the full Enlightenment vision—education versus the State, no matter what the form of its ideology. Education—comprehensive, organized, superordinate over everything; only in this way will man be truly liberated to become man, only thus will he become more than the "cleverest of the great apes." In order to accomplish this, the World Brain would have to become the standard of "reorganization and reorientation of education and information throughout the world. No less" (p. 12). "It is something that must be taken up . . . seriously—by the universities. . . . It is a super university I am thinking of . . . no less. It is nothing in the nature of a supplementary enterprise. It is a completion necessary to modernize the university idea" (p. 18).

No less, indeed. If it could come about, it would accomplish nothing less than the liberation of the university from the State. It would mean the universalization of knowledge, and the synthesis of it in the service of the distinctive energies of each new generation of youth. It would mean the triumph of reason over ideology, the triumph of the university over the State! It would fulfill the Enlightenment design for all mankind, a short century and a half after the inception of the vision. It might not bring universal happiness, as the Enlightenment thought; it remained for modern man to discover fully that the conditions of earthly existence might not permit such a thing; it remained for us to inherit the full tragic vision of the meaning of life. But it would at least release the largest possible measure of creative energies that would make us fully men, men at the height of the times. For only free men at the height of the times can wrest dignity from tragedy; should man want more nobility than that? If Diderot and Condorcet could salute us over the abyss of time, their faces would undoubtedly be lined with more care than they showed in their own. But who can doubt that their strong handclasp would be a warm approval of what we are still trying to salvage of their vision?

III. RETROSPECT

CHAPTER FOUR

The Central Problem Clarified

> ". . . without the knowledge of good and evil the use and excellence of [all the sciences] will be found to have failed us."
> —Plato

Alfred North Whitehead, who gave to our century almost as many of its epigrams as William James, somewhere remarked that the "art of reasoning consists in . . . getting hold of the big ideas and of hanging on to them like grim death." From which we can conclude that when all the leading thinkers of an age are hanging on like grim death to the same ideas, then these ideas must be the big ones. And we can further conclude, from the men we have examined, that the big idea in education, since the Enlightenment, is the synthesis of knowledge. Here was the great and central problem, got hold of again and again, from one side and another, by one great mind after another. And to meet this problem, one scheme after another was proposed, each centering on the need for economy, integration, usefulness—*moral* usefulness—of all knowledge for man in society. Furthermore, we saw how clearly the leading thinkers understood the problem in both of its aspects: the organization of knowledge from within the imperative of the knowledge itself; and the role and function of the university as an autonomous institution, free of the limiting control of any ideology—Church or State. Not everyone saw the precise historical roots of the dilemma in the Enlightenment, as did, for example, Nietzsche: "Everything nowadays is directed by the fools and the knaves, the selfishness of the money-makers and the brute forces of militarism. The state in their hands . . . wishes for the same idolatry from mankind as they showed to the Church" (1924, Vol. 5, p. 138). But, like Nietzsche, they knew that the university had to be autonomous, that knowledge had to be superordinate over the narrow passions of human ambition; that if human reason would liberate man, it would have to be universal, have to rise over crowds and nations, over any self-seeking that degrades man.

Having thus seen the problem approached in its fullness, we might also expect that it would be more-or-less solved: What about Condorcet's plan for the organization of science and education as well as the plans which preceded it, and which we have not touched upon—Bacon's *New Atlantis*? Leibnitz's Academy of Sciences? The Abbé de Saint-Pierre's Academies of Political and Moral Science? What about the gropings since then—Horace Kallen, Ortega, H. G. Wells? Why hasn't the quest been fulfilled, if the solutions were found? Is it possible (perish the thought) that the idea is so "big" that we can never find a solution, that each new thinker will have to come to grips with it anew—like with the idea of the Fall?

We might well think so; the groping continues. Listen to some more voices on the same problem. Hans Zinsser (1937, p. 805):

> Our task is to find that formula for education by which a more profound synthesis may mold the new science with the older humanistic culture into a harmonious whole. . . . We must find the formula by which the fundamentals of the entire body of modern understanding can be brought to bear on minds properly prepared for the building of a culture suitable to our age.

Philipp Frank (1950, p. 271):

> The synthesis of human knowledge . . . should be the chief goal of liberal education.

Theodore M. Greene (in Beesley, 1940, p. 69):

> The culture that the university would seek, would be successful only if it could integrate and synthesize all the available empirical data.

Or, finally, Karl Jaspers, who returned to the problem after the defeat of Germany in World War II, when it was very plain that the university had still not found itself in relationship to the State, and had once again been virtually destroyed in the process (1959, p. 88):

> The reunification of the university, which stems from an awareness of the cosmos of the sciences, cannot simply mean restoring things to their medieval unity. The whole content of modern knowledge and research must be integrated; broadening the scope of the university must initiate a genuine unification of all branches of learning.

Enough testimony, surely. It is plain that either the problem has not been successfully solved, or else that it is destined to remain an eternal problem, too big for mortal man to solve. Perhaps we shall find that it is a combination of both: that even with a successful theoretical solution, no State on earth will adopt it. We shall see. For the present let us pursue the quest for a solution in theory, and on this level we can quickly discover what was wrong: all the proposals for solving the problem of the university were just that—mere proposals. Their form was superb, but they were just that: form, without content. They solved the problem by calling for a synthesis of knowledge—but only a synthesis of knowledge could solve it. The formal spirit was there, in all its compelling beauty, but it had no body.

Each of the above thinkers gives us a glimpse of what exactly was missing: Philipp Frank was still calling for the synthesis of knowledge in 1950, which means that it was still being sought, and is still being sought. Hans Zinsser wanted us to find the formula for such a synthesis, which pinpoints the problem further. And Karl Jaspers asks for a genuine unification of all branches of learning, which reveals the insufficiency of all previous formulas. Without the formula for a genuine synthesis, there could be no solution to the problem of knowledge, regardless of how apt the formal scheme was for organizing the university as an autonomous, *univers*-al institution.

How else put into practice Ortega's brilliant idea of the "principle of economy" of knowledge? Without a genuine synthesis, how would one judge where and when to "economize"? A genuine synthesis has its own central, organizing principle, appropriate to the knowledge it integrates. It stems *from* the knowledge, and at the same time controls it: controls its size and importance; filters, selects, attributes weight to the manifold data. It is a synthesis that feeds itself prodigiously, but still moves gracefully without bogging down. With such a genuine synthesis, Ortega's "principle of economy" would be easy to apply to any student. The student's capacity to learn would still be a measure and guide for what he would assimilate. But in order to prevent anarchy or triviality, the student would have to learn *essential* knowledge, even if it were at his own pace, and according to his own capacity. And only knowledge organized with a central principle can cover all the data and at the same time be flexible without losing its own weight and imperative; in a word, without becoming trivial. This is the secret of a true synthesis, and its age-old appeal and usefulness to the human mind. It allows man to take in each and every thing in the rich manifold of experience, and at the same time, when necessary, disregard everything but the bare essential that he needs in order to keep moving forward. It gives evenness of keel without sacrifice of richness—that's its strength and justification.

The same applies to Ortega's equally excellent proposal for a "Faculty of Culture" that would be the central core of the university, and that would control the quality of knowledge by defining the guiding ideal. What is the principle of excellence by which the guiding ideal is defined? What would determine which data illuminated the ideal, and which did not? In a university run by students and for students, with the aim of imparting knowledge at the height of the times, what would determine the ensemble of such knowledge? If social awareness of the highest relevance is needed, what is to be the standard for such awareness? Question after question remains unanswered, without a genuine synthesis. The same applies, of course, to H. G. Wells's World Brain. How will the super-university pull together and control the world-wide influx of diverse data that will free man, that will put him above ideology? What will be the standard inherent in the synthesis, by which arguments among rival ideologies will be settled to the satisfaction of any open-minded person? What is to be the standard of criticism that compels all? How, in sum, will the World Brain become a Brain unless it becomes an organic synthesis that can survey the manifold of experience, and yet keep its balance and sovereignty?

All the attempts to revitalize the university, from whatever quarter they have come, have floundered on this failure. No wonder Robert Hutchins looked back longingly to the Greek metaphysical synthesis and to the medieval theological one: without a central organizing principle to put order in knowledge, the university could never revive; and since no one had come up with a new principle and order, why not go back to the systems that at least had some order. Hutchins wanted to find a formula for unifying knowledge, and in this he was correctly inspired. But he did not give us *the* formula, the genuine unification that Jaspers and others called for. The genuine unification, as we saw, had to spring from the aggregate of knowledge that *we* possess, and not from the aggregate that Plato or Thomas Aquinas possessed. The New Humanism failed because it did not present *its own* integrated world view. It was a new idealism that lacked the basic strength of all the old idealisms, even that of German classical idealism, as Paul Tillich remarked (1957, pp. 192-93). And the major criticism leveled at the New Humanism and the Great Books, as we saw, was that they skirted behind the great accumulation of knowledge—especially in the social sciences—that dates from the nineteenth century, and that has continued up to this day.

Once again our attention is forcibly drawn to the staggering dimensions of the problem of the synthesis of knowledge: it dates from Aquinas! Or from the failure of Hegelian idealism, if we prefer. But how rich was St. Thomas' attempt in terms of the needs and possibilities of the times—and how poor was Hegel's by the same standard. Small wonder that he was so quickly attacked and his system dethroned in a few decades, and that he is still bitterly slandered from certain quarters today. Hans Reichenbach called it the "poor construction of a fanatic," belonging to a period of "decay of speculative philosophy," a "primitive schematization, worthy of a freshman" (1953, pp. 68, 72-73). Hardly a merited criticism to be sure; but today we know that the new fanaticism of the logical positivists also had its ax to grind; and if it could not cut the broad swath of Hegel's genius, it has at least made its sharp little jab in the cause of science. There is the problem again, you see, and has been the problem ever since Hegel: Any attempt to synthesize knowledge will have to answer to the unshakable tradition of science. And if Hegel could not effect a genuine synthesis for the nineteenth century, surely Aquinas could not do it for the twentieth. This should be wearisomely clear by now.

Yet we must remind ourselves that Aquinas and Hegel attacked a problem that far transcends the ambition of science; and if they failed by a scientific standard, they cannot be condemned wholly on the basis of this narrow standard. The logical positivists may be content to live in a scientific world, and only a scientific world—but most people also want to live in a moral world; and we know only too bitterly that so far science has hardly helped this broader ambition. The scientists have been telling us what we *can* have—which is useful and sometimes important to know. But many others have been asking for what we *need* and *want,* even if we cannot yet quite have it. The one tradition speaks with the voice of authority and proof; the other with the voice of trust and dream. Yet one without the other is not worthy of the whole man.

1. The Historical Moral Problem

What we need and have wanted, as we saw in Chapter Two, is nothing less than a solution to the problem of community, of social morality, of ordered society. This is the great abyss at the heart of modern life that opened up with the decline of the medieval cosmology and of the medieval community that it tried unsuccessfully to hold together. The problem of the synthesis of knowledge, then, is a reflection of the problem of social reconstruction. And it is precisely here that the "tragedy of history" emerges with full clarity. I mean that if we wanted the best possible social reconstruction in any given epoch, it would have to stem from a synthesis of all the best knowledge available in that epoch. That is the ideal, and the tragedy is that it has never been realized or even very closely approximated.

Let us pause on this, else we risk skimming with the lightness of words over matters of the greatest weight. We have said that the ideal would be the closest approximation of the synthesis of available knowledge to the problem of social reconstruction. The key words here are synthesis and reconstruction. The bitter fact is that they do not stand in any necessary, close relationship to one another. We could have synthesis of knowledge without social reconstruction. We could have syntheses that are not "genuine"—that is, that do not spring from all the best available knowledge, and are not united by a single unifying principle. Or, we could have social regroupings and changes of organization that are not thoroughgoing social reconstruction. When we look over the panorama of history, these are precisely what we see: partial syntheses; syntheses drawing on poor knowledge as well as the best; social regroupings unrelated to such syntheses, or loosely related to them; or, finally, total social reconstruction undertaken forcibly and placed in close relationship to a partial synthesis. But *never* have we seen a genuine synthesis of knowledge springing from all the best available knowledge of an epoch, brought gradually and peacefully into relationship with a thoroughgoing social reconstruction. This is the ideal. And this ideal—though we may choose to overlook it or to forget it—is called democracy—*experimental* democracy, Jeffersonian democracy. It is a hope of bringing a living combination of the best knowledge peacefully into line with continuing and thoroughgoing social change.

A glance at history will show how capricious and accidental has been the relationship between synthesis of knowledge and social reconstruction; how loose or forced the union that should have been an intimate and natural courtship.

Let us take an example of partial synthesis of knowledge coming into a close relationship with social regrouping, but not a rationally controlled regrouping, simply the development of history from within its own forces. The reign of the Christian cosmology at the breakup of the Roman world is one such process. It settled rather closely over the feudal medieval communities, and brought social order of a kind for at least a few centuries. Yet the Christian synthesis, as we know, was at best partial; it excluded the tradition of Aristotelian scientific naturalism. It was a synthesis that looked almost wholly to the other world, and negated this one. When the Aristotelian tradition was finally reintroduced into the medieval centers of learning from the Arabic sources which had kept it alive, it led to the breakup of the synthesis on a conceptual level.

From our present historical vantage point, the triumph of Christianity seems natural and logical, as it has seemed to other thinkers, notably the great Auguste Comte. The Hellenistic world was breaking up, and there was no room for a tradition of disinterested science. The problem was how to survive in a world that was falling apart. Where was man to turn for support, for guidance—for morality, in a word? We know that Stoicism and Cynicism could recruit only the rare, strong person; Christianity recruited the masses as well as the rulers, and even the hardiest souls. And so some kind of social order developed independently of rational design, from the very forces of history, as it were. It was a curious union: unnatural to the world, yet natural to the times; forced somewhat by tyrannical authority, yet willing; intimate in its binding of community and faith, yet loose and increasingly strained, as social and economic changes continued their forward thrust. Small wonder that it has left some of the best thinkers in each generation since with a feeling of nostalgia, as well as of gnawing dissatisfaction. It was a synthesis of one body of available knowledge, with one kind of historically possible social order. It happened to the mass of men almost independently of their own rational, creative efforts. Which is one reason, at least, why theologians consider it a gift of grace. But it is the same reason why modern man since the Enlightenment cannot accept it: he must have some share in preparing the world for such grace.

Since the decline of medieval cosmology and community, we have been less fortunate in the historical marriage of synthesis of knowledge and social possibility. We have had splendid syntheses without any effect on social reconstruction—for example, Hegel's great work. But Hegel did not really want serious social reconstruction, he trusted the forces of history. We cannot wonder, then, that the nineteenth-century social world boomed right on while German classical idealism said nothing to the times. As for Comte's great synthesis, it had a powerful effect on men's minds, especially in the New World; but Comte soon joined Hegel in the disrepute of system-builders. Herbert Spencer offered an evolutionary synthesis of all knowledge—but it had its own curious recipe: it was *not* to be brought into relationship with social reconstruction! The great Mazzini worked a lifetime to set up a united Italy for a social reconstruction along the lines of his synthetic vision—only to see the union plunge along and forget him and his ideas. Similar fates awaited other, less illustrious thinkers.

In the twentieth century, a curious reversal of the relationship of synthesis and social reconstruction occurred. Whereas the nineteenth-century syntheses had been rich and all-embracing, those of the twentieth century ran thin. But whereas social reconstruction in the nineteenth century had been small-scale, sporadic, or half-hearted, in the twentieth it became big, thoroughgoing, and violently purposeful. In the nineteenth century, syntheses were going begging for reconstructions, so to speak; in the twentieth, reconstructions were going ahead full steam, often on the merest pretext of a synthetic world view. Imagine a social reconstruction that extended its grip over a whole society and over several other societies, that coerced almost every single life under its reign—the Nazi Third Reich; imagine further that its synthesis of knowledge was based on the single organizing principle of a world divided into good Aryans and evil non-Aryans; imagine these two unequal partners (the moronic syntheses and the complete control of society) brought forcibly into the closest relationship; and then you will understand why this horrendously unnatural union had to spawn upward of twenty million deaths.

Or, again, imagine a total social reconstruction of the great expanse of land and people called Russia taking place unrelentingly over a period of several decades, with increasing vigor and pressure; imagine too that this reconstruction takes place in close alliance with a synthesis of knowledge based on the principle of historical materialism and economic determinism: imagine further that any knowledge that does not fit into these specifications is rigorously excluded from exercising influence over the social reconstruction; imagine, finally, that the aim and goal of this unequal marriage is to make an ideal society utterly different from the materialist, capitalist societies of the West; and then you will understand why this experiment had to result in the narrowest, emptiest materialism of all—the dry-as-dust bureaucrats' paradise, the apotheosis of La Mettrie's *homme-machine:* the *société-machine.*

Unfortunately, the terrors of forced and unequal marriages do not exhaust the Pandora's Box of the problem of synthesis of knowledge and social reconstruction. We may consider, finally, what may well be the most grotesque aberration of all, the alternate route to the mechanical society, empty of living persons because empty of synthetic ideals. Imagine a society that functions without any notion of synthesis of knowledge, that at most puts such an ambition far, far into the future, considering it largely a dream; imagine that in its place the society puts the single principle of consumer self-interest that will somehow coordinate all its fragmented activities; imagine further that the society is dedicatedly opposed to thoroughgoing social reconstruction, that it shrinks with loathing from any but the most partial and makeshift social changes; and then you will understand why this society has not only emptied its people of reason, vision and ideals, but is emptying the country of its natural resources and beauty, and threatening—like a huge, lumpy, and many-colored gas-filled balloon—to blow up the entire world if it will not stand still and stop rubbing the balloon's overbloated edges.

Not happy imaginings these, I grant. But lurid does not necessarily mean untrue to life—that's perhaps the unhappiest thing. If we fan the flame a bit, it is only better to light up the problem: What is the proper synthesis of knowledge for our time—the genuine one—and what is its relationship to the problem of social reconstruction? At this point, after brushing quickly over some fifteen hundred years of history, we may feel that the question is utopian. And rightly so: it is *the* utopian question of every age. The utopian sets himself the task of imagining the union of the most complete, best developed, furthest advanced knowledge possible, with the most careful, complete social reconstruction. That is why the utopias all live in our memory, vivid with each new age, even though fantastic in their details: Plato, Francis Bacon, Sir Thomas More, Campanella, Condorcet, Charles Fourier, Edward Bellamy—these are the poets of society who have offered mankind its greatest myth: the myth of the union of reason and morality.

2. The Need for a Secular Moral Creed

No harm in the utopian question then; let us step boldly forward and ask it. In fact, we need such a question if we are to get any grip on the problem of social order. One reason that social reconstruction has always come off poorly is that the utopian question was never squarely faced and widely weighed. As a result, after twenty-three hundred years of Western history, man is as far from living the great myth as ever. Another reason that social reconstruction seems inevitably to turn against man is the paucity of available knowledge on which the synthesis of knowledge is based. The Nazi synthesis could have sprung from the head of a moron—little wonder that it sabotaged so many of the wise species *Homo sapiens*. The Russian Communist synthesis has always excluded the spiritual dimension of human life; it was to be expected that it would increasingly lose any trace of self-transcending idealism. And without a spiritual dimension to give earthly life a higher meaning; without some continued goal of self-transcendence, man is undermined from within as well as without; he becomes an insular, mechanical thing, wired according to the standard program of self-seeking desires. As for the U.S.A. and other countries of the West, the effect on man must be the very same. Without synthesis and without self-transcendence, man becomes truly a pitiful thing.

Evolution, we are learning, will have its way—on a total social level as well as on an individual level. What I mean is this: If mankind does not make the best possible adaptation to the problem of living in a world of large societies, then it is not solving the problem posed by evolution. How does *Homo sapiens* solve the problems of evolution, and how has he always solved them? Why, simply by applying the best and most that he knows to the most urgent task of adaptation which evolution has set him. For several thousand years civilization has been scrambling madly ahead, without benefit of peace or durable social order and morality. During these same years, *Homo sapiens* has gradually been building up a vast fund of knowledge. In other words, we have two distinct kinds of organic growths—society and knowledge—which need to be related to each other. And the closest possible relationship will constitute the best possible natural adaptation of evolution. The utopian question, then, is the proper question for meeting the challenge of evolution: What would be the nature of the synthesis of knowledge, and its proper relationship to social reconstruction in our time?

Now we have maneuvered ourselves into a position where we can do full justice to the question. For one thing, we see better the reason why the scientists have continued to attack Hegel and his synthesis: Our unification of knowledge must be firmly based on the whole tradition of modern science, it must draw on the *full organic growth* of knowledge developed in evolution. If it draws only on parts of the body of scientific knowledge, it cannot fully serve man. In fact, it may do him a great disservice. Modern critics of German idealism learned from two world wars how dangerous it was to base national conduct on a moral system that was pre-scientific. Hitler's race theory was the final proof. Others have blamed Hegel for being the father of Marx's philosophy of history. This kind of criticism is, of course, hardly sensible. But we can understand the gravamen of their blame: Historical materialism and economic determinism have done their own great damage to the human spirit; and a large part of the reason for this damage is that these ideologies draw only partly on science, and so represent an abuse of the scientific spirit. They do not put their trust in God's design, as did Hegel—in the ineluctable unfolding of the Absolute Spirit; but Marxism has its own belief that it can read the great design of history, and that it can read it from a scientific point of view.

But Hegel, as we noted earlier, was less concerned with the narrow questions of science than he was with the deep and broad matter of social morality. And now we have also seen that the broad matter of social morality must be brought into close relationship with the best possible knowledge. And so we can draw the full circle, and answer our large and urgent question: The synthesis of knowledge for our time will have to be fully scientific and uncompromisingly secular; and yet, paradoxical as it may seem, it is this very secular synthesis of knowledge that will have to be applied to the problem of social morality and social reconstruction. For only in this way can we have a truly *rational* social reconstruction at the height of the times. In other words, for the first time in history, man is tasked to find a secular basis for social morality!

The task is prodigious. The legacy has been ours since the decline of the theological world-view of the Middle Ages. Can we ever hope to achieve it?

When we think how many centuries the problem has plagued us, we may well wonder. When we look at the list of illustrious names who gave their best to the problem, only to be tittered at by succeeding generations, we may well despair. How to know right action from wrong, without appealing to the Church or to the Bible? The eighteenth century, which did most to undermine the final remains of the theological world view, also was most confident that it had the answer. Morality was natural, not supernatural, they said, almost to a man. If man followed nature, the chaos of society would be remedied, the masses uplifted, the tyrants deposed. We would have, in a word, the most natural social reconstruction, the fullest possible happiness on earth. The thing that had always prevented this was precisely the theological world view of the Middle Ages. Not only is a secular basis for morality necessary; it is the only one possible and desirable in order to build a society worthy of man, a society that will give him fullest freedom and happiness.

First they had asked the crucial question: If human greed and passion were not blunted by fear of divine retribution, if man's incorrigible self-love were not periodically deflated by showing him how base and vile he was in God's eyes, how would ordered society be possible at all? And they had quickly found the answer. It was no problem at all; it only seemed like a problem because theological man, cowed under the yoke of fear and superstition, failed to exercise his truly divine faculty—Reason. Reason was the key to the triumph of natural morality. Men could even pursue their most selfish and peculiar interests—it would not hurt the well-being of the whole community, provided they exercised a sagacious rule of Reason. How many illustrious thinkers supported this thesis, in one form or another, in the early part of the eighteenth century. Locke and Shaftesbury, Bolingbroke, the French *philosophes,* the Germans, Italians, and Dutch.

It was a great hope, this faith in a secular morality based on Reason. But it did not last long. First, Francis Hutcheson timidly showed that morality was not based on Reason but on feeling; then David Hume took the giant step, and showed that morality was based on unreflective public opinion. That was the end of the dream of social morality based on Reason. Was something as necessary as this to be so gracefully given up by mankind almost as soon as it was proposed? What would replace the theological moral imperative, if not a rational, secular one? How would social order ever be possible? There were other natural ways to guarantee social morality, answered Kant on the one hand, and Adam Smith on the other. Man has been blessed with a moral law within him, said Kant, which guides virtuous choices independent of Reason. Man has been blessed with a faculty for sympathy for his fellow man, said Adam Smith, which is the real cement that holds society together—albeit aided by the guiding hand of God.

And so we had the German and the English solutions to the problem of a secular morality, after the debacle of the natural morality based on Reason. Let us note merely how they too met an unfortunate end. Kant, for one, had failed to tell any of his successors what exactly the moral law told man he should do. It was only a small step for Hegel to conclude that man should do his duty, and trust God and community. And so he brought the moral problem right back to where the early Enlightenment critics had attacked it, trying to place it firmly on a secular basis; the job was left to be done all over again.

As for Adam Smith, by the middle of the nineteenth century it was more than plain that human sympathy kept people together all right, but it had a strange way of turning itself off when it was a question of increasing personal profit; nor did God's hand guide this complex process—or, if it did, God seemed to care precious little for social order and morality, especially for large segments of the population of industrial England.

Now we can return from our brief resumé, and we can see that this leaves only the French tradition open in the quest for a secular basis for social morality and we already saw in the last chapter how Condorcet summed up the whole French Enlightenment in his approach to it: Morality must become the object of science; moral facts and scientific facts must be brought together, for only in this way will intelligent social reconstruction ever be possible. Condorcet's plea was carried on by that colorful and erratic genius, Henri de Saint-Simon, by another genius, Fourier, but especially by Auguste Comte. It was Comte who crowned the whole movement by proposing what everyone had wanted: a unified world view, a synthesis of knowledge that would guide social reconstruction. The single principle which animated the synthesis is the well-known "law of three stages" of the development of civilization. Now that mankind had reached the rational, scientific stage of human development, *this* synthesis would provide exactly what was needed: a scientific, secular basis for morality—"fixed principles of judgment and of conduct." This is the synthesis we have been building for so many centuries, said Comte, the one that crowns the gradual organic growth of human reason in evolution. It is in this way that "the intellectual movement and the social crisis will be brought continually into close connection with each other" (Comte, 1848, p. 3). And it is precisely this union of the most advanced secular principles of judgment and conduct, with the social crisis, that will guarantee the most natural and happiest marriage that the task of social reconstruction has ever seen.

There is nothing for us to gain here by pausing on why Comte's great synthesis proved inadequate to the problem—we will touch on it in a later chapter. But it was thrilling in its historical importance and in its promise. It even thrilled Stuart Mill, who is said to have lacked imagination. All the more reason, then, for considering it with utmost seriousness; Mill saw right away what Comte was proposing, and how great the need of it was. Here was a possibility of a truly secular basis for morality, a "reasoned creed," as the noted but now terribly neglected historian Merz called it (1914, Vol. 4, pp. 498-99, 586). It was a way of getting back to some standard of criticism, some kind of essential principles that would uplift the masses and pull English society out of its doldrums. Neither Hegel nor Adam Smith had been able to fulfill that hope.

Uplift the masses—a new climate of enlightened opinion upon which rational social reconstruction can take place; a general system of critical education: These were the visionary possibilities that Comte communicated to Mill. But wait! There is something urgently familiar in these proposals. Of course, as we said, it is the Enlightenment program for education: a critical reasoned creed that could be made the subject of instruction in the universities of the country. It is Condorcet's plan for the union of science and education, the union that would raise man above the shackles of tradition and the State; the secular, scientific world-view that would be in the ultimate service of morality and freedom. It is also the means of implementing the great vision of Condorcet's German counterpart, Lessing: the progressive education of the human race in its march toward an unknown fulfillment. Comte's voice was one of the last and strongest for the basic Enlightenment hope.

3. Conclusion

And so we have arrived at where we began, and can draw the full and final circle on our discussion. We began with the question: How was education to be revitalized as a guide for society unless we had a genuine synthesis of knowledge? And we come back to it with empty hands—but wiser. We know that all the proposals for revitalizing education are doomed to remain empty unless they are based on such a synthesis. We know too that such a synthesis has to be "genuine" in relation to our time, which means that it must be firmly based on the whole tradition of science; it must be a true, evolutionary organic growth. We know further that the purpose of this full and rich growth is to solve the social crisis of our time; to be brought into intimate practical relationship with the problem of social reconstruction. We know, finally, that the way to do this is to make the synthesis the subject of instruction in our universities—the core of a critical curriculum that would be taught to as many as possible, because only in this way can we prepare a whole climate of enlightened opinion that will move the society. Neither the intellect of a Bacon, nor the energy of a Luther can solve the social problem, nor both added together; but only twenty-four million ordinary intellects, once awakened into action. So said the illustrious Carlyle, and so it must be. Yet it must be even more, for the world has grown in the hundred-odd years since he thunderously instructed his age. A hundred million, five-hundred million, a billion ordinary intellects must liberate man. This is the really unprecedented world-historical thunder—mankind instructing itself with a genuine New View of the World.

And this brings us to the final and most important thing we have learned in ranging over the problem of synthesis. If mankind would instruct itself, it must instruct itself wisely; and to instruct wisely is to teach morality, the right and the wrong. The synthesis of knowledge has one outstanding task, namely, to provide a reasoned basis for moral action. Only in this way can the university be revitalized, by becoming the seat of a New Moral View of the World. Nothing less. This is the heart of man, the heart of education, the heart of the social problem, Morality. This is also what has been smoldering underneath all discussions of what the university should be and do; although only a few have dared to say it. John Henry Newman did, and frankly called for knowledge of the true relations of things, knowledge as philosophy, knowledge for right choice (1852). So too did William R. Harper, in 1903, while president of the University of Chicago: "An educated man is a man who . . . by the age of thirty has a moral philosophy consonant with racial experience" (quoted in Bell, 1949, pp. 57-58). In other words, a reasoned creed, based on the whole accumulation of human knowledge. Bernard Iddings Bell said it, with his accustomed forthrightness and courage (1949, pp. 228-29, *passim;* his emphasis):

> It is obviously ridiculous to try to develop growing human beings without asking what man is to aim at and why. *We might well have a moratorium on discussion of methods and organization of education until we come to some decision about the moral ends of education.* . . . In this lies the national peril; we have no agreed-upon ethical ideology; there is nothing commonly held as imperative to be promoted or defended, nothing which compels the glad devotion of lives

> and fortunes. . . . *Make moral philosophy once more the central consideration in education.*

To compel glad devotion—even of life and fortune, this is what moral philosophy does; it teaches the hierarchy of values, what to sacrifice for what. Imagine: the university teaching the right, a right so unmistakable as to be worth potentially the sacrifice of life! *These* are the "large human issues" that Peyton Jacob had called for, the ones that would galvanize the motley crew of students; the ones that would attract youth of high social purposes. How else to do it? Morality, and morality alone as the central consideration of education; it would be a means of solving all problems at once—the phlegm of the student body, as well as the chaos of society. It is as simple as that. No, not simple; rather, the most difficult suggestion of all, says Bell, difficult but yet the one most immediately required. Without moral body our universities are literally empty. They are merely forms, like the hopeful new Italian government that Mazzini had helped bring about, but that lacked his new vision; he complained that he had "galvanized a corpse"—and by the same analogy, our universities, without a New Moral View of the World, shine over the country like a bright marble graveyard. Again, the historical tragedy: What mankind urgently needs is not necessarily what it gets.

Yet perhaps never before in history has mankind needed something so badly, and found it so terribly difficult to get that something. There is no doubt about it; the whole American experience is floundering on this failure, on the failure of the university to become the locus of the New Moral View of the World. Take the one philosopher of the twentieth century who most typifies the American experience—John Dewey. Examine his whole life and thought; weigh his philosophy well in its three major aspects; consider its ambition and aim; the whole story is contained in it: unlimited promise; irresolvable difficulty; rankling failure.

In its first or historical aspect, Dewey's philosophy was a revolt against traditional philosophy, a "reconstruction" as he termed it. It called philosophy to a new task, away from the old specialized problems, from Platonic theorizing on essences, from Berkeleyan laboring of epistemology. Philosophy had to come out in the open, become applicable to life, become pragmatic. Since knowledge is relative to human perception, and since human perception subserves human action, knowledge could not be absolute; hence the quest for absolute truth could be abandoned, and man could turn to the pursuit of knowledge that actively promotes his own welfare *now,* in the everyday world of men and not, as before, in the closed, timeless world of esoteric philosophy.

In its second or internal aspect, Dewey's pragmatism was a self-consistent logical system, based on an ontology that combined Kantian epistemology and post-Darwinian naturalism—let us say Kant and Bergson. The organism was seen to be *in* nature, striving for satisfactory experience on the basis of its peculiar perceptions and appetites, as given by evolution. What man valued, then, was relative to what he found satisfying. Immediately the objection arose: Did this mean that value was relative to appetite, that there was nothing higher than bare organismic satisfactions? No, said Dewey, it could not mean that, because man was not merely a blindly appetitive animal like all the rest. And here Dewey showed his true roots in the Enlightenment: Man differs from the other animals in that he possesses the supreme faculty, Reason. This means that for him, a value can only become a true value when it is *chosen,* chosen according to criteria formulated according to the best criticism. A human value, in other words, is a value found to be desirable for man, according to the most carefully formulated ideal about what man is and should be. And it is the community of men, in free and open inquiry and exchange, who formulate the ideal values. Thus the scientific democracy is the only one really fitting for man, because it is the only one that broadly builds the highest values.

In its third or social aspect, Dewey's philosophy and his life were dedicated to the great task of social reconstruction. And how was philosophy to find its best application to this problem? By focusing on education. Education is the "supreme human interest," in which all philosophical problems, "cosmological, moral, logical, come to a head" (Dewey, in G. Adams and W. P. Montague, 1930, Vol. 2, p. 23).

How clear Dewey's philosophy was in its historical aim, how consistent in its internal coherence, how unmistakable in its social-problem focus. How clear too the reason that it failed, in all three spheres. Like all the other great visions and proposals that sprang from the breast of the Enlightenment, it was a clarion call to action, to liberation, to a new human image. And like them, it was little more than a call—it was a form that lacked content. Let us agree that thought does not float in the stars, that thinking is grounded in an animal body; let us agree too that knowing is not absolute, but that knowledge guides flesh-and-blood action; let us accept also that values are formulated by reason, according to shared ideals that aim to further the best in man. The whole thing is empty as a wish, because it contains no standard. Where do we start? How do we get from here to there? What is better—best? How do we overcome skepticism and relativism? How do we convince by compelling proof, where is the standard of excellence, even if it is only a temporary one? If philosophy focuses on education, because all problems come to a head there, what will philosophy tell education *to do*? What truths is man to pursue for the sake of man? As we said in Chapter Two, the whole cyclone that raged over pragmatism churned on this great void.

Needless to add, a philosopher of Dewey's stature—the Kant of the twentieth century, if I may make so bold—knew what the lack was. He knew what education lacked, that it was not enough to make it "progressive," that it also had to have a critical content. The easy carpers on progressive education very conveniently overlooked the whole of Dewey's vision, as Howard Nostrand has thankfully reminded us (1963).

When Dewey, late in life, lamented the aimlessness of education, he saw that it lacked precisely a frame of reference, a unified objective, and that without it, education would continue to flounder. What framework, what ideal? queried Dewey, and answered: the democratic ideal "in its human significance"—this is the frame. Alas, as Dewey saw, it was not much of a frame—or rather, it was an empty one: "I am not implying that it is so clear and definite that we can look at it as a traveler can look at a map and tell where to go from hour to hour. Rather the point I would make is that the *problem* of education in its relation to direction of social change is all one with the *problem* of finding out what democracy means in the total range of concrete applications; economic, domestic, international, religious, cultural . . . political"

(1937b, p. 238). The democratic ideal, in other words, was an empty frame that was not at all filled in, "either in society at large or in its significance for education."

Thus Dewey joined his voice to the daring few who frankly said what education needed: moral philosophy, an agreed-upon ethical ideology; it had to become "a map and tell where to go from hour to hour." And it was the same map that we have been searching for since the decline of the medieval cosmology; it was to be drawn, not on the stars, but on the secular life, on the "concrete applications" of economic, religious, political, cultural facts. It was to be a morality based on a reasoned, secular creed. But the map was not clear and definite, said Dewey cautiously. In fact, it had only one or two ideas that were crystal clear, and these were the ideas of "equality of opportunity" and "voluntary choice based on intelligence." In other words, the two ideas that we could make out on the map were based on the moral vision of the Enlightenment: the liberation of full human energies. This means the energies of as many as possible who should be given the opportunity to learn what liberation is; and it means too that really full liberation must take place on the basis of intelligent choice.

But we know, with all respect to Dewey, that the Enlightenment map was no map at all. "Not quite clear and definite" is a great understatement. We need to know precisely where to go from hour to hour. What is the good, the bad?—these are the basic questions that we have been asking with mounting anguish, especially since the eighteenth century. What exactly would we teach in the universities? What should we learn about man and society, knowledge that would show us, by clear and compelling logic, how to *act* and how to *choose* in our personal and social life? What would show us what was good for society at large, and what was bad for it? What had to be changed, and what kept? What would settle the debate between the conservatives and the radicals, the de Maistres and the Saint-Simons—the debate that has been outstanding since that time? What was the exact content of the New Moral View of the World, a content so clear and definite that it would resolve the age-old problem of the individual versus society, without sacrificing one for the other? It would have to unmask for man anything and everything that prevents the full and free growth of his responsible powers; it would have to show the origin and nature of these constraints in the *social* world; yet at the same time it would have to be cohesive for the order and morality of the society as a whole.

If we despair of the possibility of this kind of map, then we despair ultimately of the possibility not only of "liberal education," but of democracy as well, in its ideal meaning. It is on this dilemma, as we said, that the whole American experience is floundering. And as we have now seen, Dewey, the great representative figure of this experience, also floundered on it. We can understand better what that perceptive critic, Waldo Frank, meant when he voiced his reasoned judgment on Dewey's place in American life. Dewey was the youth of America, said Frank, and not its maturity; he was the path-clearer, not the mighty problem-solver and synthesizer. And now that America had laid the design of its youth, how was it to continue further? The path was cleared, but where was the steady light?

The comparison of Dewey with Kant is then very apt. Each called philosophy to less ambitious tasks; each centered it firmly on man; each wanted to solve the crisis of morality, as well as the problem of knowledge. And yet, each left the moral dilemma wide open. Kant gave his successors a "categorical imperative," an inner moral intuition that in his time had yet to be a completely blank map. Dewey gave his age pragmatism, with its terrible relativity of values. But one great difference there was in Dewey's favor. While he himself supplied no standards of conduct, he told us where to look: in the concrete world of social reality. The mistake that Hegel fashioned on Kant could not be recommitted; questions of morality could no longer be dumbly delegated to a supernatural design, working itself out through man and history, using passive man as its helpless plaything. After Dewey, the responsibility for moral conduct fell squarely on man. He had to shape his own New Moral View of the World, and he had to find the standard in the whole panorama of life's events. A reasoned creed based on secular knowledge—that was the only way to go, no doubt about it now.

Kant had been dead for only fifty-five years when Dewey was born in 1859. Dewey lived ninety-three years of what we might now call additional groping and path-clearing. And it was in the short space of this century and a half—short, as human history is reckoned—that the great achievement was realized, the standard forged for a new morality, the map filled in for the liberation of man—The New Moral View of the World, as we have been repeatedly calling it. Let us follow quickly on the heels of these great men, pass beyond where they stopped; let us step into the promised land that they could only glimpse with a tremor: Kant with the portrait of Rousseau in his study; Dewey with his quiet faith in the natural unification of thought.

PART TWO

The Solution

"The accusation brought against it [pragmatism] of childlike trust in science omits the fact that it holds that science itself is still in its babyhood. It holds that the scientific method of inquiry has not begun to reach maturity. It holds that it will achieve manhood only when its use is extended to cover all aspects of all matters of human concern. It holds that many of the remediable evils of the present time are due to the unbalanced, one-sided application of the methods of inquiry and test that constitute everything that has a right to the name 'science.' It holds that the chief present task of philosophy is with issues and problems that are due to this state of things, including the projection of liberal hypotheses as to ways in which required social change may be brought about."

—John Dewey (1946, p. 11)

I. INTRODUCTION

CHAPTER FIVE

Alienation: A Spirit in Search of Substance

> "It may be that we too shall not recognize . . . the new, the great, and the liberating . . . when it enters the world. In the meantime, let us be assiduously listening and studying . . ."
> —Jakob Burckhardt (in Loewith, 1949, pp. 27-28)

The new, the great, and the liberating—this is what the profound historian patiently sought to decipher in the jumbled writing of the finger of history. It was a pious waiting, perhaps also a palpitating one; the scholar, quietly moving among the papers of his study, reminds us of a great cat stalking his prey, not knowing from under which sheet it would appear. But Burckhardt was not the only one to wait—hadn't Leibnitz before him hoped and waited?—and Saint-Simon, Fourier, and Comte? Only, these men were not so patient, they wanted to see the new in their own lifetime; Burckhardt hoped that the twentieth century might provide the answer, that a fresh initiative of great minds might come upon the scene at that time, and deliver the coveted prize to man. The prize: liberation from the mediocrity, the vulgarity, the wars, and the waste of the new industrial age.

Now, well into the second half of the twentieth century, the quest continues. On the surface, still no success. But behold a strange new thing. Listen and you will hear a strangled cry; something is moving and giving voice; here and there, in a novel, a play, a philosophy of existence, a scientific study of work and leisure, of mental health and illness, of religion, urbanism, politics, styles of living—even of science itself—twentieth-century man is adumbrating his *idea:* alienation. Alienation in modern society.

It seems to be *the* word that characterizes our time, or better, the one that tries to come to grips fumblingly with the problem of man in our time. It seems to be the concept wherewith man is trying to lay hold of the knowledge he needs in order to free himself. "Alienation" may well be for twentieth-century man what "Liberty" was for the Enlightenment: the groping forward into new dimensions of human existence.

Yet immediately we sense something very awry. Perhaps never before has a word which seemed so apt been so empty. People cannot agree on what exactly alienation is, or what it covers; and many simply reject it. A far cry from the idea of liberty in the eighteenth century, which became a generally accepted slogan; and even if everyone had his own idea of what it meant or ought to mean, he was agreed on the fact that it pointed to *the* human problem. Not so alienation. One popular critic, for example, says (Rosenberg, 1964, p. 15):

> To identify alienation as a universal evil characteristic of this age is neither accurate nor useful. It supports an ideology of despair and a sham profundity that repudiate the present and its possibilities. In current literature it is often difficult to differentiate alienation and dyspepsia.

Yes, the word has been used to cover almost anything. In fact, those who use it say that *everyone* is alienated in one way or another; much like the Enlightenment promoters of liberty said that everyone needed it in one form or another. And surely it would have to be distinguished from dyspepsia, unless some eager adept could prove that there was absolutely more dyspepsia in our time than in any previous age—a matter on which historical statistics are sure to be silent.

Another enterprising student tried to come to grips with the concept of alienation, tried to find out what it really means, by probing into its historical origin and career. Lewis Feuer showed how the concept traveled from Calvin through Marx and the Young Hegelians, up through Erich Fromm in our time. For

Calvin it depicted, of course, man's fall into original sin and alienation from God for all time. For the nineteenth century and for modern critics, the idea describes how man is alienated under industrial forms of social organization. Here truly was an elastic notion that could do service for religionists as well as historical materialists, for romantic socialists, as well as modern psychoanalytic critics of society. And Feuer need not have begun with Calvin, he could have gone all the way back to Plato. Man was alienated in his scheme too: For Plato, "being" was less than the Good.

Feuer reminded us that Marx himself abandoned the concept that he had flirted with in his early writings. The Young Hegelian Marx changed into the historical materialist Marx, and with this change came a more rigorous point of view. The idea of alienation was no longer attractive since it was being used by many of the romantics to express all kinds of urges for freedom: personal, sentimental, even sexual. To the later Marx and Engels, hard-bent on social revolution, the idea of alienation was even embarrassing, and they hastened to forget it. Feuer traces Marx's disillusionment with the concept, to impress on us a sobermindedness and tough testing of reality that modern users of the concept seem to have lost. He sums up his argument with these words (1963, p. 143):

> Alienation lies in every direction of human experience where basic emotional desire is frustrated, every direction in which the person may be compelled by social situations to do violence to his own nature. "Alienation" is used to convey the emotional tone which accompanies any behavior in which the person is compelled to act self-destructively; that is the most general definition of alienation, and its dimensions will be as varied as human desire and need.

What good is a concept that is as varied as human desires, that calls society into question every time man is blunted and frustrated, in the myriad ways that people seek satisfaction? Too flabby this concept, too global; shall we say, even, too easy a scapegoat? And what about the more selfless uses of the concept, for example, to give back the full ethical consciousness to socialist philosophy, to turn it into a humane critique of commercial-industrial society? Feuer sympathizes with this motive, yet it will not do; there is no getting around its inadequacy for whatever the use to which it is put: the "life history of the concept . . . suggests . . . that what it says can be better said without it; human self-destructive behavior is better dealt with without this metaphor" (p. 145).

And so we seem to have given the concept a serious blow—authoritatively, objectively, with historical insight and even some compassion—at least for serious social scientists, to whom Feuer's critique is really addressed; literary people and dilettantes can continue to play with it with impunity if they like and if Rosenberg's critique in the front-page book review of *The New York Times* does not intimidate even them. Does this mean that modern man has to abandon the one plaintive cry that seemed so apt to his historical situation, the one widely shared adumbration of our times—perhaps *the* characteristic note of the age? Will it be choked-off in mid-gorge because its articulation is too imprecise, and its accusation too broad? What then? Some are urging that ideology is dead; others that the two-party system has joined it; is our age to have no distinctive tone? Or is its distinction to be that it has no tone at all?

1. The Ever-Present Eighteenth Century

Let us stop and retrace our steps, let us once more put the question to history. Where did our idea of alienation begin? Not with Calvin, since his feelings about the matter are no longer ours. Not with the young Marx, even though we share his feelings. But back to where Marx himself had his roots, back to the eighteenth century. Yes, once again the eighteenth century—and yet again. Because, you see, the eighteenth century was yesterday, and it is today. The Enlightenment is the master key to our times, the century that started the modern epoch, the one that laid its foundation, gave it its orientation, and continues to give it its cocky spirit and its indefinable restlessness. It is our century, it is *us*. Above all, it gave us, as we shall see, the very forms, the design itself, that we are still trying to fill.

A. The origins of the idea of alienation

The characteristic thing about the eighteenth century is that it revolted with near unanimity against organized religion. And so, when it came to give us the idea of alienation—though not the word itself—it had to give us a secular one, and not an otherworldly one. The stirring began, as we know, with the Renaissance and the age of discovery; Europe discovered other ways of life, other societies, peoples large and small who lived quite well, but who did not live on the European model. In fact, they sometimes seemed to have lived even better and happier than the European himself; and that in an age when the European wanted happiness above all. And so the Europeans discovered what the modern anthropologists call "cultural relativity"—the knowledge that man can be happy here on earth in any number of different kinds of society, of ways of life, of morality. And like the modern anthropologist, the Europeans used the idea of relativity of morals as an anecdotal weapon against the morals of their own society. It happened that, of all those who wrote and traveled in that frenetic age, the Baron de Lahontan presented the strongest portrait of the pure primitive, the man of nature. Right at the beginning of the century he urged his countrymen to drop the foolish notion that the primitives were savages when they were really more advanced than the corrupt Europeans. Any European in his right mind should leave the Old World and become a Huron (Hazard, 1963, pp. 365-66).

So began a debate that was to rage throughout the century: had man fallen from his high primitive estate, or hadn't he? After the middle of the century, the word civilization itself was given its modern meaning, and applied to the difference between a savage community and the modern legal State. And so the debate was clarified further, by being given more precise words and historical and institutional dimensions. It was *ferini* against *antiferini,* those who maintained that the primitives were on a level with the beasts, and those who countered with a preference for the Noble Savage. This was really an extension of the great argument that began the whole Enlightenment itself and separated it decisively from the Renaissance, the dispute between the Ancients and the Moderns: those who claimed that antiquity was the Golden Age, which set all the standards; and those who countered that modern man not only had not degenerated, but that he was even better than the Ancients had been. The century-long debate was never really settled, and—as the brilliant and regaling historian of the Enlightenment, Paul Hazard, tells us—mixed and compromise positions were taken: Helvetius wanted civilized luxury *but with* primitive customs; the Baron d'Holbach preferred civilization, but *without* luxury (1963, p. 374). The whole business was rich and thick and well confused. But we are interested in it because it was about alienation in modern society; it was about the constraints placed upon man by the state of civilization, the blunting of natural passions and appetites, the frustration of natural desires, the twisting and corrupting of basic needs. It was a quest for an answer to the problem of how exactly society causes human unhappiness. In a word, it was *our* debate, the one we are still airing and struggling to define.

B. The new orientation of science: Rousseau and Diderot

Little wonder, then, that many voices are raised in protest against the imprecision of the idea of alienation. For two hundred and fifty years a debate has raged on the flimsiest of concepts, one that reflected the most varied personal preferences, the slightest shades of difference in character, as well as the broadest. Helvetius versus d'Holbach, or Voltaire versus Rousseau. Yes, especially the latter; here were two different natures if ever there were; even Diderot, the extrovert counterpart of Rousseau, could not *"blaire"* Voltaire. And there was Rousseau, a half-century after Lahontan, still rallying around the cry of the primitive—or at least so it seemed to Voltaire, who was obviously a staunch *ferini.* He accused Rousseau of wanting everyone to go back to the primitive state, and of course would have none of it.

Alas for Voltaire, he missed Rousseau, missed the genius that was right under his nose, so to speak. Generations of scholars have seen what Rousseau was about, from the great sociologist Alfred Fouillée to the philosopher Ernst Cassirer, right up to a few lonely voices in modern anthropology. Why did Rousseau hold fast to the idea of Natural Man, the vaguest of notions lost in the obscurities of prehistory; the most contradictory kind of concept, that covered self-sacrifice as well as child-sacrifice, manliness as well as man-eating-ness; a sentimental notion that had been bandied about inconclusively for over a half-century—why stick to it in one work after another? Let Rousseau himself tell us in his own clear words:

> For it is by no means a light undertaking to distinguish properly between what is original and what is artificial in the actual nature of man, or to form a true idea of a state which no longer exists, perhaps never did exist, and probably never will exist; and of which it is, nevertheless, necessary to have true ideas, in order to form a proper judgment of our present state.

So he wrote in the preface to the *Discourse on the Origin of Inequality,* and his meaning is crystal clear. Rousseau is telling us that the idea of a Man of Nature is a most difficult one; that even he does not necessarily believe it to be true; and yet, it is a most necessary one: if the Man of Nature did not exist, we should have to invent him, for how else can we get a critical perspective on the present, how else could we *formulate an ideal*? The concept, in a word, is an ideal one, an ideal-critical one, or as we would say today in social science, an ideal-typical one. It is an imaginary projection against reality, a projection that guides man's striving, even if the ideal is never reached nor can be reached. Either man lives with ideals that guide his efforts, or he wallows uncritically in his everyday world. Take your choice, said Rousseau. We must formulate a vision of man, and strive to approximate it.

And so Rousseau took a century that was wallowing in a chaos of criticism, in anecdotes, arguments, and sentimental longings, but above all, in a blind trust in the exercise of reason coupled with inaction, in the naive belief that all man had to do was study, think, and observe in order to find the key to happiness —Rousseau took such a century and set it up on its keel. How else save the optimism that characterized the early part of the century, after the Great Lisbon Earthquake had shattered so many illusions? The century had begun with the belief that Nature was kind and good; man had only to read its laws. The world was not an evil place, as the religious purveyors of darkness and doom had taught during the medieval times; it was not a place of sin and suffering, but a place of happiness and opportunity, if man lived in it reasonably. But after Lisbon a shadow spread on this thin faith; how many reasonable people had died in this seeming caprice of a now unlawful Nature? Rousseau took an unfounded optimism and finally spelled out the forms that it needed in order to be realized. It had to become Liberty, and Liberty had to be instrumented by the proper institutions, social and political. Above all, it had to have a well-defined ideal, a model of man. Thus, like Vauvenargues (Hazard, pp. 342-43) before him, he wanted no insipid compromise; if man wanted the good life he would have to achieve it. Morality had to be a human design, since it was obviously not a natural one. Enough, then, of this prodding around with a mute and obstinate code of Nature, enough trying to decipher the divine writing. The problem is clearly one of building a new society, and of finding the best possible model for it. What was needed, in sum, was a secular map for human moral action.

In the last chapter we saw how long and anguished the search was for such a map; how much faith the Enlightenment had that it would find a secular morality based on Reason, once it had thrown off the shackles of the Middle Ages. But we saw too how quickly the faith was dispersed when Francis Hutcheson weakened it, and then Hume heaved it down. Neither Kant's nor Adam Smith's efforts availed to save the trust in a Natural Morality. We noted too, that this left only the French tradition open in the quest for a secular basis for social morality; and how Condorcet indicated the direction in which to go: moral facts would have to become the domain of science, be brought together with scientific facts, and only in this way would rational social reconstruction be possible.

We also noted, in Chapter Three, that Condorcet's understanding of scientific method was crude and global, that he imagined that mathematics could be applied to all social facts, that moral data could be reduced to mathematical terms, and that in this way the whole State would be run by social mathematics—by the calculus of probabilities. This is perhaps natural for a mathematician, which Condorcet was; and how many scientists in our own time do not believe the same thing? Condorcet's faith was carried on by Saint-Simon, and by Saint-Simon's great disciple, Comte. Comte's was the last great synthesis that emerged from this particular tradition; and we will remember noting that Comte's synthesis was not up to the problem of social reconstruction in the nineteenth century. Let us note, now, one other thing, but one very important thing, that may seem a matter of trivial like or dislike, but that is hardly so: Comte despised Rousseau.

It is not trivial because it means that Comte, who represents the tradition of Condorcet, did not understand what Rousseau was offering to this tradition. Like Voltaire, he missed the essence of Rousseau; if it fell to us to pass judgment, we would have to consider his greater distance from Rousseau; besides, there was the matter of the French Revolution, for which he held Rousseau's rhetoric largely responsible. Rousseau was offering the Science of Society something great, unprecedented—just what it needed: an ideal type of man, a model that was quite different from Condorcet's and Comte's. Theirs was physical, mathematical—which means, ultimately, capable of being reduced to atomic particulars. It was an ideal like La Mettrie's, which is no ideal at all, strictly speaking: man as machine! With this approach you gain a Science of Society only to lose the individual man. Hardly a science that man should want to use! A science of machines, in which the scientist is the Great Winder. Rousseau's ideal type was at the other pole; it was holistic, spiritual, nonreductive, descriptive, phenomenal—use any term you will to describe man taken as a total thinking, feeling, free agent.

Where was the precedent for such a scientific tradition in the Enlightenment? Right in the Enlightenment itself. It was a tradition that set itself precisely against the kind represented by La Mettrie, and by his ancestor and inspirer, Newton. And it began with the famous *Encyclopedia* and Diderot.

Diderot and Rousseau were the true partners, so to speak, in a scientific venture that is unprecedented in the history of man. Rousseau showed that morality would have to be intrumented by man, according to an ideal formulated by him; the science of man could only have meaning as *an active ideal-type science.* But

Newtonian science did not allow for such an ideal—it was quantitative, atomic, mathematical; it had laid the universe at the threshold of the Royal Academy, but it had no room for man! What to do? Bring man back into the Newtonian universe, said Diderot; make him the center; push Newton into the background; humanity is first, science is second; make science the slave, not man. What about infinity? Not interesting, said Diderot. What about mathematics, the queen? A blight, answered Diderot—who was no mean mathematician himself; mathematics is arrogant, it falsifies—it does not give perceptible *quality*. But what about mathematical physics, the great achievement of the age? "Speak more softly," urged the *Encyclopedia,* "if the coal carriers hear you, you'll make them laugh." Existence is the thing—Man—the mass of men—Humanity; human music, not the music of the spheres, that's what interests man, the man of flesh and blood. Quality is the thing—what men see and feel—not the abstractions that they spin out of their heads. Use, that's the criterion; knowledge should be controlled by what man needs and wants; it should not be a matter of idle contemplation of infinite nature. Away with Newton and his imprisonment of the human spirit; let us have a science in the service of man; let us have humanistic science, in which central place is given to man and to the interpretation of himself. This is the spirit of our age, this is what the eighteenth century should declare to itself and to posterity. And so, Newton's great laws, that had swept all of Europe and had begun the century, were dethroned. The judgment: morally unedifying.

So spoke Diderot and the *Encyclopedia,* as Charles Coulston Gillispie has so well and urgently reminded us (1959). This is the authentic voice of the Enlightenment speaking to our time. If the eighteenth century discovered the idea of alienation, they also formulated the complete program for overcoming it: the instrumentation of an ideal by a humanistic, qualitative science, centered on man. Rousseau and Diderot left to us the integral framework for human liberation. They gave us a model of science that was truly worthy of man; its goal would be the fullest possible realization of free creative human energies; man would transform himself and the world at the same time, by placing it completely in *his* service. A subjective, value science, in a word; and not an objective, neutral science! Who could have imagined such a thing, except the most brilliant minds in an age of brilliance? What is the measure of genius, after all, if not the giving to mankind of the greatest gifts? And what are the greatest gifts for mankind, if not those that point the way to the maximum liberation of human creative energies in the service not only of the living, but of generations yet unborn?

Ah yes, but so many generations have since been born, and our age is echoing the cry of alienation almost as strongly as the eighteenth century. What happened to the breathless vision of Enlightenment science, that it is not quickening the breath of our scientists today? What happened to its great reverberation in Lessing, Goethe, Fichte, and the *Wissenschaft* ideal of early German idealist thought? What happened to Saint-Simon's attempt to revive Diderot's vision of a science of man after the French Revolution, and after he too became disillusioned with the mathematical scientists, "those sorry calculators ensconced behind their rampart of X and Z" (Manuel, 1956, p. 137). Why have we allowed Science to be spelled with a capital "S"; allowed quantities and things to get the ascendancy over man; allowed the sheer accumulation of data to block out our human vistas; allowed ourselves, in sum, to continue to wallow without direction or vision—when we already had the eighteenth century, "our" century, well set up on its keel?

C. The eternal paradox of Enlightenment science

We cannot stop here to give an adequate answer, even if we knew it in all its richness and complexity; we will get some large glimpses of it in the next chapter. It has to do with the fact that Newtonianism was a tougher nut than Diderot, Rousseau, and Saint-Simon could crack—even with the great Goethe's stubborn attack thrown into the bargain. The mathematical physicists won out, and the giants of the French and German Enlightenment died, as even giants must. In their place came the abstract professors, the "cobweb spinning flea-crackers" as Engels called them. But above all, the laboratory scientists, the careful workers, the men who make Science, but who—for the most part—lost the vision of science. No, we could surely not do without these generations of conscientious and dedicated workers; we are not implying that; but urging merely that the men whose vision could control them had no voice. Then came Darwin and Spencer who repeated Newton's feat; they again locked man into the background of Nature. When Charles Sanders Peirce and William James revived Diderot's pragmatic, man-based philosophy of science, the hope was reborn with a burst. But neither James's eloquent voice and commanding presence, nor Dewey's long life span, could assure a victory on behalf of the Enlightenment. We saw one of the basic and crucial reasons why: pragmatism contained no moral criteria by means of which a man-based value science could be instrumented. Now let us turn to the other basic reason, which is the paradox at the very heart of Enlightenment science itself.

The clue to the paradox is Marx's abandonment of the concept of alienation. We saw how he turned away from this youthful notion—it seemed too romantic, sentimental, unreal to the social problem. But why abandon a basic protest against society, a protest that had been outstanding since Rousseau? If anyone was rooted in the eighteenth century, it was Marx; didn't he appreciate Rousseau's heartfelt protest against his times, his basic moral sense which kept him in unrelenting revolt against the powers that be (1865, p. 202)? The answer is that Marx did not abandon the protest; he merely shifted the ground: from the ideal to the *possible*. Leave the dreamings of the romantics, the religionists, the philosophers; let us do what has to be done, what *can* be done in our time, said Marx. The social-historical situation calls for the overthrow of the capitalist system; it is characterized by the class struggle; so be it then. Let us have the victory of the proletariat. The Enlightenment question was not dropped; it was refined, and brought up to date: "What are the main problems of modern society; how can man's situation in the world be improved?" The class struggle was simply the most direct and forceful answer to the problem of alienation that the nineteenth century could give. Diderot's standard for knowledge was invoked: Is it useful, morally relevant, to the mass of men? And just as Newton's impersonal infinite space was morally unedifying to

Diderot, alienation and its personal, finite space was morally unedifying to Marx. The social problem was the thing.

Ah, the limpid simplicity of the pragmatic standard! But see what it hides—or, better, what it feeds on: the ideal! It devours the broader vision, uses it as fuel to the needs of the moment, uses even the thinker himself. Didn't the French Revolution consume Rousseau in the fire of its excess? So much so that future generations could no longer recognize him, dismissed him as a wild romantic, a sentimentalist, even a kind of demonic monster. As we saw in Chapter Two, when Irving Babbitt wanted a New Humanist movement in education, Rousseau (the supreme humanist) was the principal culprit! And what did the class struggle do to Marx, if not make him out a narrow and petulant tyrant; drain him dry all the better to embalm his disciple Lenin? The Russian Revolution was no less greedy than the French. In each case the Enlightenment ideal, the continuing protest against the shackles in which society holds man, the vision of full liberation for human energies—this ideal was swallowed up in revolution. If action is called for, if pragmatism is the standard, this is the result. The only *immediate* thing to do with Rousseau's ideas on Liberty and the problem of inequality was to have a revolution; likewise with Marx's ideas on alienation.

And there is the paradox of Enlightenment science. What is a scientific theory, after all, if not an agreement by many people that the thing is so? And when enough of them disagree, a new theory becomes necessary. A theory is a map for action—or at least for observation; when enough of the people who act or observe accept the theory, why, then it is a scientific theory. At least if the people who agree call themselves scientists. If those who agree are merely a crowd of people who want to cross the street at the light, then the theory that the light is green is not a scientific one in a strict sense; it is merely a tacit convention. But the price of experiment has to be paid all the same: if the whole crowd is color-blind and is run down by a bus, we can call their tacit convention wrong. The thing that makes a scientific convention different from an everyday one, is not "higher wisdom," or even greater intelligence. It is more careful control, calculation, better instrumentation, and usually greater willingness to be proven wrong. This view of science is, of course, the pragmatic, Deweyan one. But it dates from our friend Diderot. Science is based on human perception, and human perception is considered "true" to the extent that there is common agreement about it. Thomas Kuhn has recently very brilliantly reminded us of how this has been the case in the whole history of modern science, all through the various sciences.

Our point here is that it is also true in the would-be science of man. It is even especially true in the science of man; in fact, this is the largest reason why we have no such science at present, properly speaking. How can you get people to agree about people? How can you get society to agree about society? Even worse. It is hard enough to get agreement about data in an objective, neutral science. How do you get agreement about data in a subjective, value science—such as Diderot and Rousseau together envisaged? The question is overpowering in its difficulty: How do you get people to agree about instrumenting changes in their own lives? The whole matter of individual perceptions is complex enough, when all we do is ask people to look through a microscope at an objective *thing* on a slide. What if the microscope is turned back around on man himself, as a member of society? What baggage we all carry from past habits and beliefs—like a pyramid sitting on each one's brain, as Marx so aptly remarked. Each person is a rich mass of deeply ingrained prejudice; each society is a complex web of personal interests, hopes, and fears. Where could we get a theory of man that is compelling enough to draw wide agreement among men? Where could we get a theory of society that would enlist the whole society in the task of social action? The paradox of Enlightenment science is that we need to get agreement on a theory of man in society before we can begin to change the society; but at the same time, we never seem to have enough shared or compelling knowledge to get such agreement. As a result, we do not act as a whole social group on the problem of social reconstruction because we have no shared theory to guide the process. The only time we do act as a whole group on the problem of massive social change is with the ideology of revolution. Rousseau's views guided the masses during the French Revolution, *against* the aristocracy. Marx's guided the proletariat against the capitalist class. In other words, you had agreement on an *ideology* by a broad number of people who wanted to act on it; but you did not have unanimous agreement on a scientific theory.

It is obvious that the difference between an ideology and a scientific theory is not absolute: the scientific theory rarely compels the agreement of the whole scientific community. And look how scientists react against new and unusual theories! In general, we can say that people are even less objective about an ideology, less disinterested and cool, less willing to put it to the test and abandon it. It draws on human hopes, fears, passions, to a much greater extent than science, which is why it is more proper to a revolution than a scientific theory could be. But in one very important way, ideology and scientific theory are *entirely different* when it comes to the problem of social change. This is the difference that Auguste Comte taught us: ideological revolutions are bad for social-science theory because they wipe out the accumulation of traditional views; they want to start over again from scratch—and science, no matter how revolutionary its theories might be, is largely cumulative of past wisdom. Ideology is like violent religious conversion; it is a blanket replacement of world views. Science is like religious growth: it is a cumulative maturing.

The Enlightenment paradox, then, is this: It discovered the problem of alienation, the problem of social constraint on human freedom; but, in order to get agreement by society at large on the problem of social reconstruction, one would have to have a compelling theory of how society *causes* alienation. One would want a cumulative body of knowledge that enlists the support of all men of good will; and not simply a striking ideology that awakens the frustrations and passions of large groups of dispossessed people. Now we can better understand Rousseau's tragic situation. He proposed an ideal type of man who would be used as a model to guide massive social change; but he proposed this ideal at a time when very little knowledge was available about human nature. He himself attempted to fill it in with the revolutionary new views of the Enlightenment: the relativity of customs and morals; the attack against original sin and the degrading view of man; the primary responsibility of society for human ills. He showed that man was basically neutral; that he was formed by the influences of his early child training, and had no inborn evil qualities; he showed that aggression was learned in childhood, that even when it was spontaneous it was not of evil intent. His great work *Émile* (1762) reads today like a post-Freudian textbook of psychological theory; in fact, in parts it contains the most advanced intuitions on the origins of schizophrenic psychopathology. Yes, but there is the word—"intuitions." At Rousseau's time, this kind of knowledge was mostly intuition, insight, genius, but hardly a scientific theory of man's nature, shared by a body of responsible students of man. It was more ideology than science, and personal ideology at that; how many of the *philosophes* shared it? His ideal type of man, then, had to remain a form, a model without body or content. Even Voltaire, as we noted, was not compelled by it. A tragic position for a scientist to be in, alone, like Vico, with a new vision of the science of man; condemned to die before mankind could even understand it, let alone use it. At least the aged Vico received the Pope's blessing as a worthy son of Naples; Rousseau was nowhere acknowledged as a son. He skipped around Europe on the run, much like his descendant Marx was later to do, and—needless to add—for much the same reason.

But in one very important way Rousseau differed from Marx. And if we do not understand it, we miss the heart of the problem of social theory. It all boils down to this: that Rousseau laid down a design for social theory that had the ideal type as its center and guide. The ideal would instrument progress in a free society. There it was, once and for all, the only possible model for human betterment; knowledge about man would be used as a guide and critique for the progress of society; the ideal type and the social forms would always be in tension with one another, the ideal always "drawing up" the rear—the habit-incrusted social institutions. Change would be continuous, both in the ideal and in the institutions. Rousseau's ideal type, as he well knew, was merely a sketch and a hope, it was a program for science; and in the nearly two hundred years since he wrote, we have still not filled it in to the satisfaction of a large group of people.

Contrast this vision of social science with Marx's. For Marx the problem was to *get* the free society, the abolition of the class-structure. Once you got this, you would have freedom and progress "automatically," so to speak. Once the proletariat was victorious, forms of coercion would wither away, and the millennium would be realized. In other words, the ideal would somehow realize itself as a function of the new social institutions. We know why Marx slighted the guiding ideal: He was a "hard-headed" activist who wanted to see the necessary changes brought about. The whole matter of abstract ideals smacked too much of the vicious side of Hegel. Ideas are a reflection of social institutions, said Marx, social institutions do not shape themselves to ideas. The stuff of history and social process is material and not spiritual or ideal. In thus lashing out against Hegel's Absolute Spirit, Marx pushed the problem of a guiding ideal into the very background of social theory. What could be the result of this, except *the victory of expediency over the controlling vision*? And unless man has a vision to hold off and against man-made events, the inevitable must happen: He himself gets caught up and pushed into the background of the events. If the stuff of history and social progress is material and not spiritual, all the more reason to offset it by an active ideal; otherwise man himself becomes a material object of history and social process. We have seen just this happen in the Marxist societies of our time. First they eliminated their own idealists in order better to adapt to the expedient possibilities of the day; then they built a huge materialist social structure that swallowed up man. Now they compete with capitalist societies on a basis of "equality": Which of the two "equals" can more quickly and thoroughly make man a material object of history and social process?

Of course Marx could not foresee all this, nor could he be expected to. Every thinker lives within the limitation of his historical epoch and its opportunity. In the nineteenth century, the class struggle was a fact of life; it seemed destined to control history. Furthermore, there was hardly any reason to fear for lack of guiding ideals; the problem was, rather, that there were too many ideals, too many dreamers. Even if ninety per cent of them died off, there would still be plenty of humanitarian ideals on the market. Besides, the French Revolution was fresh in memory; the century was a turmoil of agitation for social justice, equality, solidarity. Who could ever have dreamed that the dust would settle so still, that commercial-industrial society would so effectively brainwash its citizens into living uncritically with its forms? No one could have foreseen how necessary it was to keep ideals to the fore; that human liberation was a continuing problem that might itself be forgotten, or cleverly covered over. The techniques of enslavement are being refined, said Gorky. It was the perfect epigram for our time.

Yet, history has the last word, and it delights in the unexpected. Today the problem of the class struggle emerges again. The individual commercial-industrial countries may have succeeded in "reeducating" their population; the parliamentary vote and the consumer product may have effectively wiped away the notion of bitter class struggle. But behold, the world as a whole has not had this reeducation! The class struggle has become international. The haves and the have-nots may not be facing each other menacingly in any particular country—but they are facing each other *between* countries. The commercial-industrial corporations of New York, Paris, London and Zurich create their slums in São Paulo, Delhi, Caracas, Bogota, Lima, Johannesburg. And so when the Chinese Communists talk about the "Asiatics" against the Westerners, they are talking about the new international class struggle that seems to be breaking down roughly on racial-geographic lines. The Marxist countries of Europe, you see, having cut away the ideal type of Rousseau, have become comfortably material in the camp of the "haves." The twenty-first century will have to tell us where it is all going to end, since we have been given the historical role of passing on to them the problem of the nineteenth. Without an ideal to guide our vision we must do as Marx and let the material forces of history play themselves out.

2. Conclusion

And so we conclude our restless probing of history. Where has it led us? We went in search of the origins of the idea of alienation in modern society, and lo! we found the stillborn forms of the science of man. There in the Enlightenment, dusted over by two centuries of neglect, lay the passionate intuitions of Diderot and Rousseau on the shape of the science of man. There was the first great protest against Newtonianism, the reorientation of science on man, the shift from objective, neutral science to subjective, value science; the change from a science that casually satisfies human curiosity to a science that actively implements human well-being; from a mode of inquiry whose gifts are accidental, to a mode whose gifts are planned and intentional; from a science that is directed toward nature, without a vision of man, to a science based on an ideal of man, and directed to its fulfillment. It is as Goethe said, life answers our wishes—but always unexpectedly, so as to give something more.

Instead of an agreed concept of alienation, we got a new vision of science, and with it, a new paradox. An ideal type science, in order to function, must command allegiance to its ideal—it must compel agreement; just as in any scientific theory, workers must agree that the theory is a proper guide for their efforts, even though all the facts are never in. But in an ideal type science based on man, this simple situation becomes an almost insurmountable hurdle: How can we get agreement on unfinished data, when the data refer to changing society and man himself? When man is the subject matter of his science, he is reluctant to act on any but the most supremely compelling theory.

So the critics of the concept of alienation were right after all, when they told us that the concept was not useful, because too vague and general. It was not compelling enough to either the eighteenth or the nineteenth centuries, since neither could set up a science modeled on it.

But they were wrong to imagine that we can do without this concept. It is the perfect concept, the only concept for a science of man in the Enlightenment vision. It holds up to man the bind in which the forms of society imprison his free human energies; it is the only concept fitting to guide liberating social change; the only concept that guards social reconstruction from falling into expediency, from losing man once again and ever again in new social forms. It is the guardian of sacred subjectivity in a mechanical, objective world.

And so history answers our question, but she does not really fulfill our wishes. Instead of a single problem, she gives us now two. The continuing problem of filling in the concept of alienation with a compelling vision of man, a vision based on hard empirical data; for only thus can we get agreement on the concept. And, secondly, the enormous and new problem of reorienting our understanding of the entire enterprise of science. We must accept the idea that the science of man is fundamentally a subjective, value science, that will be used to guide social reconstruction in the service of man. We must accept, in sum, to plunge boldly and completely into post-Newtonian science. The Enlightenment tried it and failed, right at the beginning of the craze of objective Newtonian science. After two centuries of this craze, will the task be easier or harder? This is the question that is posed to our times; and even if we disdain to answer, we will answer it with our refusal to answer.

Where could we start, if we were willing to take this bold plunge? Right with the concept of alienation itself. It would lead to immense clarification and saving of labor and energy. Look at how the research of sociologists is caught in the bind of an ideal concept based on empirical data! We must be objective, they say—and rightly so. Yet we must also be subjective if we are talking about alienation, since it is an ideal concept which refers to the liberation of human energies. It is both subjective and objective, the typical concept of a man-based, value science. We must agree that alienation is a value problem which states and sums up the fact that things should be better than they are. It answers the question "How can man's situation in the world be improved?" And it answers it by seeking out objective, empirical data that conform to human wishes. Half-objective data, if you will; and there is nothing alarming about that, since our understanding of all science is post-Kantian and Deweyan. As we said earlier, in this view, all "fact is two-faced"; in Dewey's words, "it is cosmos examined by a speck of cosmos." In other sciences, this understanding is implicit and hidden, but it operates nonetheless. In the science of man based on the concept of alienation, this understanding would be frank and explicit. We would posit an ideal type model of man, and propose the kind of changes we need to help further this ideal; and then we would gather empirical data and measure them against the ideal. In this way the basic, value nature of our science would be central at all times.

What does "alienation" mean, after all? It is from the Latin *alienus,* from *alius,* or "another." *Webster's International Dictionary* tells us that this connotes "strange, different, incongruous, owing different allegiance," "properly, therefore, belonging to another." "Not of our type," in other words; a judgmental norm based on the *idea* we have of ourselves; but also, based partly on empirical data of what we observe ourselves and the other to be like. Our agreement on both ends of this pole is partly subjective and partly objective: The judgment of "our type," and "not belonging," is a mixture of both. Since this is the case, we would have always to get agreement, in our science, both on *what we want to promote* and on the supporting objective data that we gather.

Now one of the reasons that our best professional work on alienation "slips by" this problem without making itself explicit is simply this: The type of alienation which it studies is something that we tacitly and implicitly agree is humanly undesirable.

Take, for example, Melvin Seeman's studies on powerlessness, or Ephraim Mizruchi's studies on the failure to realize coveted goals. In both types of work, the implicit agreement is the same: To be powerless, or to fail, is humanly undesirable. Mizruchi, in one of his studies, urges that the fundamental question is "one of assessing the American Dream" (1964, p. 266), because it takes such a heavy toll in people who cannot make the dream come true in their own lives. This is something we could get broad and general agreement on; a heavy toll of human unhappiness is not what we want. But see what has happened in these kinds of studies. The ideal type has not been made explicit, and no agreement on it has been sought; instead, the whole burden of winning support for the ideal falls on the empirical data themselves. In other words, a new vision of the science of man tries to rely wholly on objective inquiry, the only kind that is thought to be respectable on the old model of science.

Now we can understand more exactly why the critics of the

concept of alienation have been having such rich sport with it. It is "not accurate," difficult to differentiate from "dyspepsia," "it supports an ideology of despair and a sham profundity," "it lies in every direction of human experience," "its dimensions will be as varied as human desire and need," "what it says can be better said without it." We heard these complaints at the beginning of our discussion, and now we can see the deeper problem they reflect, what they really mean. Here is a new scientific concept on the Enlightenment model that is trying to substantiate itself wholly on the Newtonian model of science. It must, as we said, rely for its support on objective empirical data, but that is only half the story. The other half is the need to seek agreement on whether we want to promote the ideal in the first place. The critics have sensed that the concept is a frank movement in the direction of desires and critical values. But they also see that it tries to support itself with empirical data; it tries to find its justification wholly in the old scientific camp. What else can this stirring and tacking convey, except "sham profundity"? The goal is the thing, the human goal, the choice upon which all agree beforehand. The rest is just commentary, anecdote. Is "failure" a "heavy toll" compared to the many who succeed? What about "relative success"? What about situations in which powerlessness is a life-preserving adaptation, in which it is actually desirable? What about crisis situations, in which all agree that they should be powerless, and should follow a leader? What about situations in which life has to be actively sacrificed in order to protect coveted ideals? The questions are endless, and the researchers themselves are now anxiously asking them. "What is wrong with the studies? It *seems* as though what they are saying is good and true and valuable; but the critics are right too—it is all so vague and difficult to be empirically exact. What to do?"

Well, on the traditional model of science, when in doubt, redouble efforts to be exact. "Classify more rigorously; check the data more carefully; look closer, ever more closer. This is how we will silence the critics, by presenting them with rigorously controlled data and sharply clarified concepts." Obviously this is much ado about nothing, because it leaves the value half of the concept untouched. Look what happened in anthropology:

The early students of "race" bent themselves feverishly to "classify" the human types and subtypes. Every minute particular of the human anatomy and physiognomy was fair game for the most precise classification—blood type, hair type, skin pigmentation, body form, face form, foot form and what not. And what happened? Today we find ourselves deciding that even if the race concept had any validity—which we largely doubt—we should not be concerned with it: It is not *humanly* relevant! It has nothing to do with the kind of world we should seek to build for man. The parallel to the concept of alienation needs no stressing. The most rigorous classifications would go exactly the same way, as soon as we decided on goals that effaced them. Take the extreme case, just for purposes of example: Suppose we were to have a mass religious revival, and decided, like Calvin, that life *in any form* was alienated from God? Our most minute classifications would fade like beach sand under a huge wave. The human purpose is the thing, and purpose in science, like purpose in life, is a gobbler of fine distinctions, when they are not relevant to human desires. Rousseau once complained that he did not like to travel on horseback because he could not see the foliage and the wildlife close up; he missed the intricate world of nature in the blur of rapid movement. And so with science, its theories and concepts, the tacit or explicit agreement it gets on the goals that it will further. The scientist can be on horseback or on foot, depending on whether he wants to get to a destination with any urgency. And if he is on horseback, he cannot stop to classify flowers. In sum, there is no escaping the value nature of the concept of alienation, and the need to get prior agreement on the image of man that social scientists want to further. Of course, we can still do research on "goals posited," versus "cost of goals," and so on, tally up the cost and deposit the evidence in the fund of scientific knowledge about man. This is good objective science on the traditional model. But we cannot call it research on "alienation," since this word has at all times a direct value reference to *what we want* to promote.

We are pausing on the many aspects of the problem, because our task here is most serious and urgent. We are trying to rehabilitate the basic vision of Enlightenment science; and the most direct way of doing this is to rescue from iniquity the major concept on which it depends. And in order to do this, we have to understand thoroughly the many-sided problem of the concept of alienation. Let us take one final example from present theory and research; in a sense it is the most interesting because it goes back to Marx's earliest writings on the concept; it therefore pulls together most strikingly all the various threads we have been tracing here. Our latest theoretical work on the nature of mental illness, specifically schizophrenia, can be stated in language that closely resembles Hegel's speculations in the *Phenomenology of the Spirit.* Now, Marx took these speculations, phrased them in completely naturalistic terms, and in this way presented a theoretical picture of human self-estrangement. The picture is remarkably the same as the one we get from our most comprehensive theoretical work on schizophrenia. Only, this latter work is based on over one hundred years of close clinical and autobiographical study of the schizophrenic process. Marx's sketches, then, were not very convincing—in fact, they were not convincing at all, and remained unpublished for nearly a century. Today we have a picture of mental illness that makes Marx's sketches seem very convincing indeed; so, we can say that after a century and a quarter, we have succeeded in empirically substantiating the earliest writings of Marx on alienation—the very ones he himself grew away from because nothing could be done with them (see Becker, 1964b).

Now what does this mean? Does it mean that we have tied a century and a quarter of work back to its origins, and that we thereby have an *objective proof* of the reality of alienation? It seems so, because of several things: the weight of the long timespan of groping; the cogency of Marx's early theoretical insights into what we now recognize as schizophrenia; the solidity of a long tradition of research and theory in mental illness; and not least, the prestige of the psychiatric-medical profession itself, in a nation which values personal health above everything else. Have we substantiated alienation as an *empirical* problem, free of subjective valuations? No sooner put this way, than the question is answered. There can be no such thing when we use the concept of alienation. It must always be considered in reference to human desires and aims. If the theory of mental illness "seems" objective, it is only because of the several things we just listed, and because of something we noted earlier: that alienation can be agreed upon *implicitly,* when people agree that what it pictures is humanly undesirable. And human breakdown in mental illness is clearly an undesirable thing. It is perhaps the most compelling demonstration of what alienation is, and for this reason seems to be the most "objective." But we know very well that this again depends on our goals—the ever-present goals that we must decide on. Can we consider mental illness an evil in itself, if, for the price of a small drain-off of people yearly in our hospitals and clinics, most of the rest of the population are allowed to carry on in the traditional ways? What if this cost is not considered too great to pay, so long as the forms of our society can remain unchanged? Suppose that our country were to undertake a great new world-rehabilitation effort that might initially cause even more strain and mental illness? Would we condemn such a high and noble calling just for this reason? What about mental illness and its rampages during a self-protective war, and so on? Again the endless questions of value.

And again and finally our point is made, as we make contact with the historical origins. To Marx himself there was no question of a completely objective concept of alienation free of human valuations. The problem was to get a compelling concept that would serve as a rallying point for urgent social reconstruction. Marx stood right at the outer edge of the eighteenth century, and drew inspiration from Rousseau. The science of the Enlightenment had no intention of "slipping by" the respectable canons of Newtonian science. This is an ingenious tacking attempted by harassed moderns who have been under the constraints of the Newtonian victory for too long, but who have not been able to get clear about it. We lost sight of what we now might well call the "Great Historical Usurpation" of science. It is high time to rejoin our own authentic tradition, and find our roots firmly in the eighteenth century. This means that not only will we adopt a new orientation for social science, but it means especially that we will opt openly for man, and for the promotion of human values. The two are inseparable, as the eighteenth century knew, and as the nineteenth gradually forgot. Promote human freedom and the fullest possible development of human energies and talent. This is the Enlightenment legacy.

And this also draws the full circle on our discussion, and brings us back to our initial point. Push as we may, the stone keeps rolling back. Find the origins of the secular idea of alienation; rediscover the Enlightenment vision of science; opt fully and wholeheartedly for Man above incrusted forms of science and society. It is all preparatory work; we are merely fencing off the area, prior to the truly great task of excavation. The anguished question remains: How can we get agreement on what to promote—how *do* we promote "human values"? After two centuries, alienation is still a spirit in search of substance, a dream of liberation, of intelligent social reconstruction, of ordered society and natural morality—but only a spirit. It is like the optimism that characterized the early eighteenth century. What to do with it, beautiful and treacherous as it was? It had to be turned into Liberty; and Liberty, in its turn, had to find the proper social forms for its instrumentation. Alienation has to follow the same career: It has to be converted into a broad picture of human failure; we must see exactly how society holds human energies in its shackles; we must have as compelling a picture as possible, in order to begin the agreed social reconstruction. We need, in a word, The New Moral View of the World. Ah, that evasive dream: the reasoned creed that will form the mutual basis for our ideal vision. We want to succeed where everyone so far has failed. Newton was morally unedifying to Diderot and Rousseau; Rousseau was morally unedifying to Marx, except on the villainy of private property; Marx is morally unedifying to us, for the agreed ideal vision of man that we need. Will it ever end; will someone give us the moral edification, or is the dream doomed to remain just that—a figment of the Enlightenment imagination, part of the ill-fated dream of Reason governing the affairs of man?

We would surely be trifling with the reader, by inviting him to travel this far with us in our squirrel-like labors, only to lead him to an insurmountable wall. Back and forth, again and again, only for some neglected history of ideas? Only to retrace our roots so that we may more fatalistically accept our failure? No, happily, not that. We have come this far in order truly to enter the promised land. We are ready to reap the benefits of the best that mankind has been able to think, carefully and conscientiously matured over many generations. They have prepared for us a New Moral View of the World. Nothing less. It is now up to us to take possession of it.

II. THE NEW MORAL VIEW OF THE WORLD

CHAPTER SIX

The Scientific Dimension: The Solution to the Riddle of Human Nature (Psychology and Sociology)

> "Spread the facts, analyze them, debate them, make them available to all the world. *There is no other . . .* [*way*] *. . . that can possibly win the great political struggle in which we are engaged.* Truth alone can win it . . . Open the books, if you wish to be free."
>
> —Wendell Willkie (1944)

Let us then start still another journey, a new one this time, over a new landscape. So far we have been skimming along on the peaks, the high vistas of two hundred years of outstanding problems; let us descend into the valleys, where the slow and patient labor has been going on, where men have been maturing the answers to these problems. Here the going will be less rapid because the things we come to face are so rich and varied; we will have to try to pick our way carefully, yet surely and boldly through. When we finish we should have our own map, the one we have been looking for: the one that tells us where to go on the problem of social change; the one that is drawn on the concrete facts of religious, political and economic life.

The starting point of this new road is the same point from which we began at the very opening of our discussion—the American Renaissance and its great voice, Ralph Waldo Emerson. And this should be neither a coincidence, nor a surprise; for this is where the problem began, as we saw when we contrasted Emerson and Wayland. The American Renaissance was the great promise of a moral society of free men, liberating human energies up to the highest pitch of productivity and creation. John Dewey somewhere calls Emerson the greatest moralist that America ever produced; and it is fitting that he should have spoken at the height of the American hope and promise; and it is fitting, too, as we now know only too well, that he should have been a moralist, since the outstanding problem of American society has been and is a moral one. And what was the distinctive message of this great moralist, the one he drummed into the ears of his fellow Americans, the one he laid down as a basic ideal for the future, the one that all Americans, if they were to have their promised land, would try to live up to and realize? What was the distinctive moral quality that would be proper to a society of free men, the quality that would be necessary in order to make democracy work, the quality that would guarantee the freedom of others as well as of oneself, the quality that would assure excellence and initiative in the most daring undertakings, the quality that would liberate the maximum of creative energies, the quality that would permit a truly experimental democracy in the Enlightenment vision?

Self-reliance, that's what it was; the title of his most famous and stirring essay, an essay that reverberated the American hope all the way back to Europe, and made them feel stale; at least it influenced Nietzsche, who spent his life haranguing Europeans for being stale. And when I recently asked a class of students what they thought of the essay, they said it seemed "old-fashioned." Stale! the great American hope was now itself stale. In a little over a hundred years, the ideal of American democracy had been allowed to lapse. But this was not only an ideal in the sense of a "hope"—it was also an ideal in the sense of a basic program: Without self-reliance, democracy could not be realized. In other words, when this ideal was abandoned, the possibility of democracy itself was given a mortal wound. And for over a hundred years now, the life energies of America have been expiring through this gaping lacuna. Today we have a nation of souls who are being led, instead of leading; led by the mass media, led by the automatic functioning of a giant profit-and-loss economy, led by a huge military establishment, led by an enormous secret-service organization, led by a President whose powers —as Charles Beard warned—exceeded anything that Caesar could have imagined. If it were not for the bright newness and the vast array of goods, we might mistake the whole of this land for Czarist Russia. The central power is there, the military is there, the vast spy-network is there, and the fearful populace is there. And there too, is the deep hope that the Great Leader will somehow set it right, that their own energies need not and cannot help the matter.

Too strained an analogy in the interests of rhetoric? Perhaps. The one great difference and still quiet hope is the free dissemination of thought and knowledge—Wendell Willkie's hope. It can win and carry man over all those institutions, both those above ground and underground. But the one great similarity emerges just as clearly: the uncritical masses who, instead of running and leading, are being run and led. The failure of the ideal of self-reliance hinged on the failure of the development of a truly critical intelligence among the vast masses of people. Hence the fear, and the willingness to delegate power. Herman Melville saw the American problem at the same time as Emerson, and he described it in the many guises of the "Confidence Man." The Confidence Man was the American, in all his daily tasks, who had *confidence* that everything would come out all right, if only he played the game as the rules dictated and kept his wholesome optimism. Confidence without critical perspective; the everyday adjustment without the guiding vision; pragmatism without higher standards—these were the great threat to the American promise. Melville already saw that Ben Franklin could not be the American ideal: Self-reliance without critical skepticism of the everyday cultural game was a doddering creed. In a word, American self-reliance had to be based on knowledge at the height of the times, or the vision would turn to dust. Today we are in a better position to see how true was Melville's intuitive insight into the heart of the American problem; certainly his contemporaries did not see it, or would not—and so Melville had no public, and spent his later years as a customs inspector in the port of New York.

Yet, how could it have been otherwise? Here is the meat of the problem. What did Emerson's enjoinder to self-reliance *mean*—rather, what could it mean in terms of the knowledge available at that time? How can you have an ideal unless you know how to go about realizing it? And how can you go about realizing it, unless you know *what hinders it*? We might well call this the Great Historical Paradox of the American Ideal. It was put forth at a time when it could not possibly be realized. Could Emerson have answered the question "What hinders self-reliance?" Did he know why he himself intensely disliked having anyone sit behind him on the platform while he lectured? How could he have been expected to know, at that early date in man's knowledge of himself? In other words, in order to begin to fulfill the American ideal, we had to know what man *was,* and what he was *striving for;* and only when we knew that could we know what were the curbs on human freedom and responsibility. And this knowledge took all of the nineteenth century—and half of the twentieth—to acquire.

From that point of view, the nineteenth century was one of the richest in all of human history—it was the richest, we may as well say it. Not only did it tell us what hinders Emerson's enjoinder, it also gave us the key to the guiding Western maxim of over two thousand years—the parent of them all, the enjoinder of the Delphic oracle to "Know thyself." It was precisely the nineteenth century that made self-knowledge possible. No, we will not forget the eighteenth, the one that fathered it; the one that finally freed man from superstition and blind obedience to authority; the one that discovered history in the work of Vico, Gibbon, Voltaire, Hume; the one that discovered the relativity of morals, the influence of circumstances on the shape of law and government—the great Montesquieu, John Millar, Adam Ferguson; but especially the one that discovered Man. Twenty-two centuries after Socrates first tried it, man again turned his gaze from the stars to Man, to human nature and social life. And most of all, the eighteenth century, in the hopeful and tortured voice of Rousseau told the world that man was neutral, that he was made evil by society—which is the same as saying that man is good, if we can only shape society to serve him. Yes, man is good, cried Rousseau, in a frenzy of illumination that made his head swim, and made him drop to the ground; and he literally cried—wet the whole front of his waistcoat with tears of joy, as he recounts it—at this great discovery. Little wonder. It was the challenge, above all others, that the eighteenth century threw to the world. But it was the nineteenth, the giant offspring, that gave us the full Image of Man; and it was the twentieth—the elaborate footnote to the nineteenth—that tidied it up and added the curlicues.

1. Psychology

It would take volumes to tell the story, even if I could tell it with the richness it needs. But I can tell it simply, if the experts and specialized scholars will bear with massive abbreviation. Yet who is to say which is more "true" to reality—the simplification that allows man to get a grip on things—or the rich and detailed portrait that causes him to draw back in awe? Is the world ultimately more "real" than what man needs or can use? Besides, the great development of the science of man during the nineteenth and twentieth centuries, declares that same thing in all the various disciplines—tells us the same thing about man under different dimensions. Since this is so, it is possible for us to abbreviate, and to gather things together under one great truth. What was this great truth? Let us discover it by seeing how psychology, sociology, and psychiatry converged on it.

Modern psychology began when the riddle of human nature was brought up for full review at the Enlightenment. The great new discovery of modern science was that the universe was an ordered, clocklike mechanism; why not man too? Why shouldn't psychology be a science of atomism and materialism? It all began when the Enlightenment struck out at the medieval edifice of otherworldliness and superstition; where best to attack, if not at the cornerstone of the whole edifice? Man's soul and its salvation was the basis of medievalism; in that case, said the *philosophes*, let us show that man is composed of atoms just like the rest of nature, and have done with it. Let us further show that man brings nothing with him into this life, nothing exists prior to experience. All that man has inside him is what he learns from experience; and experience does not spring from the inner life or soul, but rather from the sensations we receive from the outer world. At birth man is a blank slate, a *tabula rasa;* in old age he is a bundle of prejudices, preferences, tastes, beliefs, vices, dreams, all of which gradually rubbed off on him in his journey through life. He puts together a picture of the world from all the many sensations he has received. And when he dies, he becomes again a mass of matter and atoms. An eternal soul? Well, answers La Mettrie—perhaps the father of all the materialist psychologists of the Enlightenment—when man dies we might say that he is eternal, since his atoms again become part of the great machine of Nature!

This was the psychology that took root partly in Descartes, and took full flight with Locke. And if you look at the books and journals of the discipline of psychology today, you will see that it has not fully expired yet. Now if something holds on so long, through so many generations of careful and courageous thinkers, we cannot treat it altogether casually. In fact, materialism was very important and necessary; it was the attempt to explain human experience wholly in terms of this-worldly events, since we cannot know anything about otherworldly ones. Materialism, in other words, was the great historical attempt to make man an object of science instead of religion. If man was to be given freedom in this life, he had to be turned over to science, since science was concerned with this world. For religion, the problem was never freedom in this life, but rather in the next. In a word, materialism was the attempt to free man *for* this life by first possessing him. Religion was the attempt to free man for the next life, by allowing him to remain a mystery.

Seen in these simple terms, we can understand two things: In the first place, why materialism was so necessary to human liberation; it was the only way to get prejudice-free self-knowledge. And in the second place, we can understand the long, agonizing, often vicious struggle against it. It was all about the soul, about man's career on this planet. *This* is what was behind those tedious and esoteric debates about epistemology—the idealism of Bishop

Berkeley, for instance. This protest too had its roots in Descartes, who reserved a place in his empiricism for the sanctity of the human soul; and like materialist atomism, it has also continued up to the present day, notably in existential phenomenology. These were the people who said that the inside of man's experience was a mystery; that this was the most important thing about man; and that science cannot and should not banish this mystery, even though it helps us understand what influences man, and how he works as an organism.

So there were the opposing forces in a three-hundred-year struggle. Make man an object of science, and banish entirely the mystery of his action and being. This will still allow him to be free, happy, and to fashion the Good Life, said certain of the *philosophes* and their modern descendants, many of the experimental psychologists. Not at all, said the opposition: make man an object of science if you will, but only up to a certain point: only up to the point of leaving his free subjectivity unknown.

But what is behind the plea of the opposition? Why this timidity, why this hedging about making man an object of science, a complete object? How can we liberate him, unless we see what causes all his action? There, say the dissidents, the question answers itself. The opposition to the materialists saw the danger right from the beginning. If you make man a complete *object,* you divest him of his subjectivity. And it is this that makes him noble and distinctive in nature. If you find out what causes all his action, you deprive him of his free will, and make him an automaton of nature. If you treat him like any other object of science, you reduce him to the mechanicality of all the rest of nature. You make man a *creature of* science, rather than a *creator through* science; a part of the Newtonian world machine, rather than a complete sovereign over that machine.

At this point we will hear the echo of Diderot, as we remember his fundamental protest against Newtonian science, and his attempt to make man the center of science, the center of the whole universe. But here the echo is weaker, Diderot's voice is not so strong! The dilemma in his time was just too great. If man is not material, is not determined, then—why, then, he is spiritual, undetermined, and the ecclesiasts with one mighty roar heave down the whole Enlightenment. Diderot was forced into materialism in spite of himself, even though he held out valiantly for an inner moral intuition. The whole thing was so complex, and the stakes of the battle were so high and urgent—secularism against the Church. And Montesquieu, how he did hedge between free will and determinism—he who wanted so much to show that man's institutions and laws follow the principles of natural causation. And what about the father of them all, the great master Locke, who began the careful delineation of a psychology based on sensation, who gave the model of the *tabula rasa?* After all was said and done, didn't he too say that what really moved man, what caused his action, was "uneasiness" and desire? And what of Locke's disciples, Condillac and Helvetius, who elaborated his psychology? By one of those vexing paradoxes of a system of ideas, it may come to contain at its apex the very thing it sought to exclude: It was thus that the elaboration of atomistic, materialistic, sensational psychology in the eighteenth century ended with Condillac's basic principle of "desire," and Helvetius's lauding of "passion" (Hazard, 1963, p. 363).

One after another, then, the best thinkers of the Enlightenment were caught in the contradiction of materialist psychology: What happens to the inner man when we make him an object of science? We do not want man to be the embodiment of free, undetermined spiritual essence, because this keeps him firmly under the wraps of medieval superstition. Yet, we want man to be the embodiment of free, undetermined subjectivity, because this is the only thing that keeps him interesting in all of nature. Rousseau, of course, and a few of the other *philosophes* were not caught in this dilemma, since they held firm to the belief in the immortality of the soul. But Diderot was. And that is why we have paused on it. What at first glance seems like a technical problem of psychology, an incidental embarrassment at the very beginning of the science of modern psychology, is really much more than that. It sums up the whole tragedy of the Enlightenment vision of science. Just as Socrates had protested against the atomism and determinism of Democritus, because it lost man in abstractions, Diderot protested against Newtonianism. Diderot wanted to launch the same New Socratic Celebration of Man. But in order to do this, he needed a psychology adequate to the task, a psychology that would keep man's humanity and subjectivity in the center of mechanical nature. And materialism was not such a psychology. In other words, the psychology offered by the best thinkers of the Enlightenment was not adequate to the vision offered by its great intuitive leaders, Diderot and Rousseau. And so the vision had to flounder.

As far as I can see, the rest of the history of materialistic psychology is merely a footnote to its early failure to fit into Diderot's vision of a science of man. In the nineteenth century, the laboratory psychologists redoubled efforts to atomize sensation and perception. Phrenology flourished until its journal finally ceased publication in 1912. In the twentieth century, materialistic psychology became even more uncompromising and fierce, in the work of Watson and his school. And in Russia, Pavlov trained a whole generation of modern materialist psychologists, under the name of the conditioned reflex; they are literally flourishing today. Instead of the end of materialism, we have its intensification today, in physiology, in physio-chemistry, in neurology, in the whole great medical-scientific effort to understand man.

Why this massive effort, this ferocity, this dogmatic belief, so late in the history of materialist psychology? We saw the answer earlier: Despite the heroic Enlightenment vision, Newtonianism held out and won (see Eric Voegelin's fine paper, 1948). The fear about making man an object of science has dimmed; the qualms about losing his inner dignity by reducing him to a natural object like any other, have lessened. The laboratory scientists, without the guiding vision to control them, have continued their plodding labors, and have almost buried man. On the one hand, memory dims the fundamental danger of a thoroughgoing materialistic psychology; on the other hand, habit holds firm to the old fears and hopes; there are still those who would surrender man to Science, because they imagine that the medieval view of man is *still* the enemy, they still want to capture man from God no matter what! And so materialistic psychology lingers on because the ghosts of old still haunt the charred battlefields, even though the real battle has long since moved on.

Let us then back out of this dead-end in the history of psychology, let us leave the footnote, and go back to the main text, to discover what psychology did find out about man. The fact is, you see, that materialistic psychology has still not found out anything about what human nature is, or what man is striving for, and this is the question we started out to answer.

The psychology that Diderot needed to support his New Socratic Celebration of man was largely developed during the nineteenth century; and it was begun three years before Diderot's death, in the first of Kant's great *Critiques*. Diderot wanted to rest all knowledge squarely on man, on his developing vision and knowledge; and so he oriented the *Encyclopedia* on the three faculties of mind—memory, imagination, and reason. In this way, all knowledge would become humanly relevant, since centered on man's perceptions; it would be universal, since the faculties are universal; it would be organic and growing, just like man's mind. But for Diderot, this was only an inspired vision and a hope; it remained for Kant to perfect it, by showing carefully that human perceptions were transcended by nature, that man could never know objects in all their fullness. In other words, Kant performed the enormous feat—we might almost say enormously clever feat—that defeated materialistic psychology even while keeping its gains. He centered nature on man, and so made psychology subjective; but he also showed the limitations of human perceptions in nature, and so we could be objective about them, and about man himself. In a word, man was at once limited creature, and bottomless mystery, object and subject. Materialist psychology was outflanked, then, by a new subjective tradition that could regard knowledge as given by experience. Thus it kept the best of materialism, and guaranteed more than materialism ever could: the protection of man's freedom, and the preservation of his inner mystery.

We cannot do more than note in passing what happened to Kant's beginning. The German Idealists who followed him took his model, and went on to develop it in the direction it had to follow. Fichte, Hegel, Schelling, and Schleiermacher were the principal figures in this; they laid the outlines of a fully subjective, voluntarist psychology. When Hegel's great system fell, German laboratory psychology moved in to fill the void with a new scientific vengeance, it was thus that eighteenth-century materialism was carried over into the nineteenth. As a result, the real triumph of the Kantian tradition had to wait until the end of the century, after the laboratory psychology had in its turn proved inadequate to the understanding of man. Lotze, his student Royce, Royce's student George Mead, William James, Husserl, and James Baldwin are the principal figures here. By the early decades of the twentieth century, it became apparent what had been accomplished in this century-long movement: the Kantian psychology had been elaborated into an empirical self-psychology. Idealism had been fully naturalized, as it had to be after Darwin; and the development of the self, the psyche, or the "soul" as it had been called, was completely understood: We could see how the child develops a self in interaction with adults, and how he thereby fashions an identity. In this way, we could understand how the ideas of society take root in the individual person, how the group lays hold of the individual and makes him its own, by giving him his "insides," as it were.

If we had to choose three men to characterize the high points of this whole development, we might put Schelling at the beginning. He was the one who, after Kant, developed a truly subjective psychology, that at the same time was fully voluntarist. He put flesh-and-blood striving into Fichte's subjective Self; and he opened Hegel's abstract system by immersing man into the indeterminacy of nature. Schelling gave to man the uniqueness of his ideas, the power of his will and passion, and the tragedy of his limitation and separation from any ideal within nature. He gave us, in a word, modern man.

Wilhelm Wundt would be the middle figure in this development, because his own career reflects so beautifully what happened in the nineteenth century. He began his life-work under the influence of materialistic laboratory psychology, and ended it under the banner of folk-psychology. While the materialists cheered the downfall of Hegelian idealism, Wundt tried to make man an object of laboratory research, an object reducible to atoms of sensation. While they later jeered, he saw man as a member of society, learning ideas from his social group.

In this way, materialism and idealism were fused. Man was understood as an object influenced by circumstances of birth, time, and place. Just as the materialists wanted, it was shown that man had no innate ideas, brought no knowledge into life with him; his outstanding capacity was his openness to being molded by experience. But just as the idealists wanted, it was shown that man functioned under the impetus of whole ideas, large concepts, categories of thought; his experience was not grafted onto him in layer after layer of materialist sensation, in a one-to-one cause-and-effect fashion. Rather, children learned ideas from their group, they learned modes of perceiving reality, they learned concepts and categories of thought which guided perception and sensation—and in this way helped to dictate it. The self was understood as the idealists had wanted, as in some way superordinate to the bare senses. In this way, man became an object of science, but was not reduced to a blind cog in the machine of nature. True, he was wholly influenced in his ideas by his environment; but at the same time, his ideas helped create the kind of environment he would live in. Science triumphed in the service of man, even while allowing him his subjectivity; the sense-data theory of knowledge was proven true, but its fallacious reductionism was avoided. Psychology had come of age. Or rather, had begun to come of age, since the development of the nineteenth century has still not completely taken root even to this day: over a half-century after William James chided the young Bertrand Russell for his complete sense-data theory of knowledge, the logical atomists are still waving their worn banner, still discussing the epistemology of Berkeley and Hume, as though the problem had remained at that stage.

Now let us introduce our third and final representative figure, the one who reaps the harvest of his whole tradition, and conveys to us our fully modern understanding of man. Wilhelm Dilthey was born in 1833, and died a year after William James, in 1911. The coincidence in time, and the comparison of the two men, is more than chance. Like James, Dilthey spent his whole life trying to break out boldly from the old into the new; he wanted to gather the fruit of the whole nineteenth century, decipher its distinctive message, so to speak. And what was great and distinctive about the nineteenth century? Its ineluctable thrust toward synthesis, its struggle to come to some kind of coherent world view, with man at its apex. But it wanted a synthesis based on hard science, not an airy synthesis like Hegel's; and it wanted a synthesis which left man at its center as a free creator, and not a synthesis which made man a blind creature, as had Spencer's. It wanted a synthesis, in a word, that would be a natural union of materialism and idealism. But this union was the great development of psychology in the nineteenth century, that we have just traced! And what, then, was the great synthetic truth that the century offered, the one that all the disciplines converged in, the one that told us what man was, and what he was striving for?

It was "meaning" said Dilthey, meaning is the great truth about human nature. Everything that lives, lives by drawing together strands of experience as a basis for its action; to live is to act, to move forward into the world of experience. Meaning, then—for any animal—is the drawing together of aspects of experience for action and well-being. Meaning is the relationship between parts of experience. But psychology has now shown us that man does not draw experience together on the basis of simple sensations, but rather, on the basis of concepts. Man is the animal in nature who, par excellence, imposes symbolic categories of thought on raw experience. In other words, with man, meaning has become conscious; his conception of life determines how he sees all its parts. Meaning, concludes Dilthey, "is the comprehensive category through which life becomes comprehensible" (1962, p. 105). And there we have it; the synthetic truth of the nineteenth century is out in full view: Man is the meaning-creating animal.

2. Sociology

If meaning is the category that makes life comprehensible, the category that unites the best of materialism and idealism, then we should expect that it would be a truly superordinate category that allows us to understand human behavior in all of its dimensions. And this it does, in sociology as well as in psychology. In psychology, as we saw, we were hindered from understanding man as the meaning-creating animal by the early bias of materialism and atomism, which lasted well beyond its time. It could never approach man from above, from *his* view of the world, because it insisted on approaching him from below, from the cells and nerves that compose his body. Sociology too took a long time to get at the nature of social behavior, but here the problem was more complex; the union of materialism and idealism in sociology was a long and difficult task. Let us try to sketch its history.

We might sum up the whole history of sociology in what at first seems merely a flippant statement, but is really very apt: The history of sociology is a series of attempts to overthrow fictional views of society in order to arrive at a truly fictional view of society. One after another, the mythologies of various thinkers had to be punctured in order finally to understand man as he was, as a performer of the social fiction, an actor on the stage of society, living and breathing the script for social action that is written in each time and place.

As in psychology, the first myth was the atomistic one. Hobbes was the first modern thinker here who saw man as a wholly determined atom, in a wholly materialistic universe. These atoms bumped into one another, damaged one another, they had lusty appetites and were bent on mutual rapine, and so had to be controlled by a strong authority. This authority was the Leviathan, the great society composed of atoms under the heavy rule of constraint; in this way, and only in this way, were social life and social order possible.

By now it should be "second nature" to us to peel up the corner of every theory of human conduct, in order to see what the thinker believed and wanted; there is no theory about man without a belief in what is proper for man. As always, we discover the moral problem, the problem of ordered society, and how to bring it about. Hobbes wanted social order and full individualism above all, and he put his faith in a strong monarchy in order to bring it about. This was in the seventeenth century; by the late eighteenth and early nineteenth, social theory shifted its focus. It now had to justify the new thriving middle-class merchant and manufacture society. How to permit everyone to carry on the stimulating new activity of private profit and industry, and yet keep social order without a crushing monarchy? Well, there were several ways, and we already touched upon them when we discussed the problem of natural morality in a previous chapter. One way was Mandeville's, and that was to show that no matter how selfish human behavior was, that somehow things worked out to the best interests of the social group as a whole. Like a great beehive, said Mandeville, with everyone going every which way, and yet all coming up with a big store of honey—that was society. Evil couldn't be avoided, it was part of the whole panorama; in fact, it was such an inseparable part that it was absolutely necessary. Nature was wonderful in the way it ordered selfishness to ultimate good. Yes, let us all go about our activities, said Adam Smith, and the social order will take care of itself; it will be aided by that marvelous faculty of sympathy, of fellow-feeling implanted by God. The Code of Nature will order society by an invisible design, even though men pursue their own interests. But not, of course, as Mandeville fiendishly urged; rather, with sympathy and restraint, under the control of reason; neither Hobbes nor Mandeville had counted with the powers of natural sympathy. If man would but pursue rationally that which gave him pleasure, all would be well. Tally it up, said Wollaston, at the beginning of the eighteenth century; pleasures against pains; keep a balance sheet, and you will chart the good life. Let us base our very laws and our legal reforms on this principle, said Bentham at the end of the century; the calculus of pleasure will keep the greatest number happy, and will guarantee that society functions in harmony with the desires of men.

But then came the French Revolution, and by the middle decades of the nineteenth century, the glaring injustices and human waste of the Industrial Revolution. It began to be very clear that society was composed of social classes, that their interests were not necessarily in harmony, that the honey was not spread evenly over the hive, there were too many queens who did not work, and too many workers who did not eat. It began to be very clear that power and privilege called the tune to the division of the spoils; that what thinkers had been saying for centuries was true: Money and private ownership of the land were the real evils. The medieval reformers said it, and so did Pascal, Rousseau, Babeuf, Fourier, and others, with increasing vigor, into the mid-nineteenth century; by then it could no longer be avoided; the problem of social reconstruction called for an honest theory of the social system, even if that theory no longer could serve to legitimate the social system as it was. It was evident that Smith and Bentham had honorable intentions, had left some keen insights, but that their social theory was no more solid than a house of cards.

It took no great wind to blow it down; and when Karl Marx came upon the scene he blew so strongly that we can still hear the whistle. Myths, all myths, said Marx, all fabricated to protect the new middle-class society, now that it has taken over from the deposed aristocracy. If we want a real theory of the social system, it must show things as they really are, and not the way we wish them to be. Man is not a selfish, isolated atom who needs a strong hand to control him; neither is he a natural buyer-and-seller who must handle money in order to be happy; man is a natural member of a community who dances to the tune of the ideology he learns in the society in which he lives. No, it is not as Hegel said, either; it is not the *idea* that governs society and history: it is the way in which society is set up that produces its ideology. When we look at social systems all through the history of civilization, when we cut through the veil of their mythology, we see the struggle of classes to possess power and to legitimate that power with an ideology. All else is fiction but the class struggle; and in our time, now that the Industrial Revolution is automatically assuring the continued increase of glaring injustice, now that it is forming a growing dispossessed proletarian mass—in our time, the world-historical problem will finally be righted, and the age-old panorama of the succession of exploiters will be done with. The masses will take over, and government itself will gradually be outgrown, once the exploitation and the need for it are at an end.

Here is the moralist speaking, like Smith and Bentham; but the consummate moralist, the more hardheaded one who wants to be done with the problem of social reconstruction once and for all. After the French and Industrial revolutions, Marx saw that the only way to make honest social theory was to ground it on the tradition of materialism that the eighteenth century itself had prepared; they were the real predecessors of social theory. They had begun the task of social analysis by showing that human institutions were conditioned like everything else in nature, by the hard laws of history and natural process: the bulk weight of tradition, the pressures of power, the circumstances of geography. The early materialists had shown that man was literally created by his environment, that he learned his ideas from the world in which he lived, that the main thing was the striving for satisfaction and pleasure; but that what rubbed off onto man were the superstitions of tradition, the uncritical assumptions of the society in which he lived. It remained, then, thought Marx, for the nineteenth century to marshal everything it knew, and crown the eighteenth-century beginning in materialist social analysis.

There was nothing simple-minded about Marx's materialism; it was as careful and honest as La Mettrie's, and it avoided La Mettrie's simple atomism to boot. After the German Idealists, simple atomism was not possible in social theory; it was a plain fact that society functioned as an organic whole, and Marx took this fully into account. In many ways, Marx reminds us of Diderot —forced to be a materialist in spite of himself, in order to keep his thought at the revolutionary height of the times. Like Diderot, Marx was concerned with the whole man, with the moral problem, with the unfettered development of man as a free member of society. And in Marx's time, as in Diderot's, the enemy was naive trust in the realm of the spirit.

And so we see that sociology had to repeat the career of psychology; it had to incorporate firmly the principles of materialism, but at the same time had to outgrow them. It had to fuse with the best of idealism too; and here Marx failed. His materialism, like that of the eighteenth century, was dogmatic. The fact was, you see, that just as sense-data do not produce the ideas of individuals, the conditions of human adaptation do not produce the ideologies of society. Like the individual man, the institutions of society function *under the governance* of ideas; ideas are not the sum-total of the effects of the social institutions, any more than they are the total of sense-data. They are intimately related; they are a function of one another; but they are not necessarily an exact or close function of one another. The great historical problem that Marx left for social theory, then, followed the same lines as the problem that materialist psychology left for the late nineteenth century: how to keep the benefits of an honest materialistic analysis, and at the same time allow room for the indisputable idealistic elements in human action? How, in a word, to have an honest materialism, and not a dogmatic one? A mature social theory, as we noted earlier, would have to get rid of this final fiction in social theory, the fiction of a complete materialism of the social system.

The story of its accomplishment is one of the richest and most exciting chapters in the history of ideas, in the history of man's self-liberation through ideas. It is a longer and more complex story than the history of a mature psychology, because, as we saw, that was already largely accomplished by the end of the nineteenth century; the full maturity of sociological analysis took another fifty years. And little wonder; it was not simply a matter of understanding human perception, the problem of ideas versus sense-data. This is a more-or-less objective problem. Social theory had the enormous task of understanding the very fictions that man performs in each society; the showing of man's own hand, so to speak; the self-exposure of human motives in everyday life. It had to understand the *staging* of society; it had to take Shakespeare's insight into man as a player on the stage of life, and show exactly how man did play. It was a self-exposure of a truly heroic kind, because, like all self-exposure, it left man nude and somewhat pitiful, thrown back to a position where he could no longer pretend. Little wonder, too, that very few have been able fully to digest this great achievement of sociological analysis.

It all started, as we might expect, with the eighteenth century, and their amused and malicious discovery of the relativity of social customs; the Baron de Lahontan, again, and others who called us back to the savages and their "simple and noble life," away from the otiose artificialities of civilized society. It went through Rousseau, as we saw, and others like de Sénancour, into the nineteenth century. And it was in the nineteenth century that we started really to see how man plays the game of society; the previous century had given us the spirit of criticism, now we were to achieve the letter of exact analysis. How beautifully Charles Fourier got at that original passion of man, the "cabalistic" passion as he called it. This was man's urge to intrigue, his urge to mystery, his passion for games and secrets; the original sport of human life everywhere. Without it, said Fourier, man is simply not man; it may take a million different forms in every different society, but the basic drive is the same: the drive to invest life with overriding significance. This was the key to man's peculiar nature.

By the time that other genius, Georg Simmel, wrote his original essays on human behavior, the cabalistic passion could be described in greater richness. Simmel had the German idealistic tradition to draw on, and he could show how important the "spirit" was in human perception. He described the hidden spirit, in his famous essay on the secret, and showed how man needed to hold things in awe, surround them with mystery. He described the spirit as it was enclosed in the human face, in his famous essay on "The Aesthetic Significance of the Face"; he cajoled the spirit out of architecture, in his famous piece on "The Ruin"; or out of pottery, in his essay on "The Handle." Here we could see in precise and detailed analysis how idealism blends with materialism, how inseparable was the "idea" in a world of matter. But Simmel had not finished with these breathless insights, he reserved for sociology the greatest revelation of all: that society itself is a game, that people do not play *in* society, but rather, as he puts it, that man everywhere plays *at* society.

What was now needed was some towering mind, some great genius to make a convincing demonstration of the union of idealism and materialism in sociological analysis, by showing how the whole panorama of a social system works in this way. He would have to show what Marx had shown, how power and privilege influence the division of the spoils; how invasions and wars set up the class structure; how basic is the economic problem in every society. But he would have to show too how prominent is the role of religion, of mythology, of the urge to eternal life; how man will sacrifice bread for belief, comfort for meaning; how the whole panorama functions in a gigantic interplay of self-interest, survival, splendor and display, this-worldly waste and otherworldly wonder. How important are names and titles, ranks and distinction; how man is jerked about by affiliations, loyalties, statutes;

how organizations function in the hard business of life, assuring human adaptation; and yet, through it all, how they satisfy man's basic urge to meaning, to ever-larger, ever-more satisfying, ever-more comprehensive meaning. The man who showed this was of course Max Weber, in his famous studies of India and China, of economic and social history, of capitalism and the Protestant ethic. His mind integrated such a mass of disparate data, as to stagger any lesser imagination. He showed us, in our own Western history, how we have created our world; and he even predicted our bitter future. He showed us the newest and most ruthless social game of all, the game of rational man—the game of numbers, calculation, efficiency: the uncompromising logic of modern bureaucracy. It now appeared that the whole social system was moving toward this new type of performance; this was to be the modern adaptation par excellence.

Why call it our "bitter" future, if it was so clean and efficient? Why criticize a great show that seems to minimize all unessential trimmings, an efficient performance that exhibits nothing to the viewers on stage, except the efficiency of the performance itself? Just for that reason: Here was the show to silence all criticism, because it seemed to work so well that it need not be brought up for question, its goals never reviewed or assessed. It was man performing so apparently successfully with the ingenuity of reason, that he lost all the deeper self-reflection that comes with uncertainty of success. Bureaucratic man was social play at its most tragic, precisely because the sense of tragedy has been exiled from the stage. No Stoics, Cynics, St. Francises, Savonarolas, or Pascals in our chorus, waving accusatory fingers. And what does bureaucracy do to the individual man himself, except fit him neatly into the machine; bureaucracy is the great leveler of individuality; it turns man into atoms, almost indistinguishable in one massive conglomerate of precise social movement. The forms that hold man in bondage seem right for all time, because they regulate a faceless mass of men so well: status, party, "style of life." The words become greater than the thing; and it is man himself who has become a thing. The old social cement now shows very few cracks. We are seeing Weber's prediction being fulfilled in our time, in a great managerial network that is spreading over the whole Western world, regardless of its ideological system. Capitalism, socialism, communism—all have locked man into their machine-like grip.

In this way, then, Marx's beginnings were crowned, and his materialistic bias was corrected, even while its truth was retained. Power, yes, and privilege, and the hard facts of economic determinism, the need for technological mastery in order to survive—all these called the tune to human adaptation in society. But there was more, sometimes much more: man's urges beyond the material, man's performance as a creature of fantasy, as a juggler of symbols; his response to mere appearances, to show and pomp, to awe and mystery and cabal—as Fourier had said. All this made the social system, and could even dictate the style of its economic adaptation. With Weber's union of materialism and idealism, social theory had reached maturity.

The second great fruit of the synthetic movement of the nineteenth century was gathered, and it merged with the first: Man was a meaning-creating animal who creates his meanings on the level of the total social fiction.

But Weber was not alone to bring about this maturity, there was a whole current of brilliant thinkers who showed the social system as a great "style of life." In fact, Weber's work was deficient in one important way: it lacked a sharply critical tone; it did not take a firm stance on values; it did not lead us boldly to the critical judgment of the social fiction. This final step into a fully evaluative sociology was taken by Thorstein Veblen. Veblen, who took his cue from the styles of life of primitive society, showed the great social fiction of American society: the panorama of potlatch, of conspicuous waste, of consumption for the sake of show. This was the tune to which the whole American society danced, a staging as uncritical as the Kwakiutl Indians to whom Veblen compared them. There were many differences, of course, between Kwakiutl potlatch and American potlatch, not the least of which was the fact that Kwakiutls did not go hungry, no matter how many goods were wasted. Americans, on the other hand, went hungry just to continue to waste goods, as the great depression of the 1930's proved. The more apt comparison was between the Americans and the great conspicuous waste of Roman society, and this was drawn by Veblen and by the Italian sociologist Guglielmo Ferrero. What was now needed was some fine critical mind to show how the great panorama of conspicuous waste of commercial-industrial society was becoming more efficient, more bureaucratized; how smoothly it could all function by uniting the government and the corporations with a great new war machine. How finally the most deadly mask of all could be pulled down over the commercial-industrial style of life: the mask of national survival, the mask of patriotism, the mask of unquestioned loyalty, of self-sacrifice—in a word, the destruction of men to the uncritical support of efficient waste.

C. Wright Mills showed this with great insight as well as courage; and needless to say he won no great honors from his professional colleagues in sociology in his lifetime. Very few who have followed in the footsteps of Rousseau have escaped his fate; total criticism of the style of life of one's society earns total rejection by that society; it is all quite logical, and the honest thinker can expect nothing else. The tragedy is that we have not understood Rousseau's intent, nor Carlyle's, Nietzsche's, Veblen's, Mills's: Total condemnation of the social system is a way of rousing man to action on the basis of an ideal model; it is not meant to damn men as a mass, to force them to give up their life ways and to surrender to chaos and death. History shows us that these thinkers were all honored after their death; their careers followed the model of Socrates, the first of their line, who was condemned to death and then immediately honored. The point is that they were just a step ahead of their society, and when they died it was ready to accept the spirit they proposed. Is this a law that history teaches us, the rule that man must die to support the critical vision he proposes?

I mention Rousseau and history at this time in order better to sum up the significance of this whole tradition of sociological analysis. It began with Rousseau and his century, when the relativity of social customs was fully discovered. By the time this tradition had reached its maturity with Weber, Veblen, and Mills, something truly astonishing had been achieved. Didn't Rousseau say that civilization itself was corrupt and corrupting, that man somehow had to be valued above the easy habits of social custom which tore away at his finer sentiments, at his basic inner nobility? As didn't Rousseau propose the Noble Savage as an ideal, a measure to hold up against the vicissitudes of modern artificial life? And what did the nineteenth and twentieth centuries teach us, exactly, if not that Rousseau's inspiration was fundamentally sound? By the time Marx and his successors had finished presenting their analyses, one thing stood out, one thing above all, the most astonishing disclosure that we could have imagined: Civilization *was* an uncritical style of life, which sacrificed the free energies of individuals to the perpetuation of an artificial social system, of a largely fictional pattern of social meaning. And how long had this been going on? Just as long as the *anti-ferini* of the eighteenth century had argued, since the decline of primitive, communal society! Veblen's America had drawn full circle back to Nero's Rome, and further still. It was just as the eighteenth century maintained: All the great civilizations had corrupted man—Chinese, Persian, Roman. In order to find a model for the uncorrupt society, we had to reach back to the true, primitive tribalism, before the rise of status, class, and caste; before conquest and plunder by the large mercenary armies. We had to reach back several thousand years, before the river valleys became the seat of the colorful and confused civilizations, the heavy weight of royal power and priestly class that rested on the backs of enslaved masses. In the great river valleys of the Mediterranean world, as in the New World civilization of the Incas, tribe after tribe was conquered and absorbed into the great new centers of pomp and plunder. Was this man's real fall from paradise, this process of world expansion and this welter of confusion that has sent man scrambling across the face of history?

So the *anti-ferini* maintained: When man lost his Noble Savagehood his true fall from paradise started. But what about the Greek city-states, those marvelous centers of civilization that held up to the world a model of humanistic man—and that almost in "modern times," so to speak, a short two thousand years ago? The Greek city-states, we now know, really provide the best evidence to support the *anti-ferini* cause. The thing that made their greatness, in contrast to the other Oriental civilizations of the time, was precisely this: that they moved into the Ionian cities with their patterns of communalism and brotherhood intact. This gave a combination of factors unique in world history: the Oriental sacred city, inhabited by a brotherhood of free and responsible citizens! In a setting of holy devotion, the powers of heaven were repeatedly called down to bless a union of free men. This combination created a promise and a glow that we have felt ever since. But we know too that the process was never complete, the city-state rested on a basis of slavery, and it was as imperialistic and colonialistic as its Oriental neighbors. And so the experiment had to die. As the great scholar Cornford has told us, the Greek experience could only work on the basis of a united world civilization.

Once again *ferini* versus *anti-ferini*—can't the matter ever be settled? No, it cannot, and today we know why. As the eighteenth century already knew, primitive society had its bad points as well as its good; it never was the uniform idyll that Lahontan painted it. Was man better off in the state of Nature, living in easy community, before unlimited private property, before the rise of social classes and exploitation? Was primitive society more free even than the Greek, more equalitarian, more respectful of the individual and his dignity? Modern anthropology has been able, from time to time, to answer this question in the affirmative —Vilhjalmur Stefansson (1940) for the Coronation Gulf Eskimos, Claude Lévi-Strauss (1961) for an Amazon tribe. But as Franz Boas reminded us, even primitives can have their tyrants; furthermore, not all primitive societies are the same; and most of all, even the Coronation Gulf Eskimos succumbed to change. There is the rub, and the heart of the matter: societies are always changing. Nature is in flux, and flux is greatest in man, and in his social world. Since this is so, how can we seek a stable historical model? The answer is that we can't, and should not.

Why do we need to argue about where exactly man's fall from primitive paradise started? Why do we need to find out precisely what is "true and pure," and distinguish it from what is "artificial" in man's state? The ideal depends not on the way things *are,* or *were,* but on *what we want,* on our desire to better the lot of man. This was the greatest lesson of all that Rousseau taught us, when he gave us our model of an ideal-type science of man. The ideal state "perhaps never did exist, and probably never will exist," as we heard Rousseau caution in Chapter Five. Yet, it is necessary, "in order to form a proper judgment of our present state."

And so we see how the analytic findings of our most mature sociology draw the full circle back to the Enlightenment vision of a science of man. We do not need to know exactly when or how man was "absolutely" better off than now; all we need to know is what is causing human misery now, and what has caused it in history. And so we can skirt the argument between the *ferini* and the *anti-ferini,* just like Rousseau did. Let us begin with the decline of the Greek experiment itself, with the failure of the city-state. Let us begin with the first man who saw that civilization was a new social game; who saw that it was an uncritical and debasing game; and who knew that the one hope for saving man was to awaken his critical sense, turn him against the mere forms of things. It was Socrates who saw that mass opinion and the easy praise of one's fellows unmanned the Athenians of his day, prevented them from being free and noble citizens. They were too readily playing the game of private profit and display, of power and pomp, of career and fortune; and they were neglecting the cultivation of the inner man, upon which alone the city-state could thrive. Socrates wanted man to be autonomous, to follow his own idea of justice and right, provided he reasoned it out carefully. He saw that reliance on the judgment of others was the great danger for a brotherhood of free men; and rather than stop his peculiar attempts to awaken his fellows from their uncritical sport, he preferred to die. In other words, he saw that his historical mission was to attempt to save society by making it self-critical, and he was willing to be a martyr in this unprecedented cause. And that is why we cannot talk of primitives, but must begin with Socrates—with the ideal, with the enjoinder to man to rise above the constraints in which he is held by society, no matter what kind of society it is, or where it is found. And this, as we said, is precisely what Rousseau, some two thousand years after Socrates, meant by the primitive ideal.

No wonder we still honor his name. We now have a picture of what two thousand years of this uncritical social sport has meant for man. Socrates did not put his analyses in writing himself, but Marx, Simmel, Weber, Veblen, and Mills did. Simmel described in fine detail what Socrates' intuition had told him: Man plays at society—emptily, uncritically. By the time Erving Goffman extended Simmel's and Cooley's insights with his own fine analyses, we could see exactly how the process worked, in unbelievably fine detail. Man needs to rely on the judgment of others, in order to earn his own feeling of worth. He needs to protect himself in the social encounter; he needs to save his "face"; he needs to perform, in a word, in the shared social fiction, in order to earn social honor, social approval, and social protection. Socrates intuited these things; he saw that they meant the decay of free society, because they made of man a social automaton. But one thing he could not see, and historically, it proved to be the most important of all, because it explains why his enjoinders to his fellow Athenians failed. He could not see how deeply rooted the mechanics of playing at society is; he could not see how much the individual self is a function of the social group; he could not see how deep "social performance" goes, how it is rooted in the anxiety of man, the anxiety to be accepted and honored. He did not see the crucial dynamic of the whole thing, the dynamic that a series of the best modern minds had to unveil, unveil almost tremblingly, reverently: that man's slavish devotion to the social game is rooted in the anxiety of self-discovery; that man does not know what he is; unless he is told by his social group.

And so we understand why Socrates' vision and hope had to remain just that—an ideal, an ideal unrealizable in the Athens of his day, and still unrealized in the world some twenty-five hundred years later. That is why Sorel was so violently against Socrates' teaching; Sorel saw that social order was more realistically attained by the general myth, and not the individual reason. But the intriguing question remains—why did Socrates himself not need to be told who he was by his social group? The answer is that Socrates was a true prophet, and a spiritual one at that, as Bergson so well understood. Socrates was not a secular man as we understand it today: he had his "daimon," who told him when his course of action was wrong, was against his best interests.

This helps us understand, too, another reason why modern man has still not realized the Socratic ideal. Socrates had a higher critical perspective on his life and times, even though it took the form of a personal daimon; but today, more than ever in history, the players in the social fiction are without such a perspective. In our time, the higher religious voice has been almost completely stilled. No daimon, no guardian spirits, no otherworldly religion. We are back, in a word, to the prediction of Max Weber: The mechanical bureaucratic society has drowned out everything but its own hum. Modern man earns his social honor without being able to reach for any critical perspective that might release his full manhood; even his fantasy has to work within the organized secular system.

But if Socrates' ideal was unrealizable in his day, and is still unrealized, and if man has to live under some kind of shared social myth, then, why all the fuss? the reader may ask. What about the material struggle of civilization; isn't this real? If our mature modern sociology has shown us why Socrates failed, and why he must fail—well and fine; perhaps we can use this to better accept our lot. If we know that man has been playing an uncritical social game for several thousand years, it *is* a bit amusing to ponder our fate. But knowing all this, we must live; and if the whole thing is really so ludicrous, why, then, let us do as the advertisers tell us: let us "enjoy and enjoy" the unprecedented consumer fruits of our playful and fictional society. It may be a transparent game, but its products are interesting and diverting. We cannot back off from civilization—it is here to stay. So the reader may rightfully reason.

He may object, too, that all this knowledge about playing *at* society, about the social game, the style of life that is largely fictional, the shared social myth—all of it may be true knowledge about man's conduct in society; but how deep does it really go, how much of a burden of explanation can we put on it; in a word: Does it really explain the incredible evils that we meet in our time? Isn't this all too flippant to explain the cataclysms of world war, the unprecedented sacrifice of life? What about the gas ovens of Auschwitz and Buchenwald, surely the reasons for this kind of mass slaughter go deep, very deep into human nature, into a capacity for evil that evolution itself cannot breed out? Isn't Marxist materialism much more dependable as an explanation for the bloody struggles for power and conquest; for the fight between the haves and the have-nots at all places and times; for the urge of the underdog to have his day; for the dispossessed little men to become big men, and to vent their powerful anger on the world? In a word, isn't all this talk about the play-forms of civilization quite beside the point of explaining the breadth and depth of human evil?

All this the reader may reason and object about the analyses of mature sociology; and alas, he would be wrong. These are precisely the things that we do explain, when we talk about social fictions; we explain the breadth and depth of human evil with a clarity that is amazing. Once we allowed the full place in social theory for the fictional nature of social meanings, we were presented with the most terrible realization of all: that *man's play-forms may even outwit human adaptation itself*. The fiction can become greater than physical reality; the struggle for survival becomes a struggle with the ideas one has inherited, and not with Nature itself.

Hasn't America won the struggle for survival with Nature, in this richest of lands? Is it food we lack, or shelter, or clothing? No, it is none of these; it is jobs. Jobs? Ah yes, we know the fiendish story only too well. It is not the material struggle with nature that is tearing us apart; rather, it is the struggle with our own profit-and-loss economy, our own distributional system, our money-over-the-counter game, that has lost all relationship with life. We are finally approaching the point where automation will run the whole show, and the good life will be just around the corner; but we cannot allow the good life, since the good life has to be tallied in profit-and-loss statements, in numbers of jobs, in pay envelopes. If we had to give our vast surpluses of goods away free to men who have unlimited leisure in a society run by machines; if we had to do this, it would destroy the whole fabric of life as we are accustomed to it, since we have not set up our social fiction for it. Our fiction, in other words, has crippled our rational adaptation to the real world. Better to run from job to bank to shopping center; better to dole out more and more money to the unemployed; better to subvene; better to cut down automation; better to do anything than to step into the promised land. Yes . . . there we have it: The gods have already made us mad; we have only to wait for our own fictions to destroy us.

We know the reason for all this, the reason that we allow the social fiction to dictate the means and ends of social life, instead of facing squarely up to reality to find out what we should do. We know that certain cultures would rather starve than change their diet, even with the forbidden food in plentiful quantities before their eyes; man would rather tighten his belt than raise his anxiety level. There is the heart of the matter: to change our social fiction means to change all our major accustomed habits; and for the higher primates to change habits means to arouse the anxiety of the unfamiliar. The higher primates for the most part are willing to die in the familiar, rather than survive in the unfamiliar. Man would rather sacrifice survival than change the ideas he has learned from his group. (We will see some of the basic reasons for this in the next chapter.) When whole societies do this, the spectacle is understandably grotesque. No wonder Socrates prodded his fellow citizens, accosted them wherever they could be found, hung on to them like a leech, used all his ingenuity to get them to think through the reasons for their conduct, instead of blindly following the social fiction: He lived through the whole senseless span of the war with Sparta that finally bled Athens to death. The terrible fact is that the coin of the fiction is flesh-and-blood; and this is the way it must be for a symbolic animal.

Yes, war too is a game, a play-form. This is where our thesis must lead, and this is what we meant when we said that man's play-forms may even outwit human adaptation itself. It was the brilliant Dutch historian Johan Huizinga who saw this most clearly in his important work *Homo ludens* (1955). Once we had learned from Simmel that man plays *at* society, it was only a step to realizing that "all society is a game," and that this game "is the living principle of all civilization" (1955, pp. 100-101). Like Veblen, Huizinga saw that Roman civilization was animated by a great "potlatch spirit." And like Veblen, Huizinga too took his inspiration from the study of primitive society. It was there, in their inception, that we could see most clearly that all man's activities are play-forms; they begin as simple contests, and develop their complex forms: poetry, art, law, philosophy, war—all are contests or play-forms.

When we call them play-forms, we must not imagine that play excludes seriousness, as Huizinga warns us, but as many of his critics have overlooked. In the great game of society man creates meaning, fictional meaning it is true, but life meaning all the same. This is why play awakens the sense of the holy; it is the actual creation of a realm of meaning. Only, on the scale of primitive society, these forms of meaning-creation seem to us more like true play, and are more innocuous than on the scale of civilization. What happens in the transition in scale that transmutes primitive play into grim civilized "reality"? What turns the basically innocuous contests of primitive society into the cataclysmic evils of civilized life? Well, for one thing, the very change in scale. Gone is the satisfaction of bringing back a single trophy, a single enemy head. Gone is the "trial by battle," the contest between two picked warriors that decides the victory between two sides. On the scale of civilization the primitive potlatch goes rampant, and the quality of performance gives way to sheer quantity. Not merely one sacrifice, but six thousand crosses lined the Appian Way, upon which hung crucified slaves from the revolt of Spartacus, as a gigantic symbolic warning to all. The problem of all play, of all creation of meaning, is to make it convincing; and conviction is given most forcefully by flesh-and-blood, by life and death; and on the level of civilization this is usually achieved by sheer number.

By the time we get to modern bureaucracy, as we said, this spirit wins out completely: numbers, instead of excellence; quantity, instead of quality. War today has become wholly a matter of computer calculation by numbers. The symbolism is wholly quantitative. And it is here that we best understand the first major way in which the relatively innocuous contests of primitive society become transmuted into the cataclysmic evils of civilized life. The inspiration is still the play-form, the basic urge is still the contest, but the method has assumed a life of its own: the symbol is torn out of any organic relationship with the other forms of culture. Among the primitives, as we said, one sacrifice would be enough to signal victory, one tortured prisoner would appease the gods, one life would sanctify a season, purify a whole tribe. Conviction, in a word, came easily and "cheaply" because all activities were in organic relationship; each meaning ramified in all areas. War and god, ritual and myth, song and art, imagination and reason—all formed one complex whole. The bureaucratic method, on the other hand, has a separate life of its own, and must justify itself on its terms; and these terms are abstraction and number. So we understand that when we combine the awe-inspiring finality of flesh-and-blood with the abstraction of rational calculation, the toll of evil must be high; the bureaucratic god is the bureaucracy itself, and this god, unlike that of the primitive, is unappeasable. Today we understand better than ever why primitive society seemed idyllic to the eighteenth century, and why they thought that evil increased under the forms of civilization. With the increase in scale, the play-forms become more ominous; and with the disruption in organic unity of the culture, their toll becomes devastating. The creation of meaning no longer seems like play, the cost in human suffering is no longer banal. Yet, oddly enough, and through it all, the human spirit is the same: It is still struggling for symbolic meaning, and for hard conviction.

Let us take one final example of social life as the creation of fictional meaning, and see the second major way in which man's play-forms may outwit human life itself; let us see how our mature analytic sociology can explain simply some of the greatest of human evils; let us take the thing that so frightfully shocked the twentieth century—I mean, of course, the incineration of six million Jews by the Hitler regime in Germany. When Hannah Arendt analyzed one of the principal figures in this drama, Adolph Eichmann, she called her analysis a study in the banality of evil. She met with a storm of protest that still has not died down. Surely, her critics said, human evil of this magnitude is hardly banal; surely it is lodged deep within the creatureliness of man; surely it represents a bursting through of all that is vicious and animal in the backwaters of evolution; surely man is not truly man when he accomplishes calmly a slaughter of this magnitude.

And here we ourselves can now intercede and say that surely Arendt's critics were wrong; from our foregoing discussion we already have a hint as to what she meant. Evil is banal, because evil is merely the toll of the *game* of society, and not of any basic *iniquity* in man.

When Arendt analyzed Eichmann she showed how evil is a function of the impersonality of bureaucracy, of the giving and taking of orders, of the smooth functioning of organization, of the unquestioned daily duty of basically decent men, who ask only to be rewarded by praise for a job well done. And what was underneath it all, except another great social game, a national drama by means of which Germany sought to create social order. The sacrifice of the Jews, in other words, was a great ritual purification that gave to the Germans their drama of unity and brotherhood. Hugh Duncan, in his important work *Communication and Social Order* (1962), showed this with great clarity and precision. With the analyses of Kenneth Burke and Duncan, social theory was brought to its highest point of sophistication. Man was clearly understood as an actor on the scene, at the center of the stage of a social drama, a symbolic drama in which life and death were at stake, but which was symbolic through and through. Duncan showed how Hitler adopted the techniques of American college cheerleaders, their brass band, their proficiency in whipping up enthusiasm (p. 249, note 23). Hitler himself became a great drum major, translated the "Rah, rah, rah" into the *"Sieg Heil,"* hypnotized the German masses into one great hysterical national drama which drew them together with a frenzy of conviction. Here was a unified show indeed, a fever of brotherhood, such as we see so clearly on the primitive scale; but now it was on a national scale of unprecedented scope. And as with the primitives, it drew the tribe together by washing away the impurities that held them apart: the guilt, the ambivalence, the hopeless separation of man from man, and of man from the higher divine powers. And in order to do this, it used the time-honored technique whereby a society rids itself of impurity: the ritual scapegoat who carries off the sins. The anthropologists had shown how the ritual scapegoat functions to cleanse the tribe, how the sacrifice makes a link with the divine powers, and how the impurities of each member are banished forever in the sacrificial scapegoat. Hubert and Mauss showed this in their analysis of the primitives, and Hitler actually demonstrated it in civilized Germany. Only, as we said, the primitives function more economically: one scapegoat usually, and a sacrificial ritual only at specified times; the Germans used a whole people as a scapegoat, and the sacrifice of the Jews was continual. Yet the intent was the same: to wash away guilt, and to draw the members of society together in close unity and brotherhood; again, the difference between primitive and civilized was one of scale; the national potlatch takes a greater toll than the tribal one. The human needs were the same: They were not "low," they were not on any "retarded" level of evolution, they did not spring from man's "animal" recesses.

On the contrary, they were the "highest" needs man has: the need for community, for the drama of society, the enactment of meaning on the scale of the nation-state; the need for the symbolic celebration of life; and finally, and "highest" of all: the need for the union of earthly designs with divine sanction, the need to cleanse man of sin by bathing him in cosmic power. The moral is that man's "highest" needs are those for highest meaning and conviction; and that he reaches for this highest meaning over the flesh-and-blood of other men—indeed, this is the most direct way it can be attained. In other words, even when reaching for the best, for social unity and brotherhood, for the divine itself, man will sacrifice his fellow man! We will see in Chapter Nine the only possible solution to this demonic paradox at the heart of human striving; and we will also look closer at the dynamics of the process that we are merely mentioning here.

For now we can only conclude that Rousseau and the segment of the Enlightenment that he represented was finally vindicated by the most sophisticated and mature social analysis. Man is good; evil is caused by the forms of civilization. But we must conclude too that civilization is here to stay, that societies are always changing, that it is not possible to use the primitive as a stable ideal model. And so we must understand fully and finally that, even though we may never be able to realize the Socratic ideal, we cannot avoid the call to social criticism, the call to unleash the highest possible measure of human freedom and reason. We now see that it is the social myth itself that takes the toll of human life; and the problem of social science becomes one of judging degrees of evil in the shared social mythology, of defining and criticizing the social myth, depending on its vicissitudes. We can now agree with both Socrates and Sorel: Man needs critical reason, but he needs a social myth too, since the heart of life is the dramatic creation of meaning. The problem, then, on an ideal level, is clear: What is the cost in human life and suffering, of man's social fictions?

CHAPTER SEVEN

The Scientific Dimension (Psychiatry)

What a rich legacy the nineteenth century left us. In a short twenty-five hundred years since the beginning of Western civilization with the Greeks, man had discovered his own peculiar nature: He was the animal who created and dramatized his own meanings. Plato had already told us as much, when he said that the gods were happiest when man plays. It took us a couple of thousand years to find out exactly what this meant, and to see how serious a problem it posed for the survival of human society. We now had to treat ourselves as children—we had to watch over our own careless play, in order to make sure we did not unwittingly destroy ourselves.

No matter what history does with our discovery—or rather, no matter what man now does with himself, the incredible has been achieved: In the evolution of the cosmos, on the planet Earth, the form of life called Man arrived at self-understanding, saw "through itself" and its motives. At least at one point in the universe, Life had stopped its blind scurrying; it lay exposed, pulsating, anxious, wondering whether and in what way it would again spurt on to a different development. If we were immodest, we could say that man's reason had finally given him the possibility of full possession of himself, to do with as he may. But it would be truer to say that evolution had brought Life to the point of its greatest potential liberation. Or perhaps it would be most true to speak mythically in the face of this awesome and ill-understood achievement, and to say man had finally become a potentially fully open vehicle for the design of God.

The nineteenth century did not, however, completely solve the riddle of human nature; psychology and sociology only sketched the picture in the rough. They showed us what man was about, but the picture could not be fully compelling until we saw it in precise detail. And it was psychiatry, especially the school called psychoanalysis, that showed us in microcosm exactly how man learned to strive for meaning. The twentieth century then, completed our understanding of man, by showing the laws of his individual development.

1. Psychiatry

We saw how both psychology and sociology had to go through a similar history, from a dogmatic atomistic materialism to a generous union with idealism on a higher level of synthesis. Psychiatry was no exception to this development; it helps us explain why it took so long to arrive, in its turn, at a mature understanding of man. All three approaches, in effect, were hobbled by the same early fallacy. They had to keep the benefits of a frank materialism, and yet outgrow the constrictions of its dogma. The whole problem is really summed up in the work of the greatest figure in psychiatry—Freud, who began as a medical doctor with his full roots in the nineteenth century. His bias was all toward materialism and reductionism; little wonder that no matter how much his work strained toward idealism and subjectivism, it never quite made it. With all that Freud's genius gave us, he stopped just short of giving us a true picture of man as a creator of meaning. By insisting that man is driven by instincts, instead of pulled forward by meaning, Freud kept the science of man in a frustrating bind for almost half a century, well into the middle of the twentieth. Adler gave us a much less equivocal picture of man than did Freud, because he was able to step more firmly away from the medical tradition. Wilhelm Reich also chafed at Freud for making his instinct theory so precise, even though Reich himself could not abandon the medical model, and finally succumbed to it, to the detriment of some of his best and most original thinking.

There is nothing to be gained from again repeating in detail what Freud accomplished, and what he left undone. Let us merely note here that his instinct theory reflected a large and real problem, and that this problem was one that he was unable to solve, but that has since been solved (at least to the satisfaction of a growing number of scientists): This was the problem of how to show that man was basically an organism, a physiochemical organism, without trying to reduce his behavior to motivation by chemicals and nerves. I think the new behavioral theories of schizophrenia and depression show this; they show that man is basically an animal organism, but they show it while allowing full room for man as distinctively a creator of meaning (*cf.* Becker, 1964a). And this is precisely what Freud and the tradition of medical psychiatry could not do, even though they laid the basis for it.

There is another problem in the history of ideas that we must skirt. And that is the problem of what specifically Freud added to our understanding of the genesis of the human self. The nineteenth century had already arrived at a good understanding of the development of the self in early childhood, particularly in the work of Royce, Baldwin, Mead, James, and Cooley. Interestingly, and significantly, this work took its root right in German Idealism itself, in the early speculations on the interaction of spirit and matter in the work of Schelling, Fichte, Hegel and Schleiermacher. How Freud crowned this development with his own theory of early identification, the nature of anxiety, the development of the ego and the mechanisms of defense—all this is rather technical, and need not be repeated here.

For our purposes, we need only sum up simply what Freud's basic contribution was, what he showed us about the general law of human development; even though we repeat this very briefly, it will allow us fully to understand man's striving in microcosm, and so round off our answer to the riddle of human nature.

What did Freud do, exactly? Nothing less than solve the riddle that had been outstanding since the Enlightenment pressed man's attack on the problem of morality and conscience. At the very beginning of his career, his genius whispered to him what his place in history was to be; as he wrote to his friend Fliess, he was about to discover *the source of human morality*. And so he did. He saw that the human conscience was shaped during the early years of child training, and he described the process in great detail. Man comes into the world like any other animal—a bundle of nerves and appetites; he leaves it unlike any animal that nature has known: a bundle of learned prejudices, of hates, hopes, fears, diehard beliefs. But this is what the Enlightenment discovered: the relativity of morality, the influences of society on the malleable child—it is all in Rousseau, and Diderot, and even the notorious Marquis de Sade. Yes, but it was not at all clear; it had to be laid open, as with a doctor's scalpel—and Freud was the doctor. It was easy to talk about early training, the inculcation of false beliefs, the ingraining of prejudice, and taste, and preference, and world view, and what not. But from Rousseau, through Alexander Bain, and up to John Dewey in our time, we could not get beyond the catch-all word "habit." It was all very well to talk about how habits are rubbed off in the early child training period; it was quite another matter to show why habits go so deep, why they are so hard to change, why they hang on even when the pressure of authority is lifted. And unless we showed this, we could never have a convincing theory of conscience, a naturalistic theory that thoroughly explained man's behavior as a moral agent.

And this is precisely what Freud showed. The theory of the Oedipus complex was a detailed description of the fundamental law of human development; it showed how the sense of conscience, or the Superego as Freud called it, is built into the human animal during his early training by his parents, or whatever authorities bring him up. Why does it last even after the pressure of authority is lifted; why does the adult continue to follow roughly the same rules he learned as a child, uncritically usually, and usually for his whole life? Because, as Freud showed, the early habit is built in on the basis of anxiety, the peculiar anxiety of object-loss that animates all the higher primates, and is most pronounced in man. Along with this anxiety of object-loss, the child is pulled by his inordinate need for affection, his need to feel wanted, loved, valuable in his own right. Thus, he identifies with the adults, and tries to shape himself on their model. This is the lever that edges him from the animal world into the human one. The Oedipus complex was a term that described a whole learning period, the most unique learning period in the whole animal kingdom. It showed how an animal was gradually weaned from physiological satisfactions, and taught to strive after symbolic satisfactions; it showed how an animal was taught to derive its sense of self-esteem from its *social* performance, and not from its physiological movements.

The whole Enlightenment had discovered how central was self-esteem to human conduct. All its philosophers saw that man was motivated by it, that it was the basic key to man's social nature. Man becomes social as flattery takes hold on pride, as Bernard de Mandeville very early put it. Freud showed how self-esteem grew up in the child, and how he learned to maintain it by learning modes of behavior pleasing to the adults, and by abandoning simple animal reflexes. He showed, in other words, how self-esteem comes to be maintained by a fictional style of performance, how the human animal itself becomes the locus of the social fiction. And there it was! The nineteenth century had discovered that man was an animal who strove after meanings, that society was the stage on which the drama of the creation of meaning is played. Freud capped this development by revealing in detail how man's striving after meaning is inseparable from his basic feeling of worthwhileness as an animal. The theory of the Oedipus complex gave us exactly what we needed; it revealed man's nature in microcosm: It gave us the law of the formation of an animal that thrives on meaning as its life-breath. Freud drew the full circle on the Enlightenment, then, and crowned it with unhoped-for success. It was exactly as Rousseau had foreseen. The inculcation of conscience was the inculcation of social meanings, social conventions; in a word, the artificialization of the "Natural Man."

When we understand this full circle, we can also understand why the sparks have flown so thickly around Freud and his theories. He crowned the Enlightenment, but at the same time, he betrayed it. He gave us a full picture of man as a striver after meaning; but he also said that man strived after the satisfaction of animal instincts. In other words, the Enlightenment had made plain that society is at fault for twisting man into its artificial conventions; Freud showed exactly how this twisting came about. The Enlightenment discovered self-esteem as the principal motive in human action; Freud showed how the self-esteem was made dependent on symbolic satisfactions. There should have been no doubt, after Freud, that the Enlightenment was vindicated in its censure of social learning as the primary cause of evil in human life. But Freud left the doubt; in fact, he more than left the doubt. He put the brunt of explanation of his theories on sex as an instinct that is frustrated in the child. In other words, for Freud, man harbored *within himself* the seeds of his own undoing. No matter what society man lived in, he was bound to be basically frustrated, since he was "really" an animal with appetites that were inimical to social life. Society, then, was not the culprit in human misery; rather, man's nature itself would be the cause of his eternal unhappiness. And so the full force of the Enlightenment thrust to liberate man was disarmed, even while it was crowned. For Freud, man was not the limitlessly plastic creature for which one could design utopias; he was the essential animal, who carried with him the fate of his basic antisocial nature. With Freud's instinct-theory, Rousseau and Fourier were outdone; man's passion was his fate, and society was the grudgingly best of all possible worlds.

Today we understand that Freud was hardly to be blamed for this great historical hedging (if, indeed, anyone is foolish enough to blame any historical genius for anything); we can see that he was too close to medicine, to physiology—even to the clinical situation itself—to the concrete patient and his anguished suffering. It must always be a bit incredible to the brain surgeon that the fantastic world of flesh, blood, chemistry and neurons that he lays bare with his scalpel is a world that is capable of being shaped and guided by airy symbols! Freud showed that the habits of the adult are so tenacious, because of the early learning of the child. Why did the patient fight so hard against giving up the indoctrination of his early years? To use the brain surgeon analogy, why did this concrete object struggle so violently against itself? Surely not because of any merely *symbolic* reasons: The motive must be in flesh-and-blood, in its basic animal nature. And it is here that we see that Freud failed to carry through with the logic of his own discovery: Man learns to derive his basic feeling of worthwhileness as an animal by performing in symbolic categories of meaning. His sense of worth, in other words, is composed of symbolic meanings that go to the core of his physiological organism. His world as an animal is the fictional world of his society; if he is threatened with losing this, he literally loses everything he has and is. (At least, this is what he *experiences* when he is asked to change his fundamental modes of behavior; we know that the organism can be destroyed by symbolic meanings, but also that it can rise above them and change them; man's conventions keep natural life energy in harness, but life can break out and rise above these conventions. This is how personalities change by learning new rules of behavior.)

Today we do not stop with Freud's incompleted logic, because we no longer accept his dogma. And it is this that has permitted us to understand neurosis in a new way—or in an old way, if we use the ever-present Enlightenment as our point of origin. Neurosis is not man's fate, because it is not due to the inevitable frustration of man's animal nature; it does not reflect the grip of instincts, but rather the bind of symbols. It does not refer to a constriction on man from below, but rather from above—from the realm of social meanings. It points in the direction of unlimited horizons of human life, because it points to a deficit of learning, and not one of nature. What is neurosis, then? It is the weight of early training that hobbles the independent choices of the adult; it is the past learning that is no longer appropriate to new life situations; it is the limitation on perception that leads to a certain blindness of conduct in the face of new challenges. It is the old morality that paralyzes the ability to learn by natural trial and error. And it expresses itself in the most fateful of ways for the human, symbolic animal: It results in the distrust of one's own powers of independent judgment.

And so we draw the full circle, through Freud's work, on the whole synthesis of the nineteenth century. The human animal is one who strives for meaning, and who creates meaning. And neurosis is the delegation of authority for meaning, the disbelief in one's own right to create and sustain meaning. All the terms that we have learned through Freud, and through a half-century of psychiatric clinical work, all referred to the same human deficit: Oedipus complex, the "unconscious," neurosis; all referred to man's fear of freedom in the one distinctive realm in which he could be free—in the realm of the creation of new meanings.

And once we understood this thoroughly, we could understand the great cause of evil in the realm of human affairs. Life is a continued adaptation to new challenges. New challenges call up new choices. And new choices are merely the creation of new meanings, new ways of interpreting and acting in unique situations. In this way, by man's peculiar skill, he is the one animal in nature who has not stopped evolving, because he has remained flexible to devise new solutions to the problems of adaptation. And what is evil, then, if not the crippling of the ability to be maximally flexible in the face of new problems? And what cripples this ability, if not man's fear of creating unique new meanings? And what causes this heavy fear, if not the early learning to which the child is subject? Evil, in sum, is a result of the heavy weight of authority and tradition on the ever-new challenges that each generation meets in the world. Evil is a result of man's disbelief in his right to his own independent and unique powers.

The tradition of psychiatry, then, merged into the tradition of sociology: Evil in social life results from the narrow and uncritical performance of the social fiction. There could be no doubt about it, once the whole dynamic was seen in microcosm. But in order to be seen in this way, it was necessary to show that individuals themselves cease to adapt successfully to life when their meanings become too narrow and shallow. This final and convincing demonstration had to wait until the post-Freudian era; it was then that we could elaborate theories of mental illness, theories of human breakdown, in effect, that showed human breakdown in a wholly new light: not as problems of frustration of instincts, but rather as problems of poverty in choice and meaning. Mental illness was seen to be a problem of human adaptation to the total social environment, exactly as the great psychiatrist Maudsley had urged in the nineteenth century (Altschule, 1957, p. 124).

In this way, psychiatrists, who "have always believed that their profession requires them to be social historians and critics" (Altschule, p. 137), finally acquired a fully scientific platform for their social criticism. Psychiatry and sociology had arisen as natural partners; and after an interlude of scientific separation, were finally fully joined in the middle of the twentieth century.

It had been a long and artificial separation. Psychiatry had gotten along without Marx and Veblen, even though sociology had continually strained in the direction of Freud. But now that the two merged on the same problem, the problem of social criticism, they discovered the identical thing about human failure. Marx's great critique of the social fiction of capitalism was launched under the war cry of the "fetishism of commodities." It was a brilliant and telling criticism of the new game of commercial-industrial society. It meant that man was now narrowing his meanings down to the smallest area of satisfaction, to the area of consumer goods. Everyone thrust his hands into the great grab bag of the new consumer society, drew out a handful of gadgets and trinkets, and hurried home to fondle and admire them. It was indeed a fetishism of the most vicious kind, a fetishism in which man's striving for freedom, dignity, unlimited scope, the largest possible panorama of meanings—all this was sacrificed to a single buy-and-sell fetishism. It was absurd and humanly debasing, but it went ahead full steam, until in the twentieth century man's sharpest mental skill was the quick recall of brand names, the unflinching decision between rival products.

What did this new fetishism represent, except a narrowing down of personal power and meaning? And what did psychiatry, from its side, find out about human breakdown, except that it too was due to fetishism, to the too narrow areas of meaning and choice in the individual's life! Powerlessness in the face of profuse experience—this was schizophrenia; helplessness in the face of constricted choice, this was hysteria and depression; shallowness in the undergoing of meaning, this was psychopathy. And what were the famous "sexual perversions," if not narrowness of behavior and meaning in the area of interpersonal relationships? Freud thought that sadism, masochism, and fetishism were perversions of the mechanism of instinctive satisfaction; but now it became clear that they were unique ways of experiencing meaning, by people whose powers were shallow or inflexible (*cf.* Becker, 1964a, 1965). It was all too plain: not nature, not instinct, but society, social fiction, early training of the child—these were the sources of constricted behavior, of evil in the social realm. And when consumer fetishism began to promote sex fetishism on the scale of the whole society, with all the resources of the mass media, it became plain that consumer fetishism and sex fetishism were natural allies. When man forfeits his critical powers, and his striving toward larger meanings, he is reduced to a true primate: fondling consumer things and sexual things, each in turn; trying to get the maximum stimulus of meaning out of the narrowest possible area. Sociology and psychiatry had completed their merger, and showed man as he was in the new society—not a wicked creature, venting powerful animal urges on the hopeful civilized stage of society; but rather, a neutral, powerless creature uncritically trying to weave together some little satisfactions, with the narrow materials provided for him by the great game of consumer society. Marx and Maudsley, Veblen and Freud, all took their place together.

2. Conclusion

We promised, at the beginning of Chapter Six, to show how the nineteenth century gave us the full Image of Man, solved the riddle of human nature. And now we see how it was solved in psychology, sociology, and psychiatry, as all three merged the materialist and idealist approaches to man. It was only when they had completed this merger that they attained maturity—truly scientific maturity. We also promised at the beginning of our summary account that we would try not to offend the experts, by skimming too lightly over such a vast field of esoteric knowledge. And we thought that they would not need to be offended by such massive abbreviation, since the science of man in all the various disciplines converged on the same, single great truth. Now we have seen what that truth is: that man is the meaning-creating animal; and that society itself, through the early training period in which the child is made a member of it, hobbles and distorts man's unique freedom. Too simple to be a fertile truth? Not if it allows us to get a grip on our world, not if it is exactly what we need and can use. The truth, as the great American sociologist Lester Ward knew, must be simple and nude in order to be effective. It can be esoteric while it is being developed—in fact, it has to be, or it will too easily degenerate into self-defeating slogans, as Paul Tillich observed. But once it has been fully incubated, once it has been patiently labored and brought to full growth, then it can step out in all its nude splendor, like Venus from the sea. It is no less dazzling for all its clarity; and it is surely all the more desirable because of its frank simplicity.

The limpid truth about man's nature justified any abbreviation man might give it, because it proved to be the most directly useful truth of all. It gave us what we had been seeking ever since the Enlightenment: an acute and scientific social criticism, on both the individual and social levels of analysis. Since the Enlightenment? No, since Socrates, as we saw; from his Delphic enjoinder to "Know thyself" (an enjoinder which in his time was an unspeakable mystery); and from him through all the great names that our study develops from, and constantly returns to: Rousseau, Jefferson, Emerson, Dewey, and the rest. They wanted a secular basis for moral action, and we could not get it until we could show what man's nature was, and what he was striving for. Once we knew this, it would be a relatively easy matter to show what was hindering that striving; and, finally, once we showed this, we would know what caused evil in the human realm; *this* would be our New Moral View of the World.

What does it mean to "Know thyself"? It means precisely to know what one's nature is, and what one is striving for. And the only way to know this, we now see, is to be able to examine critically the beliefs one has learned in his society, and to weigh in his own mind whether they are applicable to his life and times. It is exactly as Socrates taught. But now we know explicitly about the fictional nature of social meaning, and minutely about how this fiction is built into our very organism.

The same was true for Emerson's enjoinder in "Self Reliance." "When the good is near you," he wrote, "when you have life in yourself, it is not by any known or accustomed way; you shall not discern the footprints of any other; you shall not see the face of man; you shall not hear any name—the way, the thought, the good, shall be wholly strange and new." What a thrilling way to convey that self-reliance is the assumption of responsibility for one's own unique meanings, for new answers and choices. It is the ideal of democracy, as Emerson and Dewey saw. But in order to fulfill this ideal, in order to provide content for this framework, we had to find an answer to what hindered it. What prevents the individual from stepping where there are no footprints? Today we know it is two things. The first is in his own nature, in the form of an almost-fatal uniqueness: Man, alone among the animals, learns all his meanings from others of his kind. He has no built-in instincts that automatically guide his conduct. Everything he sees, everything he asks, every step he takes has been mapped out by the social learning. In other words, it has been mapped out by the authority of others. These are the accustomed footprints that become his own; they are for the most part safe and sure. But something paradoxical happens to an animal that learns all his meanings from others: When these meanings cease to be safe and sure, this animal becomes helpless. The tragic thing is that he does not feel that he has the right to develop his own new meanings. Among the lower animals, some are solitary, and some move with the herd. But even an animal that is separated from the herd continues to follow his own instinctual mechanisms. Man is the only herd animal who cannot stand this separation from his fellow man; the only animal who is plunged into the deepest imaginable anxiety when he is thrown back on the need to stand alone with his own meanings. What hinders self-reliance? Why is it so difficult for man to fulfill the democratic ideal? Because of the near impossibility of taking a firm stand on his autonomous meanings. The unparalleled promise of democracy took root in the deepest tragedy of the human condition. Democracy was founded on this fundamental paradox, which explains why it is the most worthy and challenging ideal that has ever been thrown out to man.

The ideal of democratic freedom, as we noted at the beginning of Chapter Six, is the challenge that the eighteenth century threw to the world, especially in the person of Jean-Jacques Rousseau.

This was the new vision of Enlightenment science, a science that would be centered on man and that would strive for the realization of moral values in society. Rousseau's challenge was the tear-laden plea that man is good, and that society renders him evil. And Rousseau's great thesis was that evil results from weakness; that self-reliance is the true strength, because it permits one to take independent ethical action. In other words, we can now see that Rousseau actually took Socrates' teaching on independent action, and made it the basis for a science of man in society; and Emerson carried on from Rousseau, and hoped that the American democracy would be such a scientific society, based on free, autonomous men.

Finally, then, in order to get agreement on this vision of Enlightenment science, we had to know the second thing that hindered man from stepping where there are no footprints. We just saw the individual dimension of the problem, that was revealed to us in intimate detail by Freudian and post-Freudian psychiatry: the individual's fear to assume the burden of responsibility for his own meanings. We had to know, in addition, the social dimension of the problem; we had to see in the concrete realm of society and history how weakness was perpetuated. In this way, we could have a fully rounded picture of what prevented the realization of the democratic ideal; and it would be, at the same time, a compelling New Moral View of the World. This is what the union of sociology and psychiatry gave us. We saw that instead of encouraging broad, new and autonomous meanings, commercial-industrial society worked in the opposite direction. It cultivated mass man and the mass mind, promoted sex fetishism along with consumer fetishism, tried with all the modern techniques at its disposal to indoctrinate the great commercial fiction like a huge blanket over the modern mind. The parents began the indoctrination, and the schools carried it on. As Alexis de Tocqueville had already seen in Emerson's time, conformity was the great danger of the new equalitarian society; and conformity is just what the schools sought. The corporations provided even the films that the children would see, to learn how to be good citizens. Progressive education tried to cultivate the uniqueness of each child, but how cultivate uniqueness except by promoting a critical attitude toward the shared cultural fiction? One hope was the university, as we saw earlier; perhaps here man would be given knowledge at the height of the times, knowledge that would make him strong and self-reliant. But the university, like the school, was a tool of the society, of the great game that all played together: it hadn't the least intention of creating spoil-sports of the cultural fiction.

Psychiatry filled in the picture in detail by showing that lack of self-reliant autonomy actually causes human breakdown. The frantic sex that the commercial society encouraged did not necessarily give the individual control over his own life, as the clinical literature proved. The shiny consumer things did not necessarily give the individual a feeling of dignity and worth, as was shown by the large numbers of "successful" people who spent time in our mental hospitals.

There was no way of avoiding it; to know himself, to attempt to be truly self-reliant, man had to learn to be critical of the automatic conditioning of his own society. And in modern times, the new civilization itself was just as antihuman in its fetishization of man as the most tyrannical traditional society. Again, it was just as Rousseau, with his unique genius, had argued the twofold truth. Civilization can be debasing; weakness causes evil. Now we knew exactly what was debasing in our commercial-industrial civilization; and we saw that weakness was essentially narrowness and powerlessness. Not powerlessness to tyrannize others, but powerlessness to assume responsibility for one's own ethical choices. And it was precisely this kind of powerlessness which led and encouraged the tyranny of all against all. We had finally fully vindicated Rousseau by giving a complete picture of the dependence of individual failure upon society. We now had the most compelling picture of how modern society, in the interests of perpetuating its own uncritical social fiction, was using man's own unique and neutral nature against him. It enslaved man through the standard fictional meanings, instead of encouraging the free development of each individual.

Why did man allow this self-defeat? It was the old story—blind habit feared the startling and the unexpected. Citizens wanted ordered and untroubled ways, courtesy rather than charisma. But now we knew that charisma was creative in the most basic way that democracy needs in order to thrive: It created the new and unexpected choices that alone can meet new and inexperienced problems. Nature, and nature alone, had the resources to further its own unfolding and continued progressive adaptation. The bottomless resources of nature, the creative depths of the ever-new—these were located par excellence in the wellsprings of the individual personality. Emerson had said that society everywhere was in conspiracy against the manhood of every one of its members; now we know that this is a conspiracy against democracy itself, and that democracy itself is the only hope for the free evolution of nature. Emerson knew only what the chains were, but now we had a concrete prescription for breaking them. We could finally begin to map out a truly experimental democracy.

When we weight this great achievement we can see how far we have come in self-knowledge in the space of a few brief centuries. The thing is truly amazing to all who have not blunted their capacity to wonder. Not only did we vindicate Rousseau, but we actually solved that dilemma of all dilemmas, the most excruciating of all, the one that took the greatest toll of anguish in the best thinkers, the one that caused the most lofty geniuses to hem and hedge, the one that pitted mind against mind, book against endless book, during the whole history of modern thought. It was the dilemma that we noted at the beginning of Chapter Six, the one that Diderot and Montesquieu were hopelessly entangled in, the same one that began in modern times in the Renaissance, and pitted the mighty Luther against the mighty Erasmus. It was the problem of free will versus determinism—and now it was solved. And it could only be solved by a union of materialism and idealism such as the nineteenth and twentieth centuries gave us in the science of man. This was a union that had to see man as determined, like any other physical thing—as Diderot and Montesquieu knew. Now we know that man *is* determined, like any other physical thing, by the world view that he automatically incorporates into himself, during his early child training. This is the materialist side of the problem. But we also had to see man as undetermined, as a total agent, capable of free acts—as Diderot and Montesquieu hoped, yet could not show. We could show it, once we realized that action was guided by ideas, and that the ideas themselves were not reducible to atoms of sensation and motion, but rather, were learned as concepts and groups of concepts.

This showed us the unique bind that man was in: He *was* determined by his early training and by the general world view shared in his society. But this was not a rigid one-to-one determinism, in which cause-and-effect were mapped out for all time, in strict mathematical terms. Rather, it was a determinism by fate, or by chance, by the accidents of place and birth, of geography and history; it was these that swept the individual blindly along the path of life so that he looked and acted very much like any determined physical thing; he had little say about how he was to see the world, and act in it. But along with this, there existed a unique possibility. Since man was determined by the accident of the ideas he learned in society, he also had the *possibility* of freedom. All he had to do was to strive to undo the grip of these ideas. If he could overcome the automatic grip of the shared social myth, and free himself somewhat of the reflexive action he learned as a child, then the possibility of autonomous action was open to him. Freedom was an *ideal* which man could strive for, the one ideal that would help him overcome the accidental determinism to which all the rest of nature was subject. Reason was his hope and his fate: If he could get a commanding grip on the ideas that reflexively filled his reason, he could overcome his fate. In a word, autonomous reason could overcome the bind of conditioned reason. Diderot and Montesquieu were right, man was determined, but he had to be free, else the human condition lost its distinctive meaning. This is what a Christian humanist like Erasmus knew, in his argument with Luther, when he insisted that man had at least a sliver of free will. Man's presence on earth could have no meaning, if he could not bring to the panorama of life a bit of his own distinctive free energies. Man was a helper of God, and not an abject slave of earthly circumstances.

But we also understand that in order even to glimpse the possibility of freedom, man must turn against the social fiction—and against himself: against his early training, and against his deep-seated fear to stand alone with his new meanings. Under these limitations freedom is almost impossible; it is a true labor of Hercules. How is man to attain it, except with the help of many accidents of fate? The man who has glimpsed the possibility of freedom, and who looks at himself honestly, must see how little his active will had to do with his life—how many accidents and circumstances conspired to push him to the brink of freedom; how he was separated unwittingly from the shared social fiction; how he was carried further and further along on his own, like driftwood tossed higher and higher upon the sand. He must admit, with Luther, that man is but a vessel, that his will is truly bound, and that only circumstances can unbind it, or, to speak mythically in Luther's sense, freedom can only come as a result of God's grace.

And finally, when this chosen man stands alone with the freedom given by this grace, to whom can he turn for affirmation and support? He must turn to the highest powers that permit and sustain his existence. Erasmus and Luther were then both right: Man can have a small measure of freedom; but freedom belongs to God alone. Man is only free to become an open vehicle for powers that he cannot understand.

This leaves us with the only question that need concern us, and to which we must now turn: How can man himself facilitate the ideal possibility of freedom? What can he do in society that will help the free release of natural powers, by making it less a matter of sheer circumstance and accident? Once we understand this ultimate challenge to man, we will have a complete New Moral View of the World.

CHAPTER EIGHT

Toward the Theological Dimension

> "Democracy . . . cannot afford to educate men for citizenship, for efficiency, or for use. Its only authority is reason, just as its only strength is criticism. . . . The superiority of its persons is its only strength. To say as much is to say that democracy lives dangerously. For humanity is dangerous, and is not to be controlled by committees of men. But the danger from its freedom—from a program which asks it what it can be rather than tells it what to do—is less than the blind risk that is run when the program is to mislead and miseducate it; or, what amounts to the same thing, to educate it partially."
>
> —Mark Van Doren (1943, pp. 38-42 *passim*)

In a work which is so frankly and fully rooted in the Enlightenment, the reader may be startled to come upon a major chapter that uses the word "theological." Isn't there some real contradiction here? We have been proposing a New Moral View of the World, and we have been proposing it in the full Enlightenment spirit, which means that the morality we seek will have to be a secular one, drawn on empirical data. Are we then subverting our whole design, by crowning our secular moral creed with an ultimate theological dimension? Do we intend to propose a map for social reconstruction that fumbles at the most crucial point—that sacrifices a fully *reasoned* moral creed for one that ultimately we will have to take on faith? Have we come this far, gone through all this elaborate long-winded preparation, only to admit defeat? Let the reader be assured at the outset: The answer is no.

In Chapter Six we said that the nineteenth century gave us the full Image of Man, and the twentieth might be considered an elaborate footnote. Largely this is true, especially if we take the nineteenth century up to its true and natural end in 1914, rather than 1900. By then Freud had written his major works, and so had William James, Josiah Royce, James Mark Baldwin, and Walter Rauschenbusch. If we place all these men in the nineteenth century, we can say that the twentieth added little that was essential to our general understanding of man. But now we must note that the biggest part of the elaborate footnote of our time is the attempt to bring theology back into its rightful place in social theory. The science of man found itself looking at theology much the same way that modern psychology finds itself looking at philosophy: Both philosophy and theology had been banished with great fanfare, and much self-congratulation, from the limitless frontier lands of science. But now that we have long since staked out our scientific claims, and mined deeper and deeper shafts into the virgin soils—whom do we come upon sitting atop the biggest nuggets? Most of us are still incredulous, and even resentful; some of us a bit shamefaced. But it is our fault: William James had already told us the lay of the land: ". . . the divorce, between scientist facts and religious facts may not necessarily be as eternal as it at first sight seems. . . ." This divorce, concludes James, might one day appear to have been a "temporarily useful eccentricity, rather than the definitively triumphant position which the sectarian scientist at present so confidently announces it to be" (1902, p. 491, n.). That was in 1902. The day that James then forecast has now arrived; his unique genius has been vindicated, as he knew it would be.

Bernard Iddings Bell has understood this peculiar task and cast of our time: "The place of the religionist . . . today is that of the scientist in the seventeenth and early eighteenth centuries; he vigorously protests against improper curtailment of experience" (1949, p. 121). But it is more than simply curtailment of experience, or rather it is more concrete than that. The scientist has always been willing to admit that religion gives experience, and that science may curtail it; he has usually held, with Freud, that this kind of experience is precisely fantasy experience, and should be curtailed in the interests of hard reality. On this ground there can be no fruitful argument.*

But what if—fantasy beyond fantasy—theology were to give us concrete data that social order is not possible, nor human freedom attainable, without a theological dimension to human experience? Religion has always enjoined man to realize his "almost hopeless condition"—to quote from Gorham Munson's fine book (1930, p. 281). What if theology were able to show us *specifically* the ways in which man's condition was hopeless, no matter what he tried to achieve in an atheistic society? And what if theology could show us further the ways in which this hopelessness could be turned to human advantage, to the realization of greater liberty, dignity, natural creativity? This is the ultimate challenge that we promised to explore at the close of the last chapter. Now we will see that this dimension of the New Moral View of the World is wholly consonant with our full rooting in the great Enlightenment. Theology has given us the most compelling rational grounds for including it as the superordinate dimension of human experience. In fact, it is only in this way that we can actually complete what the Enlightenment began, because it is only today that we can answer one of the questions that began the French Enlightenment itself: Bayle's famous hypothesis as to whether a society of atheists was possible. We shall find that our answer has to be phrased, not in terms in which the Enlightenment began, but rather in those in which it ended: *not:* Is a society of atheists possible? but: Is it a desirable ideal? We know it is possible, since we have seen it in our time. The question is—What does it do to man?—and this, too, we have seen in our time. We finally have full empirical evidence for resolving this two-hundred-and-fifty-year dilemma.

* Rather, there can be no fruitful argument here. The scientist should study James's account of the deep upheaval in his thought and life as a scientist after reading Bergson, and discovering that reason was merely one provisional aspect of organismic adaptation. And the scientist should further ponder the lasting impression that James made on Freud, after their brief meeting. Freud, preoccupied with death all his life, wished that he could meet it as bravely as the ailing James did (*cf.* Jones, 1963). See also Gregory Zilboorg's study (1959). We should now begin to see a whole series of new studies on the relationship between an individual's beliefs and the quality of his work and life lived.

1. Naturalistic Ontology: How Life Achieves Maximum Meaning and Conviction

One of the things we are celebrating, in these pages, is the comparatively short time it took man to understand the riddle of his own nature. Physics, chemistry, biology—these sciences had much longer developments; astronomy spans several thousand years. The Greek beginnings on the problem of human nature gave no spectacular results; Socrates' attempt toward humanistic self-understanding was slowly dissipated by Plato, as he tried to build a self-consistent philosophy and answer the urgent problem of social reconstruction (the problem that had already sacrificed his master). So, all our major results date from the eighteenth century—the time when man first began seriously to study himself—a short two hundred fifty years. How is it that we should know as much about man as we do, say, about the movement of the heavenly bodies, even though we have been at it a remarkably shorter period of time? A large part of the answer is that we are already inside our subject-matter; we know it more intimately, and more surely—a fact of the superiority of the human sciences over the natural sciences, at which Vico rejoiced at the very beginning of modern man's self-study. If we could get ourselves inside the atom, Heisenberg's principle of indeterminacy would probably be immediately crystal clear; after all, in the matter of human "indeterminacy," Rousseau already clearly saw why he suddenly deviated from the route of his accustomed walk, even though he did it unthinkingly and automatically. Long before Freud he understood an aspect of "unconscious motivation." The moral of this anecdote is that the honest man can see through himself even quicker than the honest scientist can see through nature.

The point of these introductory remarks is merely to say that the science of man could have understood its subject-matter even sooner than it did. What prevented this? Largely one thing: intolerance. The intolerance of method, the claims to exclusivity, the doctrine of a single valid approach to the study of man. The place where this took its greatest toll was in the fragmentation of the disciplines, the isolation of the various approaches to man. But undoubtedly the most harmful intolerance of all was the intolerance of philosophy in the science of man. The scientific world of the mid-nineteenth century reacted to the German nature-philosophy with a mighty groan: no more uncontrolled speculation, no more wild theories, no more attempt to figure out what the universe as a whole was up to, no more trying to find out what life "wanted" under the conditions of existence. The problem was, instead, what was going on *in* the organism. The results of this scientific revolt against speculative philosophy we know only too well: Psychiatry turned away from the problem of man in his social milieu, and became uncompromisingly organic. Griesinger's followers completely buried Ideler and the earlier German humanism he represented. Maudsley and his broad views died, and the medical classifiers moved in. In pathology, Virchow discovered the cell as the focus of illness; and at the same time he called on doctors to be the elder statesmen of social legislation for health! He did not see the fatal result of his own narrowing down of scope in the search for disease: The microscope is not on the scale of man's social milieu; it eclipses his total world picture, his real striving. Pragmatism, and the functional psychology of the end of the century, was a reaction to all this; and today, as we still struggle to fill out and perfect pragmatism by giving it some kind of firm standards of value, we are still fighting against the exclusion of philosophy from the science of man. We are not trying to rehabilitate the German nature-philosophy, but rather to soften the revolt against it; we are not going to entertain seriously the answers it offered to the problem of nature, but we would like to do this: We would like to make some of its questions legitimate once again in the science of man.

The fact is that we must. In order to understand man, we must understand what he is striving for—not only as a member of society, not only as a unitary organism, but as a part of *nature,* as a dimension of life. Rousseau taught us that man's nature was neutral; Fourier taught us that the passions themselves were empty vehicles, to be twisted and filled differently in each society; Simmel and Huizinga showed us how man everywhere played *at* society with these passions; Weber and Veblen showed that social life was a great game, a celebration of meaning that became inseparable from the basic problem of human adaptation and survival. With all this, we understood much about man, very much; we saw that he wanted meaning and maximum conviction, and we learned how he went about getting it. But one outstanding question remained—the most difficult and most puzzling of all, a question that is scientifically insolent: What was behind all of man's peculiar urges, what was he trying to do as a vehicle of the life force? For only if we could understand this abstract problem could we answer the greatest practical puzzle of all: What were the possibilities of life on the level of human existence; and, conversely, What was there about the human condition that was hopeless? These were the ultimate questions of the science of man because they were the ultimate questions of a New Moral View of the World. Only if we could answer them could we have a dependable and thoroughgoing map for social reconstruction. And, as we said, these were the very questions that nineteenth-century science had given up asking. In a word, the science of man had to re-legitimate naturalistic ontology because it contained the answer to the most urgent and practical needs; and this is the peculiar and daring task of our time.

It will be easy for us to understand, then, that if this is peculiar and daring today, fifty years ago it was blatant heresy. And once we understand this, we will know too how a thinker of the stature of James Mark Baldwin could be so gracefully dropped from the front rank of our preoccupations all these years. Baldwin frankly faced up to the question of what organismic life, on the level of man, is striving for. He specifically asked what the true, the good, and the beautiful meant, in terms of the human organism. This would give us a picture of the "real" world from inside man's striving. It would confirm the thesis of pragmatism by showing values to be relative to life; but it would try to overcome the hopeless relativity of pragmatism by making higher expressions of life itself the standard of value: Man would simply strive, then, for higher degrees of truth, goodness, and beauty; and both nature and human value would be satisfied.

A. The problem of freedom in nature

Before we ask whether Baldwin's work was "successful" or not, let us look briefly at what he did. The first thing we have to remind ourselves of is the tradition that he represented. Who was the first one to pose bluntly the question about the limitations and possibilities of life; that is, pose it in secular terms and not theological ones? Kant, of course; and this is the beginning of the tradition that Baldwin brought to a head during the first two decades of this century. Pragmatism was really the modern elaboration of Kant, and Baldwin's major work was completed during William James's lifetime. The point of Kant's whole work, we will remember, is that the organism is immersed in a transcendent natural world; that this immersion leads to a limitation of knowledge, because of the relativity of the organism's perspective. Man can only know that which he is equipped by nature to know. Of course Kant had immediate predecessors—Diderot, for instance—but he summed up the whole problem of knowledge beautifully for his age. Man was separated from the rest of nature, and however much he would strive, Truth would always be beyond his grasp. The world that man thinks is "real" is only a small part of Reality—a Reality that he can never fully know.

What, then, is man's fate in nature? On the face of it, it is truly nasty and brutish, to use Hobbes's often-quoted words. The materialist, atomist view of man was a pessimistic one, because it saw man as limited, a slave to selfish appetites, doomed to separation. The world that man discovered would be limited by his self-seeking appetites, limited by his imperfect reason, limited by his hopeless separation. The only thing he might achieve was a glimpse of a segment of reality, a moment's fleeting satisfaction of his appetites; and then, merciful death would still his striving, and give him the peaceful union with nature that he could never achieve in his brutish lifetime. Hardly a happy fate, we can agree.

But Kant saw a different fate, and it was this view that Schiller, Schelling, and Baldwin elaborated, as did Dewey in his *Experience and Nature* and his *Art as Experience*. Man's situation was really quite different from what the atomistic materialists had painted. It had to be, or there would be no possibility of freedom, no distinction in the human condition; man would take his place with the rest of nature, in utter servitude to natural forces. We saw earlier that this pessimistic view was precisely what Diderot and Montesquieu fought against, but not successfully in their time. The fact is that man is not a limited atom in nature, an atom with appetites and possibilities fixed for all time. He does have the possibility of a unique kind of freedom. Instead of being a mechanical atom, he is an energetic organism. This means that he does not simply relay the energies of nature, in a one-to-one fashion, from one mechanical point to another, inside and outside himself. Rather, as an organism, he can draw new energies out of himself, energies that are not completely determined by his environment.

But an organism is still transcended by nature, even though it is not a mechanical atom; still immersed in a world that it cannot wholly understand, still separated from the total truth and reality. How can it find more than animal satisfaction in such a world? How can it find a freedom which would be distinctive to the human condition? There can be only one answer: This organism would have to create a new reality of its own, and continue to create and expand it. And it could do this in two ways, each related to the other. It could open new sources of energy from within itself; and it could open new and unfamiliar views of the objects in its world.

Now we can ask: What prevents the organism from opening new sources of energy within itself? And we can give the familiar answer: the bind of habit, which seeks accustomed satisfactions, so that no new kinds of adaptation are called into play and no new sources of energy opened up. And what prevents the organism from seeing new aspects of the external world? The bind of accustomed perception, the familiar modes of thought and reason, the patterns of seeing and thinking which stamp the world out of the same habitual mold.

What, then, is the tool that man uses to break out of this rigid mold of living and seeing, a tool that only he has in great abundance? The answer is imagination, playful imagination. It is this that suspends the laws of necessity, that circles around the automatic adaptation of the organism to its hard, everyday environment. Imagination fashions a new world. Schiller called it a playful world, and Baldwin a semblant world. And it is this semblant world that becomes a new "real" for the total, energetic organism. Imagination is the link between new sources of energy within the organism and a new kind of external world outside it. In this way, imagination circles around the bind of habitual thought, and liberates new energies of adaptation; and it also circles around the accustomed facets of objects and shows them in a new light. It helps us to fashion a new, real world, drawn from the untapped energies within ourselves, and from the unexpected aspects of objects we see in a new way. Man, with his imagination, backs off from the world of the lower animals, and opens out a new one for himself. He thus becomes the only animal in nature to create a new world out of himself, and to carve out a new segment of reality, at one and the same time. Again we can remind ourselves that Plato had intuited the whole process when he said that the gods are happiest when man plays. Now we know even more exactly what that means. It applies to all of man's symbolic activities—to science as well as art—to all uses of imagination and conceptual abstraction, to all invention of new form. This is "aesthetics" in its largest sense: the creation of a new world for a new kind of total satisfaction of the human organism. This is what human freedom means, and the only thing it can mean for an organism transcended by nature, but an organism, all the same, which has boundless depths of evolution within itself. Augustine taught us that we become like the objects we love or desire; which is another way of saying that we become according to the world we strive to live in. As man merges with his new world, and seeks satisfaction in it, he *becomes* a new kind of organism.

And so we have a tradition of human uniqueness and freedom that stretches from Plato, Augustine, Kant, Schiller, Schelling, through Baldwin and Dewey right up to our time. It is ours to use and develop today. It showed us man's limitations within nature, the hopelessness of his condition, and yet the possibility of his freedom, by developing the life potential within himself. It showed us that life was bound by the conditions of existence; and yet that *in* the conditions of existence, life could attain to a kind of freedom. Life could create its own new real world, even while satisfying the strivings of the limited organism within nature. It showed us that the standard of the Real, the measure of the True, was contained within life itself. But one thing it did not show us;

the question was still left open: How do we use the standard of life *as a standard,* how can we tell which kind of "play" gives man the most freedom, the most release of the inner life force? This is the *practical* question of social reconstruction, for which we turned to naturalistic ontology for an answer. Let us continue our quest.

B. The paradox of striving versus stillness

In addition to the problem of freedom, naturalistic ontology helped us to answer a second great paradox of human striving. This second paradox is a further clue to what makes aesthetics so satisfying for the organism; and it is this clue that will ultimately lead us to a solution of the problem of a standard of value, a standard from within the life force itself. Naturalistic ontology showed us that organisms achieve satisfaction in one basic way, and that is by "merging" with nature. In this merger, the organism temporarily stills its appetites and striving, and so finds a momentary peace. For single moments, from time to time, the hopeless separation of life from nature is overcome. Augustine had expounded this thesis with his idea of *quies,* or perfect rest that gives satisfaction of desire. Hegel gave it a large place in his work, by showing how life tries to keep its own distinctive, restless quality, and yet seeks to be stilled at the same time. Dewey developed this ontology, as did Heidegger and Sartre.

This, then, is the second great paradox of our naturalistic ontology of life: the desire of life to keep its identity as a moving, feeling force; and yet, at the same time to lose this identity in a peace-giving merger with nature. This paradox is all of a piece with the problem of freedom that we outlined above: how to triumph over the limitations of nature, while yet remaining within nature. And this new paradox of movement and merger, like the paradox of freedom, is resolved in the same way: The more *complete* the merger, the more of the total organism that is included in it, the greater the satisfying stillness of temporary respite. So we might say that the "secret" of the greatest possible satisfaction of life is to bring the "largest amount" of life force into a union with nature. And this is precisely the "secret" of aesthetics. It answers the question of why man's play-forms are so satisfying.

Aesthetics gives the highest pleasure because it is the category that merges all the others, that pulls all the loose and disparate strands of experience together into one harmonious whole. Intellect, imagination, the whole organism of feeling—thought and dream, flesh and blood, emotion and nerves—all are fused into one integrating merger. The aesthetic object draws man's world together, by drawing the whole man firmly into it. In contemplating the aesthetic object, the totality of the life force is awakened and stilled at one and the same time. The aesthetic object is the *symbol* of fulfillment created playfully *by* man, that at the same time fulfills the *concrete* nature that is embodied *in* man. And it is precisely this merger of imaginative symbol and physical, pulsating life that gives the highest intensity of satisfaction to the human organism.

So we can conclude our very brief sketch of the two great problems of life that naturalistic ontology reveals to us. Even in this sketchy way, we can see how important this ontology is for an understanding of life on the human level. It reveals to us the most important thing about what man is after in his world because it shows us what life itself is striving for. It shows us nothing less than how man experiences his greatest meaning, and how he gets the unshakable conviction that this meaning is right for all time, right above all other meanings. Why the greatest meaning? Because the greatest meaning is achieved when all the aspects of experience are fused into one related whole. Meaning is, after all, nothing more than the relationships between things, controlled and understood by the experiencing organism. Why such unshakable conviction? Because, when experience is brought together and integrated, the life force attains its highest intensity; and when this intensity is fused completely with nature, via the aesthetic object, life attains its highest truth and reality (*cf.* also Becker, 1964a; 1965).

This, then, is what Baldwin meant when he said that the aesthetic object contains in itself the true, the good, and the beautiful. For an animal that strives within nature, the good must be that which is inwardly satisfying, that which stills the desire of the life force; the true must be that which is proven in experience, that which overcomes the hopeless separation of the organism and his environment, by showing man that his inward strivings can be satisfied in external nature; the beautiful, finally, is the union of both of these, because it is in this union that the life force attains both its highest intensity, and its deepest peace (Baldwin, 1915, p. 287).

C. The inclusion of ontology within the science of man

And so we see fully why pragmatism, as represented by Baldwin, used the aesthetic as the basic category of value: It was the category of life itself; it was the category of the highest True, the most Good and Beautiful, the really Real. The next step was to try to make this category a true standard of value, and we know that it is here that pragmatism failed. Let us look at the attempt in this last section before we finally judge how it failed.

We can already see what Baldwin did to the German nature-philosophy, and that was to take it down off its high metaphysical perch. The problem of aesthetics, the standard of success of the life force, could no longer be a transcendental one, but had to be a secular one, one derived from the experience of the organism itself. Thus it was Baldwin who, after Darwin, tried fully to naturalize the philosophy of Hegel and Schelling. How best to do this? Simply by merging it fully with our knowledge of man, by resting it firmly on the science of man itself (*cf.* 1915, p. viii).

This is what Baldwin did, or rather tried to do. His problem was to show what was *distinctive* about the human world that had to be fused by the aesthetic experience. Baldwin showed this in his analysis of human thought, and the genesis of the social self. We knew that man was distinctive because he had a spirit or soul, a self-identity that was a locus of conscious symbolic experience. The German idealists, especially Hegel, had already made a brilliant beginning in showing how the self-consciousness of man was developed in relationship to external objects. What Baldwin did was to take this fundamental dualism of thoughts and things, and show exactly how it arose in the child, and how the human self was developed genetically. In other words, as in the problem of aesthetics, he took German Idealism and brought it down to earth after Darwin: With the German Idealists the self was still transcendental; Baldwin made it fully empirical and historical.

When he had done this, he could show exactly the kinds of fragmentation of human experience that had to be brought together by the aesthetic. He showed that by virtue of thought and symbols, man's world is a uniquely "dualistic" one; and that in order to gain maximum meaning and conviction, these unique dualisms had to be overcome. I don't think there is any need for us here to go into detail on this problem (see Becker 1964a; 1965). Baldwin's dualisms were quite straightforward and simple: the "theoretical" versus the "practical," the "mind" versus the "body," "inner" versus "outer," and "freedom" versus "necessity." These were the basic dualisms that result from the peculiarity of human mental life, and this is what Baldwin limited himself to showing (*cf.* 1915, pp. viii, and 232). But what we do have to understand here is why Baldwin failed, why he failed to enthrone the aesthetic as a sure standard of value that would overcome the relativity of pragmatism. Now we are ready to assess this failure. It marks a great historical stage, and leads us to the most advanced positions of human thought.

D. Conclusion: the failure of organismic aesthetics as a standard of value

Simply stated, Baldwin's theory, which he called Pancalism, failed because it limited itself to the mental life, to the abstract psychological dualisms of individual striving. Could we get a standard of value out of this? What kind of standard? We would have to get the same one that Baldwin got, and this is really no standard at all. Granted that the organism achieves fulfillment in the aesthetic merger; granted that it gets maximum meaning and conviction by pulling its experience together in one harmonious whole; granted that on the human level this fusion is very complex because it includes thoughts and symbols; granted that for this reason, the aesthetic object is the human hedonic object par excellence; granted, then, that art is the highest form of satisfaction, the consummation of human striving for rich experience; grant all this—and still we must ask, what is the standard for the good, true and beautiful, what "real" is more real than any other? Suppose that each organism does find its maximum meaning in the aesthetic, what then? We have a standard that is complete anarchy, where each person is a standard unto himself. The idea of unlimited self-satisfaction is, then, no standard at all. It is an abstraction, an outline, nothing more. In itself it is theoretically important, but only theoretically, since it is empty of concrete content. What does it tell us about the practical social problem, about what we should do toward social reconstruction? It tells us, we now see, nothing more than Schiller and Schelling could tell us with their doctrine of the primacy of the aesthetic; even though it was fully naturalistic and came after Darwin, it is as unrelated to the problem of social order and social possibility as the nineteenth-century idealist anarchists were. With Baldwin's failure, pragmatism itself failed, as we have said, to be a guide to the problems of man in society in our time.

2. The Need for a Critical Individual and Social Aesthetics

We can immediately see what was needed that Baldwin failed to supply in his time. Pragmatism wanted to make the life force itself, as centered in the full human organism, the standard of value. Well and fine. But then we had to know exactly what hindered the fullest expression of this life force. If aesthetics was the category of maximum reality, then we needed to know what kinds of aesthetics were inferior to others, we needed a way of judging those aesthetic mergers that released more of the life force than did others. We needed, in a word, a way of judging "'good" aesthetics and "bad" aesthetics. And we needed it on the individual as well as on the social level.

A. A critical individual aesthetics

Baldwin's psychology, as we saw, could not help us here because even though it was an acute psychology, a penetrating study of the development of the dualisms of the mental life, it was too abstract. We needed to know precisely what there was about the aesthetic merger of individual "A" that released more of the life force than did that of individual "B." An impossible assignment? It was so during Baldwin's time, but it is not during ours. We had Freud's work to build on; and now that we are fully in the post-Freudian epoch, the whole matter has become crystal clear. On the one hand, Freud gave us the basic clue for judging "good" versus "bad" aesthetics; but on the other hand, he took it away. In effect, we had to understand man as fundamentally an "aesthetic" animal, that is, an animal who strives for total, organismic mergers with his world; but who, in some way, is prevented from releasing maximum amounts of new life energies in these mergers. Now Freud gave us just this, when he showed that the adult is bound in many ways by his early training. "Bad" aesthetics, then, would be that which the individual undertakes under the old authority, under the coercion of the old rules for behavior that he learned as a child. This would be the coercion of fear of making new and independent choices, unexpected ones, choices more appropriate to new situations; hence, choices that would take the individual out of his old world, and continually renew the possibility of developing the life force. "Good" aesthetics, then, are the choices that are not bound rigidly by the early learning, the ones that are not limited by automatic perceptions, the ones that are not a reflex of childhood conditioning. "Good" aesthetics are those which the individual undertakes, under the aegis of his own responsible powers, out of his narrow, familiar world. The thing that makes one aesthetic pattern broader and richer would be simply that it releases more of the life force in the aesthetic integration.

But as we said, on the other hand, Freud took this clear picture and muddled it with his theory of instinctual drives. As an *aesthetic* animal, man would strive for symbolic meanings, meanings that embraced a total situation; but as an instinctual animal, man would strive primarily for the satisfaction of biological instincts. We had to see man uncompromisingly as a searcher after total symbolic meanings, and not narrow neural ones; and it is this that Freud gave us, and obscured at the same time.

Once we clarified it by going beyond the narrow instinct theory, we had literally a windfall of theory on man as an animal who seeks total aesthetic mergers. We could understand sadism, masochism, and fetishism as "bad" aesthetics, as clumsy, automatic, and limited ways of relating to others; patterns of behavior used by individuals who are basically weak and shallow. We could then understand that the capacity to love, and the kind of love one could give, varied with one's powers. It could be liberating and creative, or constricting and negating. It depends largely on whether the lover is strong and free, or weak and bound by automatic habit: Is he building himself firmly into his habitual world by choosing an object that serves old needs and fears? Or is he reaching out courageously for a new world by choosing an object that leads him on to new perceptions and behaviors? It all depends on whether one stamps the world with the old, stale perceptions, or tries to look at it with new ones. Both kinds of lover achieve aesthetic mergers with their objects—the sadist as well as the stronger and maturer person; but the sadist only succeeds in choking off and inhibiting the life force in his object; the freer person brings a new unfolding in himself as well as in the object he loves. This difference in love, then, is a difference in kinds of aesthetics, and it is a difference between fearful, rigidly conditioned people and those who are more flexible and free, those who reach for new choices and responsibilities.

I have discussed this difference more fully elsewhere (1964a; 1965), and there is nothing to be gained by elaborating it here. But now we can't fail to note what it brings to the naturalistic ontology of freedom that we discussed earlier. As we saw, freedom for the life force, freedom for an organism immersed in a transcendent nature, can only come by drawing new energies out of itself. And this means releasing more of the inner life force, and at the same time seeing more of the real objects in the external world. Now we can understand further how this abstract ontology can be interpreted in the concrete individual existence! What keeps man from unfolding new natural energies from within himself? What keeps him from seeing the objects in the external world in new and richer ways? We have answered it, and answered it in terms of concrete facts in the individual life history: the automatic implanting of the child's world-view that takes place during the early training period. It is this that prevents man from fashioning new "real" worlds, and what makes one world more "real" than another, that is, more broad, rich, free, more open to the developing life force. And so we have a standard of "good" aesthetics versus "bad," of "good" love versus "bad" love, of "really" real versus "less" real—a standard inherent in the life force itself. But unlike Baldwin's abstract psychology, this standard can be approached in the concrete terms of the individual's life history: What prevents him from broadening his aesthetic mergers, from moving into freer and more liberating kinds of love?

Let us pause further at this time to note one striking thing that we will return to later in our summing up of the theological dimension. This union of naturalistic ontology with our discovery of the constrictions on freedom of the life force is one of the great achievements of human thought. It actually closes the circle on Augustine's great theory of love, and hence on over fifteen hundred years of thought on the problem of finding an empirical standard for the liberation of the life force. Augustine's theory, we may recall, was that all love was desire, desire for *quies,* or perfect rest. In other words, desire for satisfying merger with the external world. In his view, all love was of the same quality: It was the seeking by organismic life of basic satisfaction in the world. Augustine did not, then, pass judgment on love itself, since desire had the same quality in everyone. But he had to prescribe how that love or desire could be best stilled or satisfied; and here he decided that it was a difference in the object sought. It was a difference of where one's love was directed: *cupiditas* or *caritas,* to earthly things or to divine things; to things that constricted the expression of the life force and did not basically satisfy it; or to things that gave it fullest possible expression and that were really capable of quenching desire (see Nygren, 1953). Today, then, we are ready to complement Augustine's theory, from a secular, scientific point of view, by beginning to talk about the capacity to love as a capacity for larger and freer aesthetic mergers, a capacity to rid oneself of the conditioned and the constricting. In other words, we may very well be able to talk about any kind of constriction on aesthetics and love, as kinds of "fetishization" of the life force—as the great Russian philosopher Vladimir Soloviëv had already done. And then we should be able to judge empirically whether the divine object is indeed the most liberating of all. Our standard, as we shall see, would be basically simple: Is it freely chosen by responsible men; and does it lead to richer aesthetics, more liberating love—a greater outpouring of the life force, as well as a greater satisfaction of man's yearnings.

B. A critical social aesthetics

From a critical individual aesthetics we turn to the complementary problem of a critical social aesthetics. As we would expect, it is actually merely an extension into the social realm of the problem of what limits the individual freedom. So we can talk about "good" social aesthetics in the same way that we talk about "good" individual aesthetics: Does it liberate more of the life force? Only, in the social sphere, we have an additional dimension to consider: not only the early child training, that implants an uncritical, automatic world view; but also and especially the shared social fictions that reinforce and extend the early slavery of each citizen.

The social is merely the dimension in space of the individual; the social is the sphere of the object man chooses. So that, when we talk about the un-free society, the constriction of the life force on the total social level, what we are actually talking about is a society of unfree individuals. Then, our basic empirical question is just an extension of the same question we asked above: What kinds of "play" give the most freedom to man in society? What kinds of social fiction are more liberating than others? In other words, what kinds of "social aesthetics" are "good," and what kinds are "bad"?

(1) *Fragmented Society and Fetishization*

We already discussed this problem in Chapter Six, when we talked about society as a great game, as a play-form; and when we said that we needed to assess the cost in human life of man's social myths, the actual defeat of human adaptation to nature, by man's social fictions. Now we can understand even more clearly how to judge whether these fictions are constricting or liberating. When Marx accused the new commercial-industrial society of working against man, he was opting for the whole man, for the full development of human powers. In a word, commodity fetishism was just that: It was fetishization of the life force, it was "bad" aesthetics, because it was the merger of man and thing in a very narrow area of satisfaction. And as we pointed out in Chapter Seven, when consumer fetishism is allied with sex fetishism—an alliance encouraged by all the force of the mass media of the commercial society—then man is narrowed down to most reflexive, least dignified striving. It is not that goods are "bad," or that healthy sex is unclean or unworthy of man. Far from it. It is rather a question of whether man is choosing these types of aesthetic merger in free, responsible ways; whether he is flexible enough to cultivate other areas of aesthetic satisfaction; in a word, whether the new society encourages the life force to be conditioned or free. The question answers itself: There is nothing in the new society to give man a critical grasp on the consumer and sex aesthetics, or on his own conditioning. Hence, it is a thoroughly fetishized aesthetics, a *cupiditas* in the full Augustinian sense of the term. It gives us an image of man blindly and pitifully groping for satisfaction by dealing with the narrowest aspects of earthly strivings. It shows man unable to achieve *quies* because as soon as he has a desirable consumer object, or sex object, the mass media awaken new hungers for still newer and fresher things. It is a slavery of the most abject kind, a slavery that is debasing both to the man who is driven, as well as to the object toward which he is driven. In a society in which everything is a *thing* to be had, to be used, and to be discarded when no longer satisfying—in such a society people themselves are turned into objects, into things. This is a criticism of "objectification" and bureaucratic "quantification" of man that has been echoed by the best minds since the nineteenth century—by Matthew Arnold, by Scheler, by Buber, by Tillich, by countless others. Fetishized man is human aesthetics at its nadir, it is man *curvatus,* as Augustine expressed it: man bowed to earth, man looking down at the most transient things, man humbled, the human spirit constricted, almost extinguished. We need no more compelling empirical data of what constricts the life force on the level of the social fiction. It is uncritical man in uncritical society; automatic, shallow, narrow types of aesthetic merger, in place of broad, free, rich mergers.

At this time the reader may have his fill of this abstract level of discussion, and he may well ask what we might mean by "broad" mergers in place of "narrow" ones. How do we make a judgment in this difficult and vague area? This is indeed the major question, the question that brings us to the largest, most advanced problem of social theory: How do we judge the social fiction? How do we overcome the relativity of value systems? How, in sum, can we hope to approach a problem as massive as the critical evaluation of a total society? Yet, this is exactly what we must do. It is the same problem, remember, that we introduced in Chapter Six, the problem of judging what is the cost in human life and suffering of man's social fictions. And there we saw that there were indeed ways of making such judgments. For example, all societies are a conglomerate of fictional ways of sustaining and creating symbolic meanings. In terms of the fictional nature of their meanings, they are all relative, all more-or-less equal, provided they meet the task of adaptation to the hard physical world. But some social fictions take more of a toll of life and suffering than others, and this can be roughly judged. This greater toll of evil can be best seen in the transition in scale between "primitive" society and "civilized" society, as we noted. We also saw that this was a definite historical phenomenon. Primitive societies gave way to the large civilizations of the great river valleys of the world, and the peculiarly "modern" character of our world took shape: large-scale conquest, expansion, plunder, great migrations. The social fictions, in a word, became more random and confused; they lost their organic unity; societies became fragmented, where previously they had been well integrated. The symbols themselves lost their organic relationship with the life ways of the whole society, as A. M. Hocart has so well shown in his writings on India and Southeast Asia. The picture was enlarged in both scale and confusion. One way to understand this difference graphically is to compare an anthropological study of a small tribe with a sociological study of a large society or a historical study of a whole civilization. We see the difference very clearly when we compare Marcel Mauss's famous anthropological essay "The Gift" with Veblen's study of America or with Max Weber's study of India. In all of them, the social game is fictional, but there are great differences in the way it is being played. On the primitive scale, we see integration, communalism, coherent meaning extending over the whole society. On the level of the large-scale civilized society, we see fragmentation into social classes; conflict or tension between the classes or special interest groups, professions, or guilds. If we had to sum up the difference most simply and concisely, we would say that change of scale had resulted, historically, in the loss of integrated social meaning.

And this loss of integrated social meaning is a real loss of "social sense." As the social game becomes distended, unrelated in its parts, it becomes literally senseless. We see it all very clearly in the difference we noted in Chapter Six, the difference between the primitive potlatch and the Roman or American one. There is more social sense in the primitive destruction of goods, simply because it is integrated into a broad fabric of rights and duties, reciprocity and obligation, earthly and divine meanings, and so on. This means that everyone in the society is in some way benefited or enriched by the goings-on, no matter how blatantly fictional they may be. But what happens in the modern civilized potlatch—in the great consumer display of contemporary society? It is more senseless, simply because it is less related to the welfare of the total society. It is a more random "explosion" of human scurrying, a more frantic celebration; and one that does not call down divine energies or the consecration of eternal meanings—as it might have in Calvin's day. The result is that it impoverishes the society in many ways, not the least of which is that it creates dispossessed classes, and keeps them dispossessed, even though it may enhance the meaning of a small class of people at the top. This same randomness, as we noted too in Chapter Six, takes a greater toll of human life in war and conquest. The primitive can be content with hunting a single enemy head, or making a single sacrifice for the welfare of his tribe. The reason is precisely that all his activities are closely related, and have great symbolic weight or meaningfulness. But what happens when the symbols are more-or-less unrelated, as we said they were on the level of civilization? They become shallower; they no longer load a single, isolated act with great, ramifying meanings. This has one disastrous result, as we saw: It results in a loss of "control" of the symbol over the activities it represents. One life, then, no longer suffices because it loses its symbolic quality as life. Sacrifice gains significance instead in quantified terms, rather than in qualified ones. In this way, it easily runs into rampant numerical calculations; the massed army plunders and lays waste, and the count becomes the measure of glory, as already the Assyrian inscriptions so boastfully tell us. In modern times, the idea of quantification has finally achieved its full rule over all things, and in the hands of modern bureaucracy man himself has been turned into a number, a thing. The single life has practically no quality whatever, and we make our atomic war calculations in terms of "only sixty million dead."

How then, do we judge "good" social aesthetics from "bad"? Simply by comparing Mauss with Veblen and Weber. Simply by assessing the deterioration from sense into senselessness, as society changes in both scale and integration, from the primitive to the modern types. The cost in human life and suffering, as well as the impoverishment of meaning, is starkly evident. In other words, we can make the same kind of judgment of "bad" social aesthetics as we make of "bad" individual aesthetics, or sadism. As we saw, the sadist is not trying for anything different from others: He is seeking to give expression to love or desire, he too wants the satisfying stillness that comes from merger with an object. But even though he seeks the same thing as does any freer, more flexible person, the result of the sadist's seeking is more hurtful: The cost of suffering of his "kind" of love is greater; it constricts the life force of his partner, debases the total personality by manipulating it, by treating it as a thing. Now, when we move from individual to social aesthetics, we can say that every society is looking for the same thing: for the celebration of the social fiction, for the dramatization of human meanings on the level of the whole social panorama—flags, displays, parades, styles of life among the different classes, the exchange of goods—it is all one vast creation of meaning. And our judgment of society is the same as our judgment of the individual; even though societies are all looking for the same thing, and even though this creation of meaning in itself is a natural human desire, still, it takes a differential toll of human life and suffering. When classes coerce others, when military ventures engulf whole populations and continents, when the random social potlatch begins to defeat intelligent human adaptation—why, then, we can say that we are witnessing "bad" social aesthetics—a defeat of the life force by the random expression of human desires. This, then, is a straightforward judgment of "bad" social aesthetics, and it is all quite simple. We can clearly see the evil results of fetishization and of fragmented society.

(2) *Integrated Society and Scapegoating*

At this point we are forced to conclude that social unity is a desirable ideal, that social harmony and community cause less human evil than do class struggles, economic competition—in a word, the divided, uncritical pursuit of social meaning. This ideal of human brotherhood in community has been with us for a very long time, as we know. Not since communitarian socialism of the nineteenth century; not since the dispute between the *ferini* and the *anti-ferini* of the eighteenth; not since Campanella or Savonarola, or St. Francis; not since the Renaissance or the Middle Ages—but further back still, back to the very sources of Western society, back to the Stoics, with their ideal of equality and community in a state of nature; back to the prophets of the Hebrew tribes, with their ideal of a fully equalitarian society, and to the greatest communal equalitarian of them all—Jesus of Nazareth. At the very beginning of Western society the great danger was seen, the danger of senseless society; of man striving against his fellows; of self-aggrandizement and the loss of brotherhood; of the fetish of money and the empty-headed piling up of imposing goods and gains. If you have money and your friend does not, said Socrates, then your friend has money too. And when Jesus of Nazareth struck out at the money-lenders of the temple, he struck at the root of the uncritical social game that was keeping men apart, keeping their gaze bent on narrow things. It was no angry, impulsive gesture of impotent protest; it was a clear-sighted call to build a new world worthy of man; it was an attempt to halt the random rush of social forces and again make spiritual man the center of his world. The call was headed, in part, by the early Christian communities. But they were absorbed into the Roman world when it officially became Christian. Even the earlier Greek Stoicism had lost its radical force when it became Roman Stoicism. And so we see that Rome institutionalized and stifled the revolutionary protest against the universal Roman potlatch, a protest that stemmed from biblical sources, as well as from Greek Stoic visions of freedom and equality. It was revived from time to time —by a St. Francis, a Thomas Münzer, a Winstanley, a Babeuf— and in our times, by Walter Rauschenbusch, Harry F. Ward, the social gospel of Protestantism after World War I. It was a great vision, this ideal of the community of free men expressing their freedom in an equality under God. In fact, it is still our ideal type of society, the type against which all our efforts at social reconstruction must be measured, the type toward which we shall always aspire. It is the one standard that we can apply to all our social fictions, as the sociologist Peter Berger has so well understood in his important book *The Precarious Vision*.

The hope of the communal society was that it would fight against all forms of action that make men petty, mean, grasping, selfish—"unsocial," in a word. Instead of each individual pursuing his own brand of pleasure, the society as a whole would seek to assure shared meanings, communal good, the highest possible social morality. The ideal is to promote real excellence and quality in the society as a whole, instead of in those few who are favored by birth and circumstance. This is why communitarianism has been the utopian dream.

Here is where our second problem of "social aesthetics" comes in. How do you get the highest possible intensity of merger on the level of the total society? How does the society as a whole achieve the maximum generation of unity, force, conviction? As we saw above, it is the same problem we meet in the individual, and in his striving for aesthetic mergers: how to maximize meaning, and yet satisfy and still his striving at the same time? How to overcome all the tensions that characterize his ambivalent striving —the tensions that Baldwin so well described? Social aesthetics is an extension of the same problem, only instead of the individual merging himself with his world, it is the society as a whole that merges itself with the world. Individual unites with group, group with group, and the society as a whole with its guiding ideal. In this way, the hopeless separation of man from men is overcome; guilt is washed away; the "sin" of individual burdens of meaning is dispelled. Social aesthetics is, then, the highest possible release of the life force, because it takes place on the level of the whole, integrated community. And we saw above that society tries for this social aesthetics by dramatizing and celebrating the social fiction.

In other words, here is another of those paradoxes of social theory: that society will strive to celebrate maximum aesthetic meanings, whether it is truly integrated or not. The difference, as we saw, is best seen in the contrast between the primitive and the civilized scale. The primitive group generates a maximum intensity of dramatization and unity, simply because it is a truly communitarian group. The ravages of civilized society come when the society tries for its clumsy social celebration, even though it is split into hopelessly divided groups and classes. This is the difference, as we said, between a life-enhancing potlatch, and a life-dispelling one. The Trobriand potlatch and the American Christmas gift-giving are truly worlds apart in their social effects, even though they are animated by the same spirit (*cf.* Mauss, 1954, and Duncan, 1962). When we understand this, we can also understand why thinkers like Auguste Comte idolized the Middle Ages and its abundance of social ritual. Here was an example of a large-scale society that had more-or-less standardized and shared activities; it had a largely unified ritual and belief, many common social pursuits, and a tendency to value communitarianism, a tendency to sacrifice the individual will to the social good. As a result, medieval society was the closest that we have come since the decline of primitive groups, to generating a maximum intensity of social aesthetics. No wonder that it has dazzled many a social theorist with the force of its fictional drama.

But our paradox is not yet exhausted. What if we found that even communitarian society, with its highest intensity of social aesthetics, its best possible integration and celebration of meaning—what if we found that this "good" aesthetics itself had ravaging effects in terms of human suffering and death? And this of course is precisely what we do find. The members of a society draw together not only with potlatch, not only with the rituals of giving and destroying goods, but with the most effective ritual of all, the one that promotes the maximum of group solidarity and satisfaction: I mean, of course, the ritual of the sacrificial scapegoat. And as we saw in Chapter Six, it is precisely on the level of civilization that scapegoating assumes grotesque dimensions. As the group draws together in tight unity, it focuses its energies against other groups in the pursuit of war, or against minority groups within itself, in the form of discrimination and persecution. Now we have to add that, in our time, we have seen this ritual of scapegoating not only in unintegrated, individualistic societies, but also in real communitarian ones. It has hounded all our attempts to have a truly integrated society on the scale of the large civilization, from Babylon to Rome's persecutions of the Christians, through the Inquisitions of the Middle Ages, through the Nazi extermination of the Jews, up to the great communitarian revolutionary societies of today, such as China. It is a phenomenon of commercial, industrial, and primitive equalitarian society alike. Its tragedy is, as we said, that its ravages only increase as the scale of the society to be integrated increases.

This is not the place to dwell on what the scapegoat accomplishes, and exactly how it forges such intense social unity. Suffice it to say, simply, that the scapegoat gives maximum conviction to man, and draws men together, by carrying off in his flesh and blood the symbolic meanings of the social fiction. This is how man fights the fictional nature of these meanings: by grounding them in the hard, living, organic things in his physical world. It is this that gives the most convincing merger and closure to his ambivalent strivings (*cf.* Becker, 1964a, Chap. 8). Let us simply note the way Hubert and Mauss sum it up in their classic monograph (1898, pp. 102-03; see also Klapp, 1956):

> Here everything occurs in the world of ideas, and it is mental and moral energies that are in question. But the act of abnegation implicit in every sacrifice, by recalling frequently to the consciousness of the individual the presence of collective forces, in fact sustains their ideal existence. These expiations and general purifications, communions and sacralizations of groups, these creations . . . give . . . that character, good, strong, grave, and terrible, which is one of the essential traits of any social entity. Moreover, individuals find their own advantage in this same act. They confer upon each other, upon themselves, and upon those things they hold dear, the whole strength of society. They invest with the authority of society their vows, their oaths, their marriages. They surround, as if with a protective sanctity, the fields they have ploughed and the houses they have built. At the same time they find in sacrifice the means of redressing equilibriums that have been upset: . . . they redeem themselves from social obloquy, the consequence of error, and reenter the community. . . .

Little wonder that it is a time-honored technique of social unity, that gives to the great society the same thing that the primitive enjoys; little wonder that we have still not been able to rid the world of this evil, and the toll it takes in human life—all the more so because the vast and sprawling civilized nation needs unity even more desperately than does the small tribe. Before we go on to see what kind of solution there might be to this world-historical problem, let us pause and assess the distance we have come so far.

3. Conclusion

We have come fully half of our journey toward the theological dimension of our New Moral View of the World. We have seen how vital is ontology to an understanding of human striving; we have seen that human life is the groping for an aesthetics of total satisfaction, an aesthetics of integration of the restless life force into nature, an integration that would be ideally at maximum levels of intensity of that life force. We can see that human morality is a problem in aesthetics, a problem of man's striving for maximum meaning. But we have also seen that this aesthetics of human strivings is of little value to our New Moral View of the World, unless it includes an *explicit critical perspective* on the problems of man in modern society. And this is what Baldwin, for all the importance of his brilliant theoretical work, could not give us in his time. It is only today that we have a concrete picture of how man's life in society cripples and hinders the fullest possible expression of the life force, on both the individual and the total social levels. We have been able, in a word, to find human evil in those areas that are potentially under human control, and not in man's irrevocable fate within nature. We have taken a further gigantic step along the road that Rousseau indicated.

We can say, then, that man's ideal moral problems are also his ideal aesthetic problems; and we might include the moral problems under a threefold ideal for the aesthetic promotion of the life force:

1) Maximum release of intensive life force.

2) Completest closure or merger of this force with nature.
3) Greatest satisfaction of this release and merger to mankind at large.

And it is this threefold ideal that at the same time gives us our concrete, critical prescription for moral action:

1) Maximum self-knowledge promotes freer, more flexible individual aesthetic mergers. Consequently, whatever hinders the diffusion of self-knowledge promotes evil, whether this hindrance comes from the mass media of society, the constraints of custom and tradition, or the tyranny of the State; or whether it comes indirectly through the failure of the schools and universities themselves.
2) Maximum social integration promotes the highest and most intense social meanings, and the completest closure of striving. Consequently, whatever hinders the unification of society around shared meanings promotes evil, because it diminishes the life force, leads to a narrow and shallow or "fetishized" aesthetics, for example, fetishism of sex or of commodities. This problem is directly related to the first problem because a judgment on fragmented, fetishized society is also a judgment on uncritical social striving, on automatic, rigid, unreflective, and narrow life-ways of a society.

However, a group does not function as a free individual—which leads us to the next point:

3) Greatest satisfaction for mankind at large can only come when some groups of men are not sacrificed to the needs of others. Consequently, even maximum social integration has to be critically evaluated in terms of its cost in human suffering, even if the group is wholly equal, and not fetishized around sex or commodities. Whatever encourages group solidarity at the expense of other groups, whatever furthers prejudice and discrimination, nationalism, racism, and so on, is

> morally evil. And this judgment is valid, as we said, even though it leads to a high intensity of aesthetic merger for the nation as a whole.

In these three ways, we would be able, then, to assess with concrete critical data the degrees of evil of a particular social fiction. And our judgment of a society will be a neutral, scientific one, and not a vindictive, personal, or national one. In other words, our morality will stem from the understanding of the science of man itself, and not from our particular social fiction and its own prejudice and bias. Our judgment of a total social system will have to be similar to the kind of judgment which Hannah Arendt made of Adolph Eichmann. As we said earlier, Hannah Arendt showed with great clarity and compellingness, how Eichmann was merely trying to earn his feeling of human worth like any other individual in a faceless bureaucracy, and that is by functioning smoothly and efficiently with orders he receives. What did Arendt conclude? The only possible thing: that although this man was not "evil" in the sense that he harbored "inhuman" needs—still, he was definitely not a desirable person. Anyone who has to earn automatically his feeling of worth and basic dignity by unquestioningly disposing of other people's lives simply has to be banished from the pale of humankind. In the same way, the Nazi unity, which was facilitated at cost of so many millions of scapegoat lives, is a kind of social aesthetics that in itself is "neutral." We judge it, then, as Arendt judged Eichmann: We can say of social fictions that they are to be condemned, when in their promotion of social solidarity and brotherhood, they take a toll of human life and dignity. This is what we might mean by a "scientific" judgment of man's social fictions.

In these three related ways, in sum, we have a critical standard to bring to bear on the problem of social reconstruction. Historically, it is an unprecedented achievement of social theory. But it is not at all outside the bounds of what social theory has always been striving for. It is not only in the tradition of Rousseau and the eighteenth century; of Fourier, Comte, and Lester Ward and the nineteenth; but of American sociology itself: of Franklin Giddings and the twentieth century. Giddings was the one who, in the first two decades of this century, wanted to make sociology truly useful to the problem of social reconstruction; and he saw that the only way of doing this was to make its judgments compellingly scientific. It was not enough for sociologists to hope to "do good" for man in society, to try to promote human progress and welfare. They needed clear scientific criteria of what human progress was. Sociologists needed to come to grips with the problem of progress, and to try to define a kind of progress that would be an acceptable standard to human beings in many different kinds of society. It would have to be a minimum definition that would make sense to nearly all thoughtful people. This was Giddings' deep hope and lifelong aim. Only today can we see how correctly inspired he was, how well he saw the task of sociology in the service of social reconstruction—and yet, exactly where he went wrong. The question he put to his vision of sociology was: What does it cost in human energy, time, money, worry, sacrifice, and so on, to produce whatever kind of person is deemed adequate in the society under study? Today we realize that this question is wrongly put, that the index of progress cannot be put from *within* any particular society, cannot depend on what a social system *deems* adequate as its desirable type of person. And the terrible reason is the one that we have been discussing all through these pages: the social system itself, by promoting its *particular* social fiction, does not hesitate to squander human life and energy—either of its own members, by limiting their flexibility and freedom, or of members outside its group, by sacrificing them to its own unity. Giddings' vision of sociology can only be fulfilled by making human life itself the unstinting measure of value, by making maximum expression of free life energy the standard for judging the progress of a social system. This means that each social system will have to be judged from *outside* the aims and calculations of its particular social fiction. And it also means that the judgment will have to have an ontological ground, in addition to an existential, circumstantial one.

But our problem is not over. We have a crude but concrete index for judging the progress of a social system, for critically assessing the toll in human life and suffering of a particular social fiction. But this is not enough. We need a *model* for designing the kind of reconstructed society that will favor the maximum release of free life energies. Granted that social disunity leads to narrow, self-aggrandizing striving and shallow human meanings; granted that only by social integration around a shared, equalitarian value system can a society maximize the drama of social meanings; granted further that the maximum release of life force is a desirable ideal, and that the most complete "closure" of this force takes place on the level of the total integrated society; granted, too, that this comes about best by means of the society unifying itself against something, and the scapegoat has been the most effective target; granted, finally, that primitive society is gone, that civilization is here to stay, and that the social celebrations of large societies take an enormous toll in human scapegoats of all types—when we grant all this, we can see the great problem of social theory, and its greatest paradox, namely, how do you maximize the life force on the level of a total unified society, and still assure that this will not work against life itself? Is the social theorist asked to use the same ingenuity in civilized society that the anthropologist uses toward primitive groups? Does he have to try to substitute some animal—say, a pig—as a sacrificial scapegoat, in place of a human enemy from a neighboring tribe?*

In the next chapter, we shall see what kind of general model of the social system will answer to our great paradox of social theory. We have come a long way, drawn on considerable amounts of our own life energy to plow through much thick social theory, as well as through many ontological abstractions; the next chapter will crown our labors and, let us hope, give us the respite of closure on The New Moral View of the World.

* Or, another suggestion might be to do away with our mechanized slaughterhouses, and convert them from the covert sacrifice of life to a new social and public celebration of the sacrifice. As we will be able better to judge in the next chapter, this is not an idle suggestion. We could achieve maximum consecration of our social life in a perfectly natural and harmless way. We would give to our shallow, secular, one-dimensional existences a newfound transcendental perspective, a long-lost intimacy with the cosmic process. We would use the flesh-and-blood that we have to use anyway, but in newer and more socially regenerative ways. This suggestion may seem idle now, but it is one serious approach to the problem of mechanical, secular society, the problem of reconsecrating life. It may seem idle only because we are so far away from the problem of rationally guided social reconstruction, and from the need to re-sacralize our lives; it will not be idle to social theorists of the future.

CHAPTER NINE

The Theological Dimension

In the last chapter we asked how to solve the paradox of social theory, how to solve the problem of ordered society without paying the price in human life—a price that we have been paying for the support of our social fictions for several thousand years now. We also asked whether the social theorist might not follow in the footsteps of the anthropologist, and try to suggest ways of keeping a people together that do not take a toll in human life.

The question must have set many readers on edge—does the social theorist imagine that society is his to dispose of? Alas, there is the rub—it is not. Or, better—happily, it is not. The social theorist does not have a territory in trust, like the anthropological advisor to a government power. Consequently, he can't assume the same paternalistic attitudes toward "his village" or "his tribe," as the anthropologists are fond of saying. He is not able to manipulate "coordinates of social change" as the jargon might have it; he cannot "prescribe" substitute scapegoats for ceremonies that celebrate social unity; he cannot, in sum, dictate and control from some lordly seat of power. The social theorist is simply not a philosopher-king; and although Henri Saint-Simon wanted him to be precisely that, the time has not yet—and may never—come.

Every reader will have his own celebration or lamentation of the fact that the social theorist has not yet had his apotheosis.

But when we at least understand that he has not, we can see how great a paradox our problem of social order really is. There is simply no way to "solve" the problem! There is no way to dissolve the paradox by "intervening" in a society, and by setting it up according to the dictates of "right reason." This was the dream of the great social theorists of the nineteenth century, the dream of the Saint-Simonians, the Fourierists, Robert Owen, the Comtians, the Marxians; it is still the dream of revolutionary communism today. It is the dream of the social engineers, the designers of a whole society, who will set things up correctly once and for all, and utopia will be here to stay. It is also the dream that gives the conservative severe pains in the stomach, and makes him chilly with perspiration. After the Stalinist and Hitler periods in Europe, several social theorists and philosophers who had emigrated to America wrote damaging criticisms of this kind of total social engineering. They saw that it had failed, that total revolution works against man because it wipes out tradition, because it treats him like a thing to be ordered and arranged. As a result it creates a society that is different, but that is still not worthy of a humanist vision of man. The utopian promise, in a word, cannot be paid in the full measure, and anything less violates the promise. Needless to add, these same émigré social thinkers were made very tender indeed by their experiences; so sensitive, in fact, that they tended to overlook the whole problem of social theory—the whole problem of modern times: the urgent need for intelligent social reconstruction. So, to a thinker like F. A. Hayek, Adam Smith's "invisible hand of God" is still tolerably good social theory. These people forgot, in sum, that the failure of intelligent social reconstruction had made the Russian revolution itself a necessity, and that rampant commercialism had helped carry Hitler to power. The answer for us today is very clear: We must think radically about our problems, but go very cautiously with our proposed solutions.

We cannot, then, "solve" the problem of social reconstruction, because we cannot engineer a total society according to drawing-board plans. The solution, therefore, must come from within the forces of society itself. And since this is the case, our ideal model for social reconstruction must be as clear and uncompromising as we can make it. It is this model that will draw on the forces of the society as a whole, and so the problem of radicalism and conservatism in social theory will be overcome by what we might call a "radical compromise." And how will this compromise come about, how will the forces of society itself draw toward radical social reconstruction? The answer is the one we are building here: by presenting a New Moral View of the World, and using it as the basis of instruction in our universities. And what is the ideal at the core of our new view, the ideal that will draw on the forces of society, and so will not coerce man—the ideal that defeats the manipulations of social engineers, even while it achieves what the engineers want? The answer, of course, is the one we have never left: the ideal of freedom. It is this that we are now ready to probe more fully; it is here that the greatest paradox of all lies—the one we might call the root paradox of social theory. And it is this very root paradox that carries us frankly into the theological dimension of our problem, as we shall see shortly.

It is not a new paradox in our discussion—we already discussed it in Chapter Seven: It is the root paradox of social theory, because it is the paradox of democracy, of democracy as the ideal type of society. It is the paradox of self-reliance, the quality democracy needs most, and the one that comes least naturally to man. As we saw in Chapter Seven, man is the one animal in nature who, par excellence, lives and thrives on the creation of meaning. But the tragic thing is that this peculiar animal, the one who lives and breathes symbolic meanings, does not feel that he has the right to develop his own new meanings as an individual separate from the herd. The tragedy is simply this: that new meanings can only come from the creative depths of the life force within each individual; but the individual is the last one who believes in his right to develop unique meanings. He takes everything he needs uncritically from the society at large. As a result, man's meanings, instead of being free and open, are in fact "instinctivized"—hardened into the mold of a standard social pattern. Thus, the one animal in nature who is the potentially open vehicle for the life force actually closes up that vehicle by his fear of standing on his own original meanings. This is the tragic paradox of man, freedom, democracy, and social theory—and, in the present stage of evolution, of life itself.

The psychoanalytic word "transference" is the one that sums up this whole situation very well. Transference simply implies "seeing the world in terms of uncritical, automatic meanings," either those meanings the person learned in his past or those he sees in the world around him. But "transference" means that *both* types take precedence over the person himself. He gives in, in other words, to the reality that has been imposed upon him by others, to the "reality of the stronger person"—as the psychiatrist Helm Stierlin put it.

And so we see the paradox in somewhat more richness. Man cannot bear standing alone with his own meanings. Therefore, it is *natural* for him to lean on the meanings of others. But this leaning on the meanings of others is "transference"; it is a surrender of his individuality to the authority of the world. Therefore, we must conclude that "transference" itself is "natural"—that the "humanly undesirable" is the "humanly necessary."

The problem is, then, how to overcome, or rather mitigate, such a devilish paradox, a paradox that supports man but that defeats the fullest possible expression of the life force contained within man. The answer (on one level of abstract conceptualization) is very simple. Society needs individual aesthetics, new definitions of the true, the good, and the beautiful, new meanings in order to meet new challenges. But the individual himself does not feel he has the authority, and must lean on others, must lean on stale, traditional, authoritarian meanings. Society, then, must cultivate individuals who encourage each other to develop their own meanings, autonomous people who encourage the autonomy of others. This is the Enlightenment definition of freedom as an ideal type. It seeks to accomplish what is nearly impossible, by enlisting everyone in the venture, since only if the maximum amount of persons are enlisted does the venture have a chance at all. And the reason for this is precisely that only autonomous people encourage the autonomy of others; if most of the people are slaves to standard meanings, they will suppress any new meanings which threaten them. This is why freedom can only function in a thoroughgoing democracy, because it uses the vast body of men to realize an ideal that can only be realized by a vast body. When all are free, freedom is assured.

Now this is one answer, as we said, on an abstract level, and on that level it is indeed quite simple, elegant, logically apodictic. But on a practical level the problem is enormous; it will probably always remain an ideal out of reach of man's efforts. The point is that we can only promote free men by giving them self-critical knowledge. Here is the core of the difficulty. For in order to free oneself, in order to "know" oneself critically, one must already be somewhat freed, somewhat "loosened up" by favorable circumstances. The organism has to have had certain life chances, a certain life career, which predispose it to self-examination and self-reflection. This is what we actually mean, in a secular sense, by "grace." That is, the carrying-forward of man into new circumstances, independently of his own effort and volition; but which circumstances make it possible for him to come into new modes of experience, reflection, awareness. We noted this at the close of Chapter Seven. Unless we have this kind of "grace," no amount of hard, critical self-knowledge will help release new life energies in the individual.*

1. The Inadequacy of the Secular Ideal

If we had to leave the problem on this level, it would surely be almost impossibly visionary. Does the ideal of freedom need hun-

* The reader may ask why we have eliminated psychoanalysis from our discussion of freedom. One answer is that as a technique for the liberation of large masses of men, psychoanalysis is inadequate: It is too time-consuming and takes too much specialized training. Nor is money the problem. Even if people could be found who would be willing to teach the technique and give the sessions free, the problem of numbers would remain. Freud already saw this in his time, and he said that the application of psychoanalysis to large numbers would mean that it had to be diluted from gold to silver—which is a euphemism for saying that it would have to become authoritarian, and give up its ideal of fostering freedom. Hardly a solution to our problem! There is one way that the liberation of man might be facilitated, and that is by a general education which introduced self-critical reflection as a part of the school curriculum, as soon as feasible. This solution is something that stems logically from the whole argument of this book; but of course in itself it is also utopian at the present time. Besides, as I have written elsewhere, it is to be preferred over psychoanalysis on many counts, not the least of which is that psychoanalysis is itself largely a distorting, tyrannical dogma over the minds of its initiates. I hope we will be able to conclude from the pages that follow that there is no substitute for free men finding their own freedom.

dreds of centuries, as well as the preparation of "grace," in order to be even approximated? Is man so helpless in the face of this problem that it is taken entirely out of his hands? The answer is both yes and no. Yes, in the terms that we have just described the problem. No, in the sense that man can aid the progress of freedom in other ways than merely the propagation of self-critical knowledge. If we are to have a truly New Moral View of the World, then we must be able to lay down some definite suggestions for the reorganization of society that will not depend wholly on the unknown span of evolution, on the workings of nature that transcend man. This is, after all, exactly where Herbert Spencer left social theory: Man had to trust evolutionary nature, and not upset it by his meddling action. But we need a plan for the new society, and Spencer already failed in the nineteenth century.

The fact is that the problem of freedom cannot be answered on a wholly secular level, can *never* be answered entirely on this level. The hope of educating as large a group of free men as possible, in order that they will sustain and encourage each other's freedom—this hope is only a beginning of the problem. By itself it could never succeed, and this is precisely where the theological dimension of our whole discussion enters in. This is the other part of our answer to the problem of freedom, on an abstract conceptual level.

The theological dimension answers the question of how to help men become free, and remain free, and how to attain to a maximum of freedom. Now freedom, as an ideal, means several things, as we saw. It means flexibility of behavior in the face of new and unexpected choices, the ability to break away from the bind of accustomed objects and actions. It also means progression to larger and deeper meanings, and not being tied to narrow and shallow ones. And finally, it means—again ideally—the ability to stand alone with one's choice and decision, the willingness to assume full responsibility for the new and the unexpected.

Here we can see how beautifully and necessarily religion comes to the aid of freedom. It overcomes the paradox that is not resolved by the purely secular ideal, and it overcomes it in "hard, empirical" terms since those are the ones we prefer. For example, we said that free men need the encouragement of other free men in order to sustain each other's original meanings. But this leaves the paradox of how to be truly free, if you need the support of someone else for your freedom. In other words, even the quintessentially free man cannot stand alone. And this is not because of "weakness." Nothing like that, as Augustine and Tolstoy attest. Even the strongest person cannot stand alone, because the finite creature has to get his meanings from outside himself. No, let us even say that especially the strongest person cannot stand alone, because he, above all others, is not bound to any automatically sustaining meanings. Nothing holds him or chains him, nothing fetters his view. As a result, he looks about for the largest possible horizon of action and meaning. And when he does this, he finds himself alone in the universe itself. In order to keep his action meaningful under this kind of horizon, he must then turn to the object of highest contemplation and meaning—God. God alone can make sense of a free horizon of meaning. Without God, such a horizon is absurd; which is just the word that Sartre finds to describe the feeling of atheistic existentialism.

Augustine was one of the first strong, free men who faced up honestly to this problem. He saw that man is "empty" in himself, and that he must reach outside himself for meanings. Usually, he turns to immediate objects of his world, to the "goods" of his society, to the support of his comrades, to the sustenance of the earthly career. He does this because he cannot remain satisfied with his own emptiness. Today, we understand that man is "empty," because he is almost totally devoid of instincts; he is the only animal in nature who does not have instinctive patterns of reactivity built into his organism. As a result, he is literally "empty" of natural "meanings." And it is precisely when he turns to the immediate objects of his world that he gets the substitute for what he lacks as an animal, namely, automatic meanings; or, as we said above, a new kind of automatic "instinctivization"—a "symbolic instinctivization," but an instinctivization all the same, because it is uncritically bound to the circumstances of birth, time, and place—just like those of any other animal. Under these conditions, even though man uses symbols, he is as unfree as any lower animal! And this is precisely why Augustine made the distinction between *cupiditas* and *caritas,* between "fetishized" man who is *curvatus,* bent narrowly on earthly things, and man who stands nobly erect, looking out toward the horizon of free, maximum meaning—man who lives by *caritas,* or love of God (*cf.* Nygren, pp. 536, 537, 540, 541). Thus, Augustine discovered the problem of "transference" fully fifteen hundred years before psychoanalytic theory; and his answer to the problem is one that psychoanalytic theory has still to discover, since it leaves the person still fixed on narrow things, or on the analyst himself as "god."

Max Scheler reintroduced Augustine's thought into the science of man, and for him the problem was very clear: Man believes either in a God or in an idol; there is no third course open (1921, p. 399; *cf.* also 268-69). How else meet the problem of transference, if transference is the surrender of individuality to the authority of the world, of others? If transference is natural to man, how can he find support for his meanings in the freest possible way, except by leaning on God, on the unconditional ground of being? Only in this way can he leave his own meanings unfettered, because even the presence of other free men will act as a fetter, since they are definite objects to him. As Scheler so well put it: "Any man who examines himself or his fellows will find that he identifies himself, or they identify themselves, with a particular good or kind of good in such a way that his (or their) personal relationship to that good may be summarized in these words: 'Without thee, in which I believe, I cannot be, I will not be, I ought not to be. We two, I and thou good, stand and fall together' " (1921, p. 399). How to overcome this bondage to a good which consumes man, to a value which limits his nature? Only by fixing on a good that does not constrict, and that cannot fall. This is what William Ernest Hocking meant when he said that the tragedy of human life is "the law of entropy as applied to value": man's capacity for love and joy run down, in proportion as they remain confined to narrow things (1944, pp. 78-79). Recently, this Augustinian moral was drawn with great force by Jean Anouilh in his *Beckett:* one man's freedom was consumed in the object of his desire and friendship; but Beckett, the friend, gained maximum freedom by making God his object.

And why, finally, is God the sole object that does not limit man's freedom, that meets his natural need for transference without fettering him, that sustains his grounding for meaning independently of other men, without exercising a counter-freedom, as men do, even with the most autonomous intent? The answer, as Hegel so well saw, is that God is the only object who is not a concrete object: When we reach for God, we do not come over and against another self-individuality. God is abstract necessity, the unconditioned, and this is liberating rather than opposing or confining, even though we submit our energies to it (1832, p. 310). Man achieves his highest freedom when he allies his energies with the unconditioned cosmic process.*

And so we have a forceful, empirical argument, based on ontological problems of man's striving, for using religion as a support for the ideal of human freedom. Free men must turn to God as ultimate support for meaning because the truly free man has nowhere else to turn; only in this way can he remain free, and only in this direction can he find a maximum of freedom. Earthly authority is limiting, unavoidably coercive. The whole historical problem of sin is contained here, and is really the problem of personal freedom understood in ontological terms. Sin is man's fate, and the release from sin is the only way to freedom. But what is sin? "Sin" is "unsupported meanings," separation from a grounding in higher authority, aloneness of the individual with his own meanings. What are these "unsupported meanings" if not the thousand-and-one daily acts that seem unconnected with any larger framework; the minor happenings and accidents of one's action that seem unconnected with any self-transcendent justification. It is just these that threaten one's meaning, because they are torn from any coherent framework that sustains and transcends one's own self. The weight of sin is the need to relay the burden for oppressive private meanings to some dependable transcending source. And that is why theology has always understood sin as a "turning away from God."**

* In addition to Scheler, Georg Simmel reintroduced these Augustinian ideas into the science of man (1959, *cf.* p. 35).

** I mean, Protestant theology, of course, which is based on the ideal of freedom. Catholicism took its stand against freedom as an ideal at the time of

This is also the reason that "sin" became a world-historical problem in the West, during the Greek and Hellenistic period. It was at that time that the integral framework of self-transcending meaning was gradually torn apart. Man began to act and think "on his own"; he lost the protective cover of myth and ritual that governed all his daily activities. After all, what do myth and ritual do except "sanctify" one's daily acts, which means that they infuse one's action with a sure authority, an authority of timeless meaning, a support from beyond in almost everything that man does and contemplates. When we say that the primitive "lives" in a wholly sacred world, we mean that his everyday secular life is intimately related to a pattern of divine meanings; he is bathed, refreshed, sustained, by objects, acts, and rituals which give his life a deeper dimension. This is what the medieval cathedral signified in the daily life of the Middle Ages. It was the place where daily occupations were sanctified, refreshed, and renewed in always-present transcendent powers, in the eternally present body of Christ. In the Greek world, man was gradually cut off from this deeper grounding for his private acts. And to complicate the problem, the old community of equals launched after the pursuit of private gain; as a result, men were further separated from the automatic support of their fellows. When life became gradually secular, it became "accidental" instead of divinely necessary; instead of being *timeless* in its significance, it became *historical*. And this is where the "terror of history" began, and what it meant (to borrow Eliade's fine phrase). It meant the anxious fear of unsupported and unsanctioned meanings. It was Christianity that answered the problem of sin in the Hellenistic world because it answered the problem of support for accidental

---

the Counter-Reformation; and logically, it turned against Augustinian thought. Logically, too, the problem of sin could no longer be a global problem, but became a problem of certain individual acts which violated the law of the Church. Sin, in other words, became a problem of freedom within earthly authority (the Church), and not a problem of truly transcendental support. Freedom within limited authority is a fundamental contradiction, of course, and it is justified as only it can be: namely, by making salvation of the soul in an afterlife the true problem of freedom, rather than the transcendental support for earthly meanings. Thus, the decision between Protestantism and Catholicism is basically a decision for what earthly life means.

personal meanings; Christianity filled the void left by the decline of coherent myth, integral ritual, and organized community. And it did this in the most unique and necessary way: How was it to overcome the terror of history? By sanctifying historical time itself, by making that which was most accidental, most meaningful. In this way, Christianity answered the problem of sin, and answered it in a way that primitive Greek society could not: by making possible an ideal freedom—a freedom in history, and above any uncritical earthly community. Christianity provided a God who gave a new critical perspective on every society of the Hellenistic world.

This, then, is the problem of related sin and freedom, and it is still very much ours today: God as the highest ground for meanings, and God as the uncompromising critical perspective on earthly authority; God as divine support, and God as the possibility of true freedom. It is only with such an ideal that we can have maximum support for personal meaning, as well as maximum possibility for new meanings. The ideal remains very much an ideal, very much a tragic paradox. The whole history of religion testifies to the tragedy: Men band together to support each other's meanings, but they band together against groups of other men; they try for freedom in opposition to tyranny, and so they themselves tyrannize. They draw down the perspective of God to criticize earthly societies, but they do this to show that they are an elect group who are divinely inspired, as the Evangelical radicals did. In other words, freedom itself becomes fetishized, and love itself feeds on a scapegoat: God is perverted to earthly needs and designs. Here is the paradox which we all know, and for which we can all supply our own historical examples. But man must continue to try for God as the pinnacle of meaning for a society of free and equal men. How else can he ever hope for liberation from narrow earthly meanings, for a source of strength not even to be found among free men? The ideal of freedom, in a word, is not a guarantee against perversion and slavery; but without this ideal of freedom in God, slavery and perversion must always remain the usual human condition. And who will deny that in our time the techniques of slavery and the gamuts of perversion are being refined, precisely in those societies which have abandoned the quest for the divine meaning of life?

2. Freedom to Do What?

This answers half of our question of how to make freedom possible, how to do what a secular ideal of freedom could never alone hope for. But it is, as we said, only half of the question. The second half of our answer is even more decisive for our argument about the inadequacy of the secular ideal. The fact is that the secular ideal could never succeed because it could not answer the really crucial question, namely the question about what man is to do with his freedom. This has been the terrible problem of freedom in secular society ever since the Enlightenment. We might say that at that time the ideal of freedom came to the great crossroads of history. There were three main paths—which one would it take? Would it follow the path of the Catholic Counter-Reformation? In that case, man was free here on earth only to guarantee the salvation of his everlasting soul. He was "free" to comply with Church authority. Would it take the path of Zwingli and Calvin, and their version of the Protestant Reformation? In that case, man was "free" here on earth in order to prove that he was elected and predestined by God. And the way to show that one had merit was to pile up the visible earthly signs of that merit. The result of this path we know only too well. As Troeltsch and Max Weber taught us, it gave the fullest possible impetus to the development of capitalist society. And it was not very long before the majesty of God was overshadowed by the glitter of consumer goods. The tragic end of this development was that freedom came to be equated with freedom to buy and sell in the new society; as a result, freedom became completely secularized and perverted to the uncritical social pursuit of private gain. The prophet of this tradition was Bernard Mandeville, and his famous *The Fable of the Bees,* with its "new moral message" that the pursuit of private vices brings public benefits to all. It shocked the intellectual world of the early eighteenth century, and provoked critics to rise up in indignation and disgust. What was this chap Mandeville saying—that man's aspirations be limited to upholding the new merchant society? That if we try to arrange our social world according to cherished moral ideals, we are bound to fail? That man is a selfish creature in any case, and the best we can do is not meddle with his selfishness; because if we do meddle, then we scuttle the possibility of any society at all? These were the anguished questions; and as it turned out, the protests gradually died down, and Mandeville went into many editions. We should not be surprised that his work influenced Hume and Adam Smith, and so prepared the great utilitarian philosophy of laissez-faire society: Whatever kept the new society going was relatively good, because it was relatively useful. John Locke had already seen the danger of where all this might end when he proposed that we tolerate many things, but not atheism: The new society could not function to man's benefit if it lost the idea of God. Well, it did lose it, and today we no longer question Mandeville's proposition: Man will be used to promote the sale and distribution of merchant goods. By following this path, in sum, Western man defeated himself from the start. By limiting freedom to finitude, he allowed finitude to triumph over freedom.

But there was a third major path—the path of Luther and the beginning of the Reformation. It was the path we have alluded to several times—the path that seemed like no freedom at all. Man's will was bound; nothing depended on him, he was a mere mask for the workings of God, as Luther so powerfully put it. The most that man could hope to become, he could only become by grace: an open vehicle for the workings of the divine spirit. Luther's tradition found its apogee in Lessing, Herder, Hegel, and Schelling: The meaning of all of history is the record of the divine design, working itself out through man.

We know that this path too, like the Calvinist one, grew over, and man strayed off into meaningless wastes. The trouble with it was that it really didn't go beyond Luther because it did not succeed in incorporating the eighteenth century. After the eighteenth century, it was no longer possible to proceed upon the course of history without incorporating the best of human reason. The new problem was: What had man learned about himself that would help him become a free vehicle for the divine plan in nature? In Hegel's day the answer was: Next to nothing, and so Hegelianism fell with a great crash in the mid-nineteenth century. The most that Hegel could do was to urge the continuation of ordered, traditional society; a creative union of the secular and divine authorities that would provide the only possible way for the full expression of the spirit. But this was no way to allow for the incorporation of the radical self-knowledge of the nature of man and the workings of society that was being developed by the Enlightenment spirit. So Hegelianism was attacked and naturalized by Feuerbach and Marx. In other words, the vision of social order had to give way to the continued pursuit of critical knowledge. The only thing was that the naturalistic tradition succeeded only too well; and thus, as with Calvinism and capitalism, so with Marxism and socialism: The idea of God dropped out entirely, and there was no more role or room for the divine spirit within secular society.

I am presenting a very sweeping version of the modern career of freedom; but it helps us see the high points clearly, so let us conclude the sweep by noting that the Lutheran third path had a small trail following alongside. It was a trail that dated from Luther himself, from his own political conservatism—I mean of course the trail of the Evangelical-Radical sects. They saw that in order for man to serve as a mask of God, as a vehicle for the divine spirit, his social institutions had to come under radical criticism. There could be no compromise with corrupt society and its earthly designs. Now this "trail" of Evangelical Radicalism, especially in America, proved to be the really vital path along which the ideal of freedom could be developed. It overcame the conservatism of Luther and Hegel; and at the same time, it embraced the socialism of the nineteenth century. As a result, it was the one tradition that could fuse social criticism with man's religious quest. And this it did, in the work of Walter Rauschenbusch, Harry F. Ward, and the social gospel movement of before and after World War I. It used the self-critical naturalism of the Enlightenment, but it did not sacrifice the spiritualism of the Reform tradition. The only problem with the vital tradition of religious socialism was that it, too, was somewhat premature; it was only toward the middle of the twentieth century that the scientific dimension of the New Moral View of the World was developed fully enough to be able to merge naturally with the theological dimension. And this is precisely the story that we are telling in these pages. If we are not wrong, and if this merger is now ripe, we can proceed to see at this point what true human freedom would mean for man.

The answer is already clear. It would be freedom to realize the divine design in nature, a freedom in which man would serve as a vehicle for higher powers. And, true to the post-Enlightenment, man would bring his best reason to bear on the problem of man in society, in order to help make himself a perfect vehicle for these powers. The Reformation would find its apotheosis in human Reason, and the Divine Logos would come fully into its own.

All this may appear frightfully abstract, but it really is the only *concrete* way to answer the problem of human freedom. As we said earlier, freedom is—for man—an ideal, and can only be an ideal. Consequently, the "best" freedom must be the embodiment of the highest possible ideal, along with the best critical knowledge that man is capable of, to help realize this ideal. In other words, when we answer the question "Freedom to do what?" the answer must point to the greatest possible problem which confronts human life, and the answer must draw on the best possible energies that human life disposes of. Human freedom, then, can mean nothing less than the freedom to keep the universe going and evolving. And, since the Enlightenment, and the great vision of Lessing, keeping the universe evolving can mean nothing less than developing human powers to their highest potential. Finally, since the nineteenth century and its final destruction of traditionally organized society, we know that human powers cannot be developed to their highest potential without a thoroughgoing social reconstruction.

This is the true problem of freedom and of education in our time. How many discussions of freedom have missed it completely? How many arguments about academic freedom, and about the freedom of the student to learn, have not even approached the real problem. And the *real* problem, like all human problems, is the *ideal* problem. Perhaps that is why we have been missing it by so wide a mark in our society and in our time: We live in an epoch that has almost wholly abandoned the quest for the ideal. Yet, our best thinkers have perfectly understood what man needs and wants, and what education must provide: nothing less than a sense of helping out the birth throes of creation and the continuation of life. Paul Tillich saw that humanist education failed precisely because it did not show the direction of the full development of human potentialities; and that this direction could only be the "initiation into the mystery of being" (1963, Vol. III, p. 249). The individual must be taught what part he is to play, and with his own free energies, in furthering the life pulse of the universe itself. This, and only this, will give him the idea of the absolutely serious, something great and transcending to which he can willingly subordinate himself, and give his life the highest and most abiding meaning. It is this *absolutely serious* which has dropped out of education in modern commercial-industrial society (Tillich, 1964, pp. 149 ff.); and with this dropping out, the student has been cheated of the possibility of realizing his manhood and basic human dignity. How else are we to get the sense of high responsibility back into life, a responsibility that transcends all the selfish and petty purposes that now characterize our commercial-industrial society? Freedom, in education, must be freedom to be "on the fighting edge of the cosmos" as Gorham Munson so well put it (1930, p. 281). Otherwise, education is not real liberation because it does not enlist our highest manhood for an ideal quest. This is what M. L. Jacks also stressed when he called for a true synthesis in a total education, and said that this could only be found in religion (1946, p. 83):

> The full synthesis for which we have been searching is only to be found in religion, and it is a Christian philosophy of life and of education which alone can justify the inclusion in a curriculum of the subjects we teach, link those up with the other experiences of school life, answer the innumerable "Why's" which children ask, and make sense of the whole. The Christian faith in a personal God, the Creator of the universe and the Father of mankind—a God with a plan, for the carrying out of which He needs the co-operation of every human being at his best—this faith provides our final synthesis.

Let us not pause here on whether the Christian faith alone is adequate to this problem; perhaps we will be able to return to this problem in Part III, when we outline the curriculum proper to our New Moral View of the World. But one thing we here must agree upon, and that is the need for education to hold up to man the vision of the *absolutely serious:* the awesome, the mighty, the all-transcending, the divine mystery in all its unspeakable magnitude—this, and only this, is fit to call upon the energies of free men. This, and only this, gives life its dignity and its tragedy, its joy and its weight, its sense of abysmal limitation, and somehow its limitless opportunity. The all-transcending mystery of the cosmic process is the only possible direction of the thrust of life, and hence of the possibility of freedom—whatever it may ultimately mean. Again, we are reminded of Augustine's idea that unless man looked in this direction, he was hopelessly *curvatus,* somehow less than fully human, festishized and bent upon narrow and ignoble things. This was the difference between *cupiditas* and *caritas,* of love for things and love for God. And what is "love" for any living creature, except the sentiment that the universe is alive and significant,—alive and significant in relation to the creature's own living energies? And so a cat "loves" a twig and a sparrow; and man's love of God stems from the same sentiment of aliveness and meaning (*cf.* James, 1902, pp. 464-65). But by this we do not mean that God is man's twig or his sparrow, but rather that love of God is the "highest" love, because it is the only way man has of attributing the most significance to his life, and thus of making the whole universe come alive.

The thrust of life, as Augustine wanted to show, was always in the direction of "more life." In this way, Augustine was able to argue that the quest for God was both a natural principle of biological life, as well as the highest possible ideal. And it was just in these terms that Leuba and James again broached the problem at the beginning of this century (*cf.* James, 1902, p. 497). How does man find the maximum expansion of his organism, his being, his freedom—how does he satisfy the urge to "more life"?—if not by extending the range of his striving and meanings up to the highest possible level of gravity? When we understand this against the background of a tradition that stretches from Augustine to modern pragmatism, we can also understand the problem of meaninglessness in modern life. It is not a problem of absolute meaninglessness, but of relative meaninglessness—of constriction, narrowness, limited scope and horizon; of a world-view that calls upon energies that are too shallow, too facile, too inverted to a humdrum daily quest. Modern man's meaninglessness is a problem of what to do with life, what to do with it beyond simply living it out in a completely fetishized way. It is a problem, to use Augustine's example, of not looking up, of not looking deeply. It is the peculiar problem, as we said, of modern man, and when we read the lives of our most creative people, we can see how they struggled with it—"What am I free to do, that will give me the maximum amount of meaning?" Carlyle, James Hinton, William James, Tolstoi—each struggled in his turn. As that great modern writer Nikos Kazantzakis confessed, he too was launched in this same search for peace of mind through highest possible meaning, and he did not find it until he found that his work and life were grounded in the deepest purposes of creation (1958, pp. xxiii-xxiv). This is the logical and only possible answer to the problem of freedom; and it is at the same time the only possible answer to the problem of happiness in life. What can happiness mean for man, except to realize that life is a gift, and not a burden? And how can modern man convert life from a burden into a gift, except by consecrating it in the service of a self-transcending cause? As Gabriel Marcel has so acutely understood, it is only in this way that life becomes a gift because it becomes something that man can give to meanings and purposes that transcend his own (1962, pp. 242 ff.). The individual finite life is intimately linked with ultimate concern.

This is why modern man whines so pitifully with the burden of life—he has nothing ultimate to dedicate it to; nothing infinite to assume responsibility for; nothing self-transcending to be truly courageous about. He has only himself, his dazzling and diverting little consumer objects; his few closely huddled loved ones; his life-span; his life-insurance; his place in a merely biological and financial chain of things. When we understand this lack of a self-transcending purpose in modern life, we can also fully understand what Nietzsche meant and wanted in his great tirade against modern life and modern bourgeois man. And we can also appreciate the real thrust of Nietzsche's work, its real meaning and power as a critique of the basic failure of our time. It is all eloquently stated in his *Birth of Tragedy*. And it is as Karl Löwith has so penetratingly seen—the key to Nietzsche's whole philosophy is that it revives the dispute between paganism and Christianity (1949, Appendix II). Only, in this dispute, Nietzsche takes the side of paganism against Christianity; it is as though he were

Sallustius, holding forth in defense of the ancient views, against a world rapidly spinning into chaos. Why was paganism to be preferred to Christianity? Hadn't Christianity answered beautifully to the great problem of the disintegrating pagan world, hadn't it met the problem of the "terror of history"—the problem of a world that had lost its religious groundings, and had left man exposed in the anxiety of uprooted meanings? Didn't Christianity specifically fill the void left by a disintegrating myth and ritual, and did it not give the new secular history a transcending holy meaning? Yes, all this it did, as we noted earlier. But by Nietzsche's time, as he said, "God was dead." It was exactly as Locke had feared: If the new society lost the idea of God, it would become a monster. And this is what happened in the nineteenth century; and the monster was the new secular "idea of progress," in a society that lived for the most immediate and petty satisfactions, a society literally gone mad with the fetishism of commodities, a society that had lost contact with the divine ground of nature, and lived trivially on the surface of a hope that "things were getting better all the time." But as Nietzsche saw, the idea of a "better" life was utterly senseless when it was no longer grounded in the deepest purpose of creation. Christianity had once filled a historical calling, but when it allied itself with the commercial-industrial bourgeois society, its historical mission had failed; its God was dead, its reason for being was at an end.

Back, then, to the pagans, back to a life of integral myth, ritual, fellowship in community; back to men whose very lives are a part of the great cosmic rhythms of nature; back to a share in eternal time, and in eternal tasks—this was what Nietzsche called for. Back to real, responsible, manly religion, religion which calls upon man's highest individual energies and socially shared sacrifices, in order to keep the universe itself running. Back to the Greeks, then, and to their vision of human destiny, of human tragic destiny, in a cosmos that transcends man, and yet that needs man. For this we need a new man, a superman, not the humble Christian slave, the willing plaything of history; we need a man who will inject his own will into nature, lift it up with his purposes, fashion it to his design, assume his own responsibility for its continuation. Even the Greek man will not do; our new superman must be even greater than anything that has ever existed. Not only must he insert his will into the cosmos to keep it running; but he must also take command of history, keep it moving in a meaningful direction. And not only this, but he must now shoulder the new self-critical knowledge, be able to bear the self-understanding that modern man has gained in his disillusionment. In a word, the new man must truly be a superman, because he must bear the sole responsibility for keeping the cosmos running in history; and the whole awesome, inscrutable meaning must now rest upon him alone, upon him *as man*.

Thus Nietzsche, and the full circle on a saga of two thousand years: the pagan terror of history; the Christian taming of history; and finally, in the nineteenth century, what we might call the new terror of a tame commercial, atheistic history. Nietzsche's philosophy, we now see, was the true post-Hegelian philosophy of history. Hegel had taken the problem of history and Christianity, and showed how the whole cosmos evolves according to the laws of the Absolute Spirit, across time, and through man. But in Hegel's thought, as in Luther's, man is not the willful helper and mover of cosmic energies; he is not the responsible agent of meanings shouldered by him alone; instead, he is God's vessel—the passive Christian slave. As Luther put it, in his own humble admission: "As for myself, I frankly confess that I should not want free will to be given me . . . because . . . I should still be forced to labor with no guarantee of success and to beat the air only. If I lived and worked to all eternity, my conscience would never reach comfortable certainty as to how much it must do to satisfy God" (Erasmus-Luther, 1524-1525, pp. 135-36). "Comfortable certainty"? Decidedly, Luther is not Nietzsche's existential man; he was not man trembling in the uncertainty of his own imputation of meaning; nor, three hundred years later, was Hegel. But unlike Luther, for whom the world alternated abruptly and painfully between salvation and chaos, Hegel's system set history nicely in its groove, and allowed it to evolve serenely and surely. Luther at least had an agonizing consciousness of the individual man and his doubtful destiny; but with Hegel, the individual's destiny was at all times right and reasonable, since it fitted into the historical scheme of things. No wonder he had to be attacked so hard by those who wanted again to find a place for man in history—by Kierkegaard, who wanted to give the individual back the agony of his own personal destiny, and by Nietzsche, again, who wanted to give the individual back the responsibility for a willful part in the panorama of creation. This post-Hegelian philosophy of history found one of its clearest expressions in Josiah Royce's *Philosophy of Loyalty:* Man must devote his highest energies to a cause that transcends his personal existence; he is free to be loyal and decisive, to do his deeds in support of world-life. This is what human freedom at its best means, and what it can only mean. "If my deed were not done, the world-life would miss my deed," said Royce (1908, p. 395). This is post-Hegelian philosophy of *active human history;* and with Royce, this philosophy entered American thought as a problem which is still ours to solve.

And so we rejoin our discussion of freedom and education, after having glanced at another aspect of what the nineteenth century did with it through Hegel, Nietzsche, and Royce. The task for education, and the meaning of freedom in the new society, should now be even more clear. Education would teach the individual how "the world-life would miss his deed." Nothing less. An impossible task? Perhaps an unprecedented one? A utopian assignment for a dream of freedom and social order? It only *seems* that way to modern man—modern man who alone is cheated of his basic right to manhood and dignity; modern man who alone is deprived of the end of education, the end that awakens his full manhood and utilizes his highest ethical energies. Because, you see, the fact is that every child who was born into what we now call primitive society knew this end; he knew what part he was to play with his creative energies, in furthering the very life-pulse of the universe itself. He had an integrated world map; he knew how the world began, how light triumphed over darkness, how life itself sprang from chaos. He knew the great and awesome myth of the origin of things, how the hero-god dismembered the monster, and from his parts threw up sun and moon, and laid down plants and stones, and fashioned man and woman. This origin myth of his people was his most treasured possession, the lifeblood of his tribe that connected his very existence with the ground and abyss of being itself. He had, in fact, what we now call an ontology of being.

But a myth is not scientifically accurate; it is a creation of fancy; it is grotesque to speak of the dismemberment of dragons by heroes, as if this were palatable knowledge to mature men. Yes, perhaps true enough; and yet . . . what is modern man learning above all, after these three centuries of fervent faith in science, and in the scientific answer to the problem of life? He is learning that science can give no answer to this problem, that the more science progresses, the less sure it is of what life is, the more ignorant it is of the origin and meaning of things. And if science despairs of answers, where are we to get the vital world picture that we so desperately need to give us manly and dignified ends? We are learning, belatedly, that a fanciful myth is better than no myth at all; and that all knowledge is itself somewhat fanciful. Where do children come from—from the union of sperm and egg? Does this explain how a full-blown human identity springs out from the void? Only to those who willfully limit their curiosity, who are content to remain on the moronic level of understanding of the puzzle of the living object. As an answer to the total question of how life springs from the void, the sperm-and-egg answer is really not better than "the stork brought it." This is what Oscar Wilde meant when he said that the true mystery of the world is the visible and not the invisible. It is things as they are —why they are here, and not the microscopic mechanics of the process.

All this is by way of affirming that man needs ontology in addition to science, and he needs belief to encircle his ontology with. And this the primitive had, and modern man has lost. All this is very well known, this difference between modern man and the primitives and ancients; yet we fail to realize that it is at the very core of our problem of education, and of basic human dignity. Man everywhere had an ontology of being, a belief in the myth that represents it, and a knowledge of what *he* had to do to *keep* creation running. This was provided by public and private rituals and celebrations, in which the individual learned how his best powers fit into the destiny of life itself; as he performed his sacred ritual acts, sacrifices, penances, he was actually helping in the continual birth throes and in the ordering of cosmic life, community life, human destiny.

Today we realize that if primitive ontology and religion can no longer be our own, we at least know that we are not relieved from developing our own. This is the great new realization of the twentieth century, of the epoch of post-scientistic man. Already at the time of Socrates, the pagan mythology was not adequate to Western understanding and was gradually ousted by Christianity. But Christianity, as we said above in discussing Nietzsche, had already lost its mythical force in the nineteenth century. Today we need to develop, from within the forces of our own individual and social aspirations, a new guiding mythology, a mythology that will be compatible too with our most advanced scientific knowledge, and with our most elaborate descriptive ontology. It is not enough that we know how our best powers fit into the destiny of life itself; we must also have knowledge that was not possible on earlier levels of living. We must also answer the question that the primitive never dared answer, and that Greek society at Socrates' time also did not dare, namely: "How do I develop my own personal and unique powers to their fullest?" This, as we said, is the problem of post-Nietzschean society. We need a unified world picture, founded on a living myth and vital belief; and we need in addition knowledge that is personally liberating, that makes our action less automatic and more free within the society that follows that belief. This and this alone will solve the modern problem of education and freedom. It will unite the best of traditional education as it existed, say, during the Middle Ages. It will initiate man into a self-transcending mystery handed down by society and tradition; but it will unite this with a fully post-Enlightenment tradition of liberating scientific knowledge. It will teach man all he needs to know about the self-constraint and the social constraint to which he is subject as a member of the human family, as one who grows up and learns to think from his fellow man.

This is The New Moral View of the World that will answer to the problem of education—and through education, to the problem of social reconstruction. It will teach us that human freedom in its fullest and most ideal meaning can only come about by the highest development of each individual man in the community of men. It will point toward the building of a community where unlimited knowledge is the goal, and where the mystery of life is the guiding principle of communal action. Its highest concern will be to help nature and life by freeing the energies of all men; and its communal life will be a celebration of the broadest and deepest meanings of the universe. Man will rediscover the value of his own soul, of his precious individual energies that he has lost in mechanistic, commercial society; he will find, as Max Scheler wanted, his own divine self; he will meet, as Martin Buber wanted, other "Thou's" to encourage and enhance his "I." By making the mystery of life the guiding principle of communal life, man will resanctify himself and his fellows which, as Gabriel Marcel sees, is the only hope for rediscovering human dignity. And by doing all this in the celebration of community, fellowship, dedication to self-transcendence, man will permit the fullest possible liberation of the life-force, the highest intensity of striving for "more life" that Augustine wanted. Only in this way can fetishization of commercial-industrial society be overcome.* And not only commercial society, but also the vast Communist collectivities of Russia and China: human dignity cannot be achieved merely by feeding great numbers of people who dedicate themselves in turn to feeding other great numbers. In this way we have what Rousseau foresaw in his tirade against medicine, against doctors who inculcated a fear of death only in order to cure illness: In this way we have societies of healthy, walking cadavers. It is not enough to feed man, and to treat him as an object of solicitude in a mass of objects. His full individuality must also be liberated, and this can only be done, as we said, by a fully critical education, and by a community that lives in and through the most intense religious concern. Today Russia and China have neither. A society dedicated to serving the mystery of the cosmic process needs *full* persons who embody part of

* Only by making the human community itself the basis for true vitality, will man be able to orient his education "around the native poetries of life"—as Baker Brownell wanted (1950, p. 292). Brownell urges the small community as the ideal group, and modern sociology is finding that Fourier's proposed community of 1600 persons is an ideal number! But the problem of the small community, its ideal number, model, and so on, cannot concern us here. It is a problem which will have to be solved, and can only be solved, after enough people have accepted The New Moral View of the World as a compelling argument for education and social reconstruction.

that mystery. For over three hundred years we have been gradually emptying man, making him a manipulator of the world, but one who gained it only to lose its significance to him, and his deep significance to it. This is the tragedy that Western commercialism and communistic collectivism share in full and equal partnership. Each has lost man in its own way because each has lost the full meaning of the individual life.

Man, then, needs a living and daily concern with ultimates, with the mystery of being, and with his role in the perpetuation of being. And rational, technical knowledge, as we said, cannot give this. When we thus understand the problem of man as the problem of vital life of whole persons in a real equalitarian community of men, we understand fully the great world-historical task that has been left to us since the decline of the Greek Stoic ideal; or, since the decline of tribal Hebrew society. If we combine equalitarian Hebrew society with Socratic rationalism, we have our ideal of freedom, and the challenge flung out by twenty-five hundred years of Western history. We also see how inadequate is that oft-quoted phrase of the great scholar Gilbert Murray—the "failure of nerve." Murray used this term to describe the disintegration of Hellenistic society after the great surge of scientific rationalism that began with the Ionian philosophers and ended with Aristotle. But now we see that the decline of scientific rationalism is no mere "failure of nerve." Rather, it is the stark inadequacy of the scientific quest to the problem of social order and community. Man lives in a cosmos of transcendent, divine meaning, and not under a microscope of disinterested scientific investigation. I would say that it is a tribute to the basic vigor of Hellenistic society that Aristotelian rationalism was swamped by a new surge of Neoplatonism and the Alexandrian world picture. Man needs nothing less than a full world picture; and ancient man—unlike modern man—had not yet lost his awe of nature and being.

We can also understand, as we look back over this panorama of history, how all the great stirrings for a true community of man in God that took place from the Middle Ages until our time could not succeed. At no time until our very own did we have the potential command of nature and the self-critical knowledge that would make a true community of free men possible. It was only when we could combine a scientific view of the world with a theological one that we could truly hope for a union of Hebrew humanitarianism with Socratic self-development. It is only today that the great ideal of Western history can perhaps begin to be approached. Perhaps we can at long last begin to realize the vision of St. Francis, of Gioacchino da Fiore, of Thomas Münzer.

3. Conclusion

Perhaps. One thing above all which the theological dimension of The New Moral View of the World teaches us is that the ideal of freedom is an ideal. Education for fullest possible self-critical liberation—yes; the best possible models for social reconstruction —of course; the most courageous planning for the new society— nothing less will do. Yet—no manipulations, no brash engineers, no raucous ordering and declaiming. The ideal of freedom, if it means anything at all, must be realized from within the free energies of men, men who take their destiny and shape it from within their lives.

The great lesson of the theological dimension of human striving is that the ideal of freedom must be realized by finite man, by man under the conditions of existence. And our best descriptive ontology of life tells us that striving beings can never achieve fulfillment while they remain living beings. If we harken back to our ontology in Chapter Eight, we will remember that it is ridden with paradoxes: how to strive and be still; how to release the maximum amount of living energy, and yet achieve the most complete closure and satisfaction; how to keep the world rich and diverse, and yet how to pull it integrally together; how to be an intensely private individual, and yet how to bask in the full brotherhood of the great public life; how to get intense meanings from objects, and yet how to avoid fetishizing our action to a narrow range; how to get the maximum closeness of social unity, and yet not destroy others outside your own group, or suppress minorities within it—how, in sum, to have the greatest intensity and satisfaction of life, within the limitations of the conditions of life and history.

It is not surprising, then, that theology above all teaches us that freedom must remain an ideal within the unresolvable paradoxes of finite striving. No society can achieve more than fleeting human fulfillment. It is not surprising, either, that the most penetrating, powerful, and challenging explanation of the paradoxes, or "ambiguities" of life, should come from the pen of a theologian—the great Paul Tillich. In his world-historically important *Systematic Theology,* Tillich has given to our age a monumental tribute to what the human mind can achieve in analyzing its own condition. It is already safe to call this work the greatest work of apologetic theology since Thomas Aquinas. It does nothing less for our time than Aquinas did for his, but it does it for a much more complex and vast accumulation of knowledge—of seven additional centuries of human achievement in reflecting on man and the world. This is Tillich's unmistakably great feat: that he did nothing less than make Christian theology compatible with the full development of human self-critical reason since the Renaissance and the Enlightenment. This means that he had to combine the best theological, ontological, sociological, and psychological knowledge into one coherent and self-consistent picture of the human condition. And this is summed up in his *Systematic Theology,* in an almost unbelievably acute discussion of the ambiguities of human life in all its dimensions.

When we appreciate what Tillich did, we can bring together our whole discussion of the previous two chapters, and better understand the importance of what Baldwin began, and exactly how he failed. When Baldwin discussed the "dualisms" (or ambiguities) of man, he limited himself to psychological ambiguities (1915, p. 232), as we saw in Chapter Eight. But these are hardly the only ambiguities of the human condition. How could we use aesthetics as a standard of value, if this standard illuminated only one area of human striving? We need also to understand the ambiguities of social or group life that Simmel introduced into sociology (1959, pp. 47-48). And we need to understand the basic ambiguities of ontology, of the conditions of being of life itself in the universe; and Baldwin had ruled ontology out of his discussion (1915, p. 224). But Tillich included all these ambiguities, as we said—ontological, sociological, psychological—

and he included them with an unparalleled penetration of thought. He set himself the task of understanding how the whole gamut of human ambiguities could be overcome, the ambiguities of *life,* embodied in *man,* living in human *society.* The answer was by a perspective of theonomy, a perspective of the unconditional, that would govern all of our striving. This was the true and natural superordinate point of view that crowns all our knowledge of life. It is the perspective of the ground of all being, of the unconditioned creative abyss of life. Only by means of a theonomy can man hope to overcome the many ambiguities of life without sacrificing individual and social freedom. We must go directly to Tillich in order to study in detail why this is so. Here we can only say that theonomy permits a meaningful ideal of human freedom because it throws the perspective of unambiguous life onto human ambiguity. In other words, it opens the only vista that does not oppose and constrict finite man. Therefore it offers the only direction in which life can strive for maximum intensity and most complete closure, without feeding upon other life. It is the answer to our anguished ideal of freedom that would avoid fetishization, automaticity, destructive scapegoating. It is, in a word, the ultimate perspective on our social fictions, and on the human relationships they embody.

And so we can finally see what it offers. It gives us nothing less than the ultimate standard of value that pragmatism could not give. Pragmatism, as we saw in Chapter Eight, told us only half of what we needed most to know. It told us what the "real" was —that the "real" was the world as integrated in the perspective of the striving organism. But we had to know what makes one "real" *more real* than another, we had to have a norm that would tell us which aesthetic integration was more valuable to man than another. This other half of the answer was provided by the perspective of theonomy. It told us how to realize the highest expression that is the natural norm of all value. The norm, in other words, must spring from the essence of life itself, from the ground of freedom in the inexhaustible source of life. And the theonomous perspective alone illuminates this ground, and so overcomes the atomistic relativity of pragmatism, as Tillich also has argued (1963, Vol. III, p. 29). Theonomy crowns pragmatism by pointing to the source of life as the ideal of freedom and the measure of value; and this is why pragmatic realism, as represented by Baldwin, must now become what Tillich calls "belief-ful realism."

William James once referred to Baldwin, with his accustomed warmth and generosity, as "such a growing person." Today we realize that Baldwin performed the great feat of grounding the science of man on philosophy, which was growth enough a half century before its time. He could hardly have been expected to take the necessary next step and ground the science of man on theonomy. This is the step we must take in our time, if we too are to be "growing persons." Because only in this way will we give to pragmatism a norm of value that makes social reconstruction possible; and only in this way will we have a social reconstruction that permits the full expression of man's essential spirit and potential freedom. When we combine the theonomous perspective with our critical scientific New Moral View of the World, we have the fullest map that we need to proceed to an education for social reconstruction that alone would be truly worthy of man. We have a map that gives us a critical individual and social aesthetics, and that makes the fullest expression of the life force itself the measure of value. This is how the scientific and the theological dimensions merge in our New Moral View of the World.

After having come all this way, is it all too neat—or somehow uncomfortably and anxiously less than neat? Use the inexhaustible source of life as a standard of value—a source that itself is always partly *hidden* in the depths of being? Judge the success of aesthetic realization of life in a particular social fiction, in a *concrete* human situation? Surely this is more than many can safely do; this is a norm that is no sure norm at all! Yes, quite true; it is, as Tillich himself avows, a "venture and a risk" (1963, Vol. III, p. 30). But surely we did not expect that life is a light burden, to be gracefully handled by clumsy primate hands? Life—this awesome thing, which sends its mighty groan out of time into the eternal; do we expect to be "comfortable" with it! Life in the lap of modern man is akin to fire in the hands of Prometheus. It is a dangerous theft and responsibility, for which he may well expect to be struck down by nature's wrath, for some "human" error of calculation. And yet he must move forward with this great burden and cosmic charge.

Now we know the full import of our epigraph to Chapter Eight, and can draw another full and final circle on our discussion: It is indeed as Mark Van Doren says, "that democracy lives dangerously. For humanity is dangerous . . ." Democracy lives dangerously because it is the only form of government that has willingly undertaken the unfolding of the cosmic process itself.

III. RETROSPECT

CHAPTER TEN

A Theory of Alienation as a Philosophy of Education

"To a sound judgment, the most abstract truth is the most practical."

—Emerson

It is time to take a lingering look over our shoulder to see exactly the way we have come. We began Part II of our study with the great historian Burckhardt, and his patient waiting for that "something"—whatever it was—that would liberate the human spirit in the modern world. It was a "something" that would have to work in opposition to the world that the nineteenth century left us: that bare and efficient world that was crushing the human spirit, and that would soon try to mash it to a pulp with World War I, II, and if necessary, III. What a world it was! It was intent on forgetting completely the mystery of the cosmic process, the presence of divine purpose in human destiny. It was a world intent on enthroning mechanistic science in all the affairs of man, even in the science of man itself. It was a world of business and commerce, of goods and more goods, of the uncritical pursuit of private gain—no matter what this pursuit did to the human spirit. It was a world, too, of revolution against much of this, a world of socialism and communism, of mass movements in the new nations that wanted to begin all over again where the French Revolution had left off. But alas, the revolutions themselves took a heavy stand right on the human spirit—

as revolutions will; they held up to the world their own peculiar ideal, which was as grotesque as the one they revolted against: well-fed man, all stomach and no free spirit.

Could there be any solution to this incredible world-picture of the twentieth century? The passage of time seems to aggravate it impossibly. Especially today, with the immense growth of population, the problem of feeding the sheer numbers of men seems to forbid the development of the human spirit. This was the terrible vision that Dostoevski had, in his story about the Grand Inquisitor: that the masses would always prefer bread to freedom, that freedom will always have to be a possession of a courageous elite, who will lead and guide the obedient and well-fed masses.

Is there "something" which can work counter to the Grand Inquisitor; is there some hope of offering to man at least a countervision—even though all the forces of human nature and history seem to be intent on defeating our ideals? Is there something which can work against the death grip of both commercial and communist ideology, and mechanistic science, and maybe even history itself? One thing, perhaps—one thing alone. It was the thing supplied by the depths of the human spirit itself, and it found its expression through man's mind: a theory of alienation, a broad and compelling theory, which showed what man was, what he was striving for, and what hindered this striving—in himself, in society, in nature. We needed a theory of alienation that was composed of the best knowledge in psychology, sociology, ontology, and theology, and this is what the hard-pressed human spirit itself supplied. It was a theory of alienation that was at the same time a thoroughgoing New Moral View of the World. "Alienation" was the strangled cry of modern man, the key word of our times, the epigraph to our whole age; and as the eighteenth century responded to the deep urge for "Liberty" by finding a way to translate that urge into law and action, the twentieth responded to its helpless feeling of alienation by translating that feeling into a compelling prescription for education and social reconstruction.

Yes, there were many critics who tried to stifle the cry by arguing it away, by questioning its logical consistency, its compatibility with the habitual scientific quest, its suspicious alliance with ideologies of dreamy frustration. But the weight of knowledge and evidence was too formidable; modern man supported and grounded his cry of alienation in the only way it could be grounded: by redefining science in the original Enlightenment vision of Diderot and Rousseau, and by supporting the idea of alienation with the best knowledge in all the social science disciplines. As Emerson reminds us in our epigraph above, "To a sound judgment, the most abstract truth is the most practical." What makes a judgment sound, if not the broadest array of fact upon which to base a decision? And this is just what we got on the problem of alienation. Does the word lend itself to too many different meanings, as its critics say? If it does, then we will deal with all of them in the only way we can: by supplying a veritable "encyclopedia of the social sciences" to support our criticism of alienation in our time (*cf.* Eric and Mary Josephson, 1962, p. 13). And this is just what we have supplied. It will no longer do to discredit the idea of alienation, as one of its critics does, by pointing out that "what it says can be better said without it; human self-destructive behavior is better dealt with without this metaphor" (Feuer, 1963, p. 145). And the simple reason that this will no longer do is that our encyclopedia of the social sciences tells us that human behavior is not "self-destructive"; that the human spirit is defeated not from within, but is constricted and baffled from without, from the range of habits that make up our ponderous social fictions. In a word, our New Moral View of the World is just that, a view of the whole panorama of life, of all the dimensions that make for immorality, for human evil. And that is why it is most abstract, and yet most practical, most liberating to the human spirit.

1. The Natural Solution of the Problem of Liberal Education

This means that the general theory of alienation is what I have elsewhere called it—an "anthropodicy" (1965). It is an explanation for the evil in the world that is caused by manmade arrangements; and as such, it points out those evils which could be ameliorated by human effort.

When we take a retrospective glance over Part II of our study, we can see how splendidly it answers the problem posed in Part I: What is a "liberal" education? A general theory of alienation, an anthropodicy. It features a body of knowledge that teaches man how his human freedom and responsible choice is constricted. It teaches him the "good" by showing him the causes of evil. And what can good and evil mean for man except in terms of the liberation of responsible human powers? This is what Emerson understood when he laid down the challenge of self-reliance as the keynote of American democracy; whatever limits self-reliance works against man. And the great historical task, since Emerson's enjoinder, was to develop a comprehensive theory of the limitations of self-reliance. If we could get this, we would answer the problem of education in a democracy.

We saw that in order to get it, the nineteenth century had to find out what man was striving for, what was distinctive about his action; and it found out that man was peculiarly the animal who strived after meaning, and the creation of meaning. The problem of self-reliance, then, the problem of human liberation, was how to permit the self-creation of meaning. Then we saw that as each discipline reached maturity, it was able to deal with a dimension of the restriction of meaning. Sociology was able to study the whole social system as a dramatic social fiction; psychiatry could understand mental illness as the constriction of action and meaning; ontology allowed us to deduce a critical individual and social aesthetics which showed that man needed integral meaning and intensity of conviction for his meanings; theology confirmed psychiatry, and showed us that man cannot stand alone with his meanings; but theology also showed us something more: that the truly free man will reach for free fellow men, and ultimately for a theonomy on which to base his highest strivings. In this way, from all fields, we could understand all the dimensions of human striving as a search for rich and secure meanings; and we could see that evil was not due to "inborn" hates and aggressions, but that it resulted from the natural use of one's fellow men to satisfy one's urge for meaning. And one thing we could see above all: that if weakness was greater, evil was greater; and weakness for man means shallow and narrow meanings, and lack of critical awareness of who one is, and what he is striving for.

In other words, our anthropodicy confirmed the search of the Enlightenment: By developing his critical reason, man can free himself from a large measure of the evil that exists in his social world. Most of all, Rousseau was vindicated in his belief that evil stems from weakness and not from strength. It results from the fear of free choice, from the inability to assume responsibility for unique action and meanings. On the individual level this means that the weak man is the empty man, the manipulated one, and the manipulator of others—the masochist and the sadist. On the social level it means mass man, the frightened scapegoater, the warmonger. On both levels it means clumsy, shallow, uncritical, rigid aesthetics, destructive ways of satisfying one's strivings, ways that take a toll in the lives of one's fellow men.

In this way, when we have filled in the program of the Enlightenment, of Rousseau and Emerson, we have a natural solution, as we said, to the problem of education. General education would simply be an anthropodicy of alienation, a study of the constriction of human powers in the search for meaning. This is exactly the view that one educator is now putting forth; Philip Phenix sets the new keynote for general education when he says: "Since the object of general education is to lead to the fulfillment of human life through the enlargement and deepening of meaning, the modern curriculum should be designed with particular attention to these sources of meaninglessness in contemporary life" (Phenix, 1964, p. 5). And those sources, we now know, are anything that hinders self-reliance, the assumption of responsibility for new and unique meanings.

A. The solution of the New Humanist contradiction

We can now understand better how right the critics of the New Humanism were. No wonder they took it to task so vehemently: The one thing that man must criticize above all is the social fiction which calls the tune to his uncritical aesthetic performance; and here the New Humanists were never on target. No wonder Everett Dean Martin was against commercialism, and spoke approvingly of Nietzsche: how else work toward a truly "free spirit," how else get true community of cooperation in pursuit of an ideal? Commercial society created the herd opinion, frustrated self-criticism and self-mastery, by making man a puppet in search of consumer satisfactions (*cf.* Martin, 1922, esp. pp. vii-viii). No wonder C. H. Grattan, in his evaluation of the New Humanists, said that the burden "of all sensible critiques of modern society must be against its economic structure" (1930, p. 9). Otherwise, how can we begin the retreat from mechanization of the person, quantification of the human soul, the separation of man from man in the individual search for shallow satisfactions? How can we overcome fetishization of sex and commodities, reorient our earth-bent strivings to higher and nobler visions and ideals, to greater intimacies with meanings that transcend our own petty lives? The New Humanists, for all their worthwhile idealism, failed to see that education had to be education for intelligent social criticism. As Gorham Munson put it: "My own view is that capitalism cannot be whitewashed, and for the reason that it is founded on only a comparatively narrow portion of human psychology. It is a function of Practical Man or Instinctive Man: it enormously stimulates greed and virtually debars the entrance of any generous motive. It is guaranteed to make men acquisitive. . . . For my life, I cannot see how it can admit within itself any forces of regeneration" (1930, p. 234). And it was only when we saw that man was not Practical Man, but aesthetic man, that we could see how far commercial industrialism fell from satisfying truly human strivings; and it was not until post-Freudian psychology that we could see man uncompromisingly as a striver after meanings, and not as a creature of instincts. The critique of commercialism does not rest on any counter-ideology, but rests on a mature understanding of man himself. And this understanding the New Humanists did not yet have. They gave us classical ideals, but what could we do with them? We needed to judge the forces that kept us from realizing those ideals; we needed a science of self-study, as Munson pointed out; and we needed a standard for scientific evaluation of the institutional panorama of a given society: How does the social fiction constrict and hobble man's search for ever "more life"?

Once we had this kind of anthropodicy, we could provide the positive things that the New Humanists wanted: We could begin to realize the nobler ideal of man. A New Athenian Celebration of the person? Human dignity? A new willfulness based on the strengths of cool reason? The overcoming of childish emotionality, stupidity, blind trust, superstition? The fullest development of the individual subjectivity, in all its depth and uniqueness? All these things the New Humanists wanted, and all these things the new anthropodicy of alienation can give.

B. The solution of the Great Books problem

As we saw in Chapter Two, the Great Books proposal was born out of the heart of the New Humanist protest; in fact the New Humanists had their own lists of suggested books. Do we want to achieve what the Great Books tried? Do we want a record of all man's critical adventures in his long past? Do we want to study his history to see how his humanity developed, how his mind and soul were shaped through the buffeting of time and fate? Do we want really to read the pageant of the human spirit as the greatest story ever told? Do we want to fulfill Lessing's program, and Kant's, Herder's, Condorcet's, and Vico's? Do we want, in a word, the noblest human self-assessment? If we do, the way to get it should be more than clear and compelling: We must reread human history just as the Enlightenment tried to do, as the record of man's alienation in society. Only now we can give what the Enlightenment could not: a truly social-critical self-appraisal, in place of a merely ideological and hopeful marshaling of the record of human superstition and stupidity. This will give us what the Great Books wanted: the truth of history full in the face; a record of man's struggle against the forces that constrict him. It will make him the kind of fighter that we need—a fighter truly at the height of the times: humble, yet hopeful; knowledgeable, free and energetic, yet restrained and wise.

Furthermore, with this kind of reading of history, the problem focus would always be on the present—on problems in the present social and historical world. It would overcome the fatal weakness of the New Humanists and the Great Books, the fundamental fallacy on which they fell: antiquarianism. It would be a looking back from the heights of the present, from alienation and evil in the modern condition; it would give the best and highest organizing perspective to the search for past wisdom. In his attempt to overcome alienation, modern man would have the heaviest emotional investment in the quest for knowledge, an investment he could never get with the kind of dispassionate antiquarianism that the New Humanists offered. There would be no danger of dragging the past down to the level of present mediocrity, the danger that Nietzsche warned us against, the real abuse of history. When freedom itself is at stake, when human energies and full development are the prize, we would give the highest passion to our search, we would uncover the past with the utmost care, our archaeology of the intellect would be a dusting off of precious facts with trembling hands. Our perspective is nothing less than a New Moral View of the World, drawing on the very energy of life—life constricted, life baffled, life belittled, life trivialized, fetishized—life seeking to surge out and move forward.

Hutchins wanted something else that the New Humanists did not imagine they could give: namely, a truly mass education for excellence. How can we permit elitism in a democracy? said Hutchins quite truly. But everyone cannot be excellent, objected the New Humanists, otherwise the word has no meaning—and education must be for excellence, and excellence alone. But now we see the simple and lucid answer: Teach everyone the basic anthropodicy of alienation, and you will have "mass-elitism"! What is more excellent than teaching everyone the causes of their lack of freedom? What is more democratic than freeing the energies of all men? Does this mass-elitism threaten to diminish the excellence of knowledge? But what is excellent knowledge, except knowledge that has a truly critical quality; and what has this quality except the most thoroughgoing theory of alienation? Is the whole floodtide of mass society seeking to express itself, as Ortega warns us? Then give the floodtide its say: Give everyone as much critically excellent knowledge as he can digest. (As we will see in Part III, this allows beautifully for the application of Ortega's principle of "economy of knowledge," without blunting the value to the individual student of even small amounts of knowledge.) How better to awaken the interests of broad masses of students than by making their own life and freedom the stake of their education? Their own lives become their "intellectual positions," to expand and defend, to sally out from in search of richer and richer nourishment. How better to expand the base of "scholarship" and "expertise" than by making life itself the problem frame of knowledge, by giving to each the task of throwing light on his own liberation, of weighing and choosing from accumulated wisdom for the purposes of his own soul? This is what we mean by "mass-elitism," and what we can only mean. It gives us fully what Horace Kallen wanted; it allows us to fit "the works and ways of the schools to the powers and needs of the pupils, thus humanizing rebellious futility into free, self-ruling, cooperative personality" (1949, p. 86).

Where would be our problems of "student apathy" then? Of student rebelliousness and destructiveness? How can he bite the hand that feeds him manly food, or turn away from it in disdain? One look at his fellows, and he will see how they thrive, and how he starves. Everything that Whitehead proposed in his classic essay on "The Aims of Education" is now possible: The student will understand the application of all knowledge, "here and now in the circumstances of his actual life"; all knowledge will be directed to "an understanding of an insistent present," and will equip him for that present; all the knowledge will be alive; curiosity, judgment, and power of mastery will come from the vitality of the knowledge itself, and not from a "schedule of examination subjects." And this will be possible because the alienation curriculum finally eradicates "the fatal disconnection of subjects which kills the vitality of our modern curriculum." The student will be studying because, as Whitehead said, "for some reason, he wants to know it. This makes all the difference" (1959, pp. 192-205, *passim*). And the "reason" is no longer "some" reason—but the reason of the student's very existence itself: his own liberation as an individual.

Do we want Hutchins' "Great Conversation"? Is the Great Conversation impossible in our time, because of specialization, fragmentation, trivial knowledge? Are vocationalism and professionalism ruining the university in its quest for higher truth? Are the everyday needs of society baffling our search for an ideal that would unite scholars into a body, and raise them above the separatism of special, professional, and vocational work? Is this what has destroyed our community of interest, our common problem, our unity of knowledge, our Great Democratic Conversation? Then make the Great Conversation—Man! Make it the mass of men, make it their life, and the raising of it to the highest possible intensity. Make it an anthropodicy that all can share, that they can exchange insights into, that they can modify and improve, that they can use as a means of drawing together and of raising each other up. This is what experimental democracy means, and what it can only mean: the mass of men drawing together to improve the quality, intensity, nobility, and freedom of their lives.

Was our true unity of knowledge hindered by lack of a natural ordering principle? What would this principle be that would unite the truths that a university would teach? Would we have to stop, with Hutchins, at the metaphysics of the Greeks, at the theology of Aquinas and the Middle Ages? No longer. Our anthropodicy of alienation gives us a completely up-to-date hierarchy of knowledge; it is a hierarchy that takes its roots both in secular, social-critical knowledge, and in ontology and theology. It rests on all the truths that expose the limitations of the human condition and that call man to the highest possible intensity and range of meanings. It calls man to his best development in a community of man, a community transcended and infused with the mystery of life, and charged to develop it, love it, and serve it. In this way our community in Great Conversation will be had: by asking the big questions, the questions of ultimate concern, the questions of human destiny in the cosmos. What is the principle that we have been seeking, that tells us what truth is "higher" than another, what knowledge is "more significant" and fundamental? What principle breaks through the hopeless relativity of pragmatism? Nothing else than the principle of life itself, a standard that stems from the depths of the life-force as it is manifest in man and society. How do we judge this abstract manifestation? As we saw at the close of the last chapter, this judgment is a dangerous, courageous, and tentative thing. And yet at no time have we been better equipped by reason and experience to venture it: We have a critical individual and social aesthetics on which to base it, as well as a sound descriptive ontology, and a most mature argument for theonomy. We will venture our judgments on the concrete facts of social life: Do they or do they not promote the development of the individual personality and freedom?

Finally, we can now see that Sidney Hook was wrong when he criticized Hutchins for championing an "ideal" curriculum. There is such an ideal, there is a "one best" body of knowledge that all should learn. But it would be accomplished not as Hutchins foresaw, not by "Truth pursued for its own sake," but rather, by truth pursued for *man's* sake, for the students' sake. This would provide for what the New Humanists and Hutchins wanted, it would allow us to begin to realize a nobler ideal of man; it would call into question any social fiction that constricts human energies and free choices.

C. The solution of the progressives' dilemma

We can already see that by answering the paradoxes and shortcomings of the New Humanists and the Great Books proposal, we have also automatically met the desires of their major critics —the progressives. They wanted truly "liberal" education, a liberating education worthy of man; an education that would make *new* men, Promethean men, capable of carrying on the dangerous venture of democracy. Not education for indoctrination, not education for servitude, not education for the status quo, but the education of men who will bring needed change into the world—the kind of education that was championed by the men we reviewed in Chapter Three: Emerson above all, who wanted a "manworthy" education; Everett Dean Martin, who wanted an education that would emancipate the student from herd opinion and vulgar self-interests; A. D. Henderson, who wanted a student who had a critical understanding of social dynamics; Theodore M. Greene, who wanted a mind "that can function powerfully, creatively, and wisely under its own steam"; Kenneth Burke, who asked for an education that would expose the motives of secular ambition, cut through the uncritical use of symbols with which each society brainwashes each generation; C. Wright Mills, who wanted an education to produce a mind that would not be overwhelmed by events; and Horace Kallen, finally, who called for an education that would set the world into "transforming perspectives." (See also Sargent's courageous book, 1945.)

How would we make this kind of education, that Henderson so aptly called for, the kind that would give us the social leadership we need? It would have to be an education that gives us the larger whole; that ties the university in with the community; that allows the student to play off his education against the contemporary scene: an education dealing with live people, everyday hard experience, controversial problems of the broadest import—religion, moral, economic, political; it would be an education in which immediate problems were judged against higher aims—an education that posited an ideal of man, and a conception of the good society; it would have to be an education which was "a continuous exploration for the best way of life" (Henderson, 1944, pp. 25-35, *passim*). In order to have this kind of education, we would have to center on the vital problems of society, study the whole panorama of human progress and measure it against our ideal values; and this would be done not in the interests of propaganda or ideology, but under the unflinching discipline of science, and the highest standards of the critical scientific intellect. The student would use this frame to probe into urgent moral and social problems. It would thus give a combination of both comprehensiveness and intensity, the perfect combination of general education and special education within one framework (p. 83). In this way, and only in this way, would we develop what Alexander Meiklejohn called for, an education that would create the national intelligence (in Henderson, p. 169).

It would have to be an education based on the unity of knowledge from within the imperatives of knowledge itself—exactly as Dewey wanted. Knowledge would grow by seeing the interrelationships of subject matters; the student would no longer be able to say that he "has had" a course—over and done with a meaningless segment of fact. He would not have to resort to petty grade-seeking, because he would not be cowed by meaninglessness. On the contrary, he would himself be able to break down the dividing walls that are suffocating our curriculum; he would be able to see a subject matter "which takes account of out-leadings into the wide world of nature and man, of knowledge and of social interests and uses. . . . Theoretical subjects will become more practical, because more related to the scope of life; practical subjects will become more charged with theory and intelligent insight" (Dewey, 1931, pp. 38-39). In these words, Dewey himself saw why progressive education was not adequate, but he knew the times were not yet ripe, and he did not want to force the natural unity of thought. Wise visionary, supremely patient and noble scientist. More recently, J. S. Bruner called for the same organic unity of knowledge from within knowledge—the only way it can lead us out of our educational confusion (1962, pp. 120-21). It is the only way too that we can possibly get started on the problem of social reconstruction: We would have to have unified knowledge that linked the university intimately with the immediate problems of the social world. This is what George S. Counts called for in his challenging and inspired book of thirty-five years ago: *Dare the Schools Build a New Social Order?*

Today we know that they did not dare; but we also know that they *could not* dare, because they did not have a natural unification of knowledge that tied the school constructively into the community. Only a New Moral View of the World could do that. Only a New Moral View of the World could give us the framework necessary to undertake the gigantic task of social reconstruction. This, and only this, was able to "create the national intelligence" necessary to the task. This was the map we needed, the frame for the democratic ideal, the one that Dewey wanted, that would show us where to go "from hour to hour." This was the map that would find out "what democracy means in the total range of concrete applications; economic, domestic, international, religious. . . ." (Dewey, 1937b, p. 238). This is the world-historical significance of our anthropodicy. It has "filled the frame in," as Dewey wanted; and it has filled it in both in society at large, and "in its significance for education." The frame is "democracy" —democracy as an ideal of the maximum liberation of free human subjectivity. No longer "dim" as Dewey lamented in 1937; but clear—compellingly clear.

Compelling? Yes—there is the problem. As we saw in Chapter Five, no theory is ever "finished," because truth itself is never finished. Scientists accept a unified theoretical framework because it is compelling. In the science of man, this problem is especially aggravated, because the theory deals with man himself; and we are burdened with tons of prejudice which hinder our agreement on even the most basic facts. Just as we do not "see" under a microscope without training, so too are we blind to man, until the scales have been painfully pulled from our eyes. But when we deal with man, the scales cling tenaciously. This is one of the reasons that we have been so relatively long in getting agreement on the facts of human alienation: our own deep-grained ideologies keep us from seeing clearly. But the anthropodicy is there—starkly there—no matter how we may at first hedge. It is exactly what Walter Lippmann has been calling for these many decades. It is the true "Public Philosophy" of our democracy—of any democracy. Lippmann wanted us to get broad rational agreement on a public philosophy; and he saw that in order to get this, we would have to be convinced by concrete facts, we would have to *see* the values we want. Only in this way can we have moral advance, by getting rational agreement on things that can be seen and understood. And as we have seen all through these chapters, at no time in history have we had an anthropodicy so compelling to rational man, so much an outgrowth of the concrete experiments of history itself. It would not be difficult to get agreement among men of good will on the theoretical principles of alienation, simply because we have seen in the laboratory of history what they have caused, the evil that they have unleashed upon man. We know that when freedom is equated with the right to buy and sell goods it fosters a nation of sheep under the control of the mass media—just the opposite of the self-reliant man that Emerson hoped for; we know that when revolutions make success their only criterion, and when they lose their guiding humanistic ideals, then they make societies of new consumer puppets —as in Russia—or of well-fed, obedient citizens—as in China; we know what fetishization means; we know that scapegoating by empty-headed masses could consume the entire world in gas ovens; we know that most mental-illness is not caused by brain chemicals gone astray, or by microbes in the nervous system: it is caused by social arrangements that constrain man, that deprive him of a broad, critical command of his life and experience; we know that atheism is the last barrier to true freedom, because it turns man in upon himself, makes him slavishly dependent on others, separates him from contact with the great cosmic mystery; we know that it narrows his life, and so deprives him of the highest purpose, the deepest and most lasting possibility for self-realization and self-transcendence. We know all these things: They are our national propositions of alienation for which we would turn for agreement to our fellow men. They are natural, empirical, historical data which allow us to design a new ideal of human freedom, and work together to realize it.

2. The Natural Solution of the Problem of Education Versus the State

This, then, is the solution to the problem of liberal education, seen from both sides—from the side of the conservatives, and from the side of the progressives who criticized them, and yet who themselves could offer no true solution of their own in their time. But wait. What about that other great problem, that insoluble one—the keystone to the whole progressive program, the heaviest artillery in their attack. I mean the problem we discussed in Chapter Three, the problem of education *versus* the State. The chief enemy of education, said Horace Kallen, is the "economic-industrial-financial-political powers that happen to be." The State itself is thus the enemy of academic freedom, said Bernard Iddings Bell; this freedom is threatened "by no other source as it is by organized secular government." This is what keeps education from effectively changing the society; this is what prevents our experimental democracy from being truly experimental; as each new generation is brainwashed anew into the shared social fiction, our best educative efforts are subverted. Education is little else than indoctrination, said Kallen, and the reason is that the "democratic ideal of education for democracy never quite broke away from the authoritarianism which has pertained to education from its beginnings." The problem, then, is how to permit education to work actively against the prevailing ideology, how to get it out from under the heavy hand of the political and economic powers that control it.

We saw in Chapter Three that the problem of authoritarianism versus education really began anew with the French Enlightenment, at which time education broke away from the Church, only to be safely tucked away under the arm of the State. It was simply an exchange of hard masters, and not a true liberation at all. We also saw that Condorcet proposed the great solution to this problem, the logical and necessary solution: The answer to the control of education by Church and State must be the establishment of a truly autonomous, self-governing community of scholars, protected from encroachments from all outside authorities. Only in this way would we prevent the citizens from becoming docile instruments in the hands of those who seek to use and control them. And this could only be done by placing education under a supreme body for the direction of science and education, who would thus be custodians of progress and human liberation.

Condorcet's program was swept up in the French Revolution, in the fruitless debates about an education that would be proper to the new society. No one could agree on what was needed. As we saw, in modern times, Condorcet's challenge was again taken up—by Nietzsche, Ortega, H. G. Wells. In order to get the "culture" that Nietzsche called for, Ortega proposed a new university organization: it would teach knowledge at the "height of the times," the best self-critical and social-critical knowledge. And in order to do this, in order to give the really "vital" ideas of the age, the university would have to be run *by* students, *for* students: They would direct its internal ordering, impose discipline, be responsible for morale, guide their own self-development. What they would be offered is a hard critical body of knowledge that would give the highest social awareness. The autonomy of this knowledge, the integrity of the university, would be guaranteed by making a "Faculty of Culture" the nucleus of the university. This would be a true synthesis of knowledge at the disposal of a student-run university. In this way, Ortega hoped to fully enfranchise the university along the lines envisaged by Condorcet. The university would be freed from within, and given over to the students; it would be freed from without, by making its knowledge independent and above the everyday shared social fiction. The free university would hold up to society itself the guiding ideal of the progress and freedom of man.

H. G. Wells's proposal for a "World Brain" or "World Encyclopedia" was a similarly inspired vision. It would achieve much the same thing as a superordinate and independent "Faculty of Culture." It would be a true synthesis of knowledge that "would hold the world together mentally." It would provide the mental background of every intelligent person in the world. As a true synthesis, it would unite scientific facts and moral facts; in this way, it would act as a clearing house of misunderstandings. It "would *compel* men to come to terms with one another," said Wells. This common world vision would provide a scientific solution to the problem of social and moral order. It would be a "super-university" that pointed the way out of social confusion: it would be the standard, superordinate overall education throughout the world. The "World Brain" would guide man from the heights of the best knowledge, from heights that look down and judge the times. In this way, and in this way alone, science would overcome ideology. The super-university would be the central pillar of society, and would allow man to fashion the best critical vision of truth. Without it, said Wells, the world remains prey to all the "isms," all the conflicting and narrow ideologies, all the confusion of self-interest. Only with a body of knowledge set against the cleverness, narrowness, and confusion of our fragmented societies—only with such a body can there be hope for human survival. In sum, only with an education set over and above the State can man attain his full dignity and nobility, his full step away from the apes.

Condorcet, Kallen, Ortega, Wells—the independent university uplifting the society, vitalizing it by working actively against the uncritical, everyday world views of the mass of citizens; the independent university, the autonomous body of science; the World Encyclopedia!—what are we to say of it? A hundred-and-fifty-year-old lost cause? A splendid dead dream? A noble empty hope? A fantasy fitting to overcerebral apes? Yet another vision stillborn in the womb of time?

Or . . . ?

Incredible hope against hope, promise matched to promise, awakening joined to dream—a vision that can be realized? Yes—a vision already realized, a vision made body, the word made flesh: for the last one hundred-and-fifty years the finest minds of man have fashioned the answer to their dream; they have given us the means for its realization—*the New Moral View of the World.* Condorcet's great proposal can now be our own; the problem that has been outstanding since the Enlightenment can now be fully answered. We can have a self-governing educational community, a free scientific community autonomous within the society. We have our World Encyclopedia; its framework is *the general anthropodicy of alienation.* Education need no longer be beholden to the powers that be; it need no longer "truckle to the times"—to use Emerson's words. We can begin the fight against "un-culture," against the ideologies that shackle the spirit of man. Rousseau, Emerson, Nietzsche, Jefferson—the great spirits have been vindicated in their hope.

Now the temperate voice of caution breaks in, and blunts our jubilation: "Not so fast," it urges. The structure is weak; worse than weak: It has the rotten pillar at its core, the danger that has been there since Condorcet first made his proposal. Are we suggesting a State within a State? An authority unbounded within an authority unbounded? Irresponsibility enclosed within irresponsibility? Is this our "great historical solution" to the Enlightenment problem? What about the danger from within? What about the human greed and passion for power *of the scientists and educators themselves*? Here, surely, is the Trojan Horse in our midst. Condorcet may have thought he answered this problem, when he proposed his best "guarantee" against the ambitions of the scientists: namely, full publicity of their elective lists and their scientific work, publicity to an increasingly enlightened public; in this way, thought Condorcet, the broadest opinion would always be called into play to check the enterprise of science itself.

"Alas," continues the voice of caution, "today we know better." A paper guarantee is no guarantee at all. We have seen the hard facts of scientific *hubris,* in the hundred-and-fifty years since Condorcet wrote. We have seen the "Utopias" that science has proposed, as well as the world that it has helped to deliver. We have Skinner's *Walden Two*—a vision of the future in which man is controlled by science, made happy by technique, *rendered well-adjusted* by the manipulations of others. Emerson's vision? Only the *hubris* of science could take Thoreau's *Walden,* and dare to appropriate a word with such noble connotations, for such a vile vision.

We have seen the world that scientists helped bring to birth: a world armed with weapons that they fathered—thermonuclear weapons, bacteriological weapons—the "gifts" of science to man! If they made them so willingly for the ideology of their national politicians, what would stop them from making these weapons to protect their own scientific elite?

Furthermore, we have the proposals of social scientists themselves, who would "engineer" our social paradise: the psychiatrists, who would set up "mental health" centers in each neighborhood, and see that we all conformed to the standards of "normal behavior" outlined in their textbooks. And if we did not, they would take care of us—with generous dosage of drugs, with stimulating shocks of electricity, or with loving confinement in closed wards. We have seen how the Marxists have "engineered" their social paradises in Russia and China; we have seen how readily American sociologists sell their services to Madison Avenue, to the sprawling enterprise of consumer commerce; how they give over their techniques to help manipulate man; we have seen how willingly they hire out their talents to the Department of the Army, to assess the "internal situation" in foreign countries.

Yes, we have seen all of this, Monsieur Condorcet, *citoyen et savant*. We have seen too what William James would have called "new, low forms of cunning": Rorschach tests, and TAT's, and tests of all kinds that seek to discover man's "hidden motives"—so that a "scientific" judgment can be made about his insides! Tests devised by smug little men that would make a smug little world for their comfort. In sum, we have seen science that would objectify man, turn him into a thing, deprive him of his free and unpredictable subjectivity, quantify him, control him, predict him. This is a science that would create an authority *for* science *against* man, because it is a science that seeks to know what man *is,* because it is intoxicated with the *hubris* of science. It is science as Antichrist: the true Antichrist that entices man with the sweet promise of utopia, only to enslave his freedom. All these centuries mankind has been wondering what form the Antichrist would take; it would have to be a form that would lure and attract man, only in order to destroy him; it would have to be an enticing form, a dazzling one—not a ferocious or ugly one. As the theologians in Europe very soon saw, Hitler was not Antichrist, because he was so transparently evil. Nor was Stalin Antichrist, nor Mao, nor yet the Pentagon—all too patent in their deception of the human spirit. But science, yes, science is the new world Lord that would seduce all mankind to its promise of the millennium.

So concludes the voice of caution. What are we to reply? It is all too true. Science has betrayed us in all branches of knowledge because it became an end in itself, and forgot that it was to serve man. But the science we hoped for was one that would be interested in something quite different: one that would be occupied in promoting the free human spirit, one that would further the development of the life force in its highest embodiment—in man; a science that would seek to help the unfolding of the cosmic mystery, even if that meant willingly limiting its power to know and control man. The science we wanted was one that would serve the growth of the individual subjectivity, serve the birth of mystery. But, then, we have our reply to the voice of caution! Science is not Antichrist; we have seen through the false vision of mechanistic, quantifying science—and we have seen through it in our time! We have seen that Condorcet's vision of science was erroneous because it was based on mathematics as the queen; we have been able to go back beyond Condorcet, and pick up the true Enlightenment vision of science, the one that began with Diderot and Rousseau. It was Diderot who protested against Newton, against mathematics, against the quantification of nature and the human spirit. It was Rousseau who offered a new basis for science, in the form of an ideal of man that science would serve and help realize. In other words, in our time we have seen that false science failed because it sought its unity in a false principle, in the principle of mathematics and quantification. Mathematics was a false unity, because it forced qualitative nature into its own constrictive mold. Thereby it constricted the human spirit, and thereby it has progressively effaced and objectified man. In its place, we wanted a science based on true unity, on the natural unification of knowledge. And by natural unification, we mean a unification stemming from the nature of the knowledge itself, and not from any principle or model imposed from the outside. In a word, we needed a unified science that would stem from what was unique about man, that would stem from *quality and value.* And this is precisely the science that we now have. We have a New Moral View of the World that is based firmly on man's urge for the free creation of subjective meaning. This is our world-historical answer to the problem of scientific *hubris.* We have a science that gives us a moral imperative.

From this vantage point we can see very clearly the immensity of this historical problem. Not only did Condorcet's vision fail because it was premature, because it was based on an erroneous idea of science. We now see that it *had* to fail, that it was a *good thing* that it did fail. If the successors to Condorcet had been able to set up an autonomous body of science based on Newtonianism, it would merely have meant exchanging one tyranny for another. The human spirit would have been thoroughly controlled and mechanized by this kind of science; and what is worse, an autonomous body of coercive science would have no one to control it—not even the State. At least today the democratic legislative process does serve as a control on the fantasy of scientists, even if it uses their techniques in its own interest. This is why nineteenth-century critics of Saint-Simon and Comte were so bothered, and why a present-day critic like F. A. Hayek denounces the utopias of the social engineers who sprang out of the French Revolution. Their mechanistic science left no room for any moral principle, and it would have choken off man, even as modern science has almost succeeded in doing.

The great default of the eighteenth century was the default of a subjective psychology, a psychology which would center on man as a free creator of meaning. Diderot's and Rousseau's program for a reorientation of Newtonianism had to fail for lack of an adequate psychology. It was the Newtonian psychology itself that won the day, because it had no mature competitor. As a result, Condorcet picked up the atomism and determinism of La Mettrie; Saint-Simon and Comte carried on this very tradition. The whole thing was fought out in the nineteenth century, and is summed up in the debate between Cousin and Comte.

Comte stuck to the reductionism and physicalism of La Mettrie's psychology; Cousin reached for a subjective, nonreductionist approach to the mind. Stuart Mill ultimately fell out with Comte because of Comte's uncompromising loyalty to reductionist psychology, even in the form of phrenology. Finally, at the end of the century, the new subjective psychology of the creation of symbolic meanings was matured. And this ended the theoretical problem that had begun with Diderot's protest against Newton, but could not be solved by him in his time.

All this is now history, but we can see how intimately it is related to our problem—the problem of education versus the State. If Condorcet had set up his National Academy of Arts and Sciences, controlling the whole educational establishment, and if he had set it up on the psychology of his day, why, then, it would have brought about possibly a greater barbarization of man than we have today. This is also what very rightly kept the educators of the French Revolution from agreeing on a program of education: They could not agree on an image of man.

So now we can ask the great question: If we have a New Moral View of the World that gives us a compelling image of man; if we have a unified science that is firmly based on the human subjectivity, on quality and value; if we have a unification of thought stemming from the nature of knowledge itself, and not imposed from the outside by dogmatic scientific beliefs or fads like Newtonianism; if we have a unification of knowledge that gives us a standard of *human* value; if we have all this, what is to prevent us from instrumenting, at long last, Condorcet's vision? If we have a naturally unified body of science, a framework that gives us a moral imperative, then we no longer need fear the tyranny of science, or the tyranny of an educative authority that would work against man. In other words, we can have an independent university, an autonomous body of science that links the process of education constructively into the community. This means that the State no longer needs to guard man against the authority of science within it; it means that the university can be independent of the State, without being socially destructive; it means that the ideal of experimental democracy can begin to be realized. It means nothing less than the world-historical resolution of the problem of education versus the State: a natural resolution, not an artificial one; a peaceful resolution, not a revolutionary one; a humanistic resolution, not a coercive one. There is no longer any need for the State to fear the autonomy of the university—unless it fears the fullest development of its own citizens.

With this great question we can let our theoretical solution to the problem of education rest, and we can close the middle part of our study. We began Chapter One by juxtaposing Emerson and Wayland, by showing how well Emerson saw the problem of fragmentation of knowledge, and consequently the problem of man in society, the problem of moral order. We also showed that Wayland championed the fragmentation of the curriculum, because he thought society still rested firmly on a shared idea of God. It was the same hope that Locke had expressed over a century earlier: that man could follow most any whims in the new society, providing he did not lose the idea of God; if he lost that, social order would no longer be possible. Well, as we saw, shortly after Wayland, Nietzsche pronounced his famous sentence of the Divine Death. The result was that we could see our world without any veil, without any illusions. We no longer had a society in which human dignity and true freedom were possible; we had fragmentation without unity, science without morality, pluralism without order. What we needed was a new unity, a unity that would bring the whole man back into a divine cosmos. On my life, we have it now, or we will never have it. There is no need for any State to fear an education that will fashion whole men, and direct their loyalty to the highest principle of all. Unless, of course, the ideology of the State imagines itself to be this divine ground. In that case, it will continue to have subjects, and not citizens, "so many walking monsters—a good finger, a neck, a stomach, an elbow, but never a man." It will prove that Emerson was truly the great prophetic voice of our democracy.

PART THREE

Conclusion: The Special Problem of the Curriculum

". . . affairs cannot remain unregulated, chaotic; but must be regulated, brought into some kind of order. What intellect were able to regulate them? The intellect of a Bacon, the energy of a Luther, if left to their own strength, might pause in dismay before such a task; a Bacon and a Luther added together could not do it. What can? Only twenty-four million ordinary intellects, once awakened into action. . . ."

—Thomas Carlyle (quoted in Gascoyne, 1952, p. 21)

CHAPTER ELEVEN

The Orientation

> "Instruction should embrace the most suggestive truths. The more important and comprehensive the knowledge is which a student is acquiring, the more likely it will be to exercise his thinking powers. . . ."
>
> —Lester Ward (in Chugerman, 1939, p. 485)

Let us try to answer one more question before we bring our study to a close. So far we have been dealing with a theoretical solution to the problem of education. Let us suppose that our New Moral View of the World is really the acceptable answer to a philosophy of education for our time. The question, then, is: How do we link this theory with the more special problem of the curriculum? In answering this last question, the most that we could hope to do at the present time is to suggest the general shape that a curriculum would take, if it were frankly based on a general anthropodicy of alienation. It will be easy enough to spell out the exact shape and detail of the various courses, once we accept the general curriculum program; so that, we may hopefully leave the detailed curriculum problems to a more widespread, give-and-take discussion. For now, let us see what the curriculum would look like in terms of its basic orientation; its general body of knowledge; and its relationship to the organization of the university. These three questions will form the content of three brief concluding chapters in Part III.

Lester Frank Ward, who supplies the epigraph for the present chapter, was one of the last great American sociologists to take social science seriously: He was one of the last to use it for answering problems of human conduct. Ward's classes, according to his biographer, were "a sort of mental electric-bath for the students" (Chugerman, p. 36). Imagine it: a mental electric-bath; this is the problem of education in a nutshell—how to bathe and vivify the mind. Ward's technique is what we are interested in; and it will come as no surprise that his real technique was the avoidance of technique. The important thing for him was not *how* to teach, but *what* should be taught. The mind is hungry for food, said Ward—naturally hungry; and food is food, no matter how conveyed to the mouth: by chopsticks, cutlery, or greedy and unwashed fingers. What truths, then, are the most suggestive? For Ward, it was nothing less than the survey of all knowledge for the sake of humanity; what has happened in the world, and what it all means for the future of mankind—the tabular view of all knowledge, for each and every hungry student.

We do not have to strain to recognize immediately that Ward was firmly rooted in the Enlightenment. His program was a continuation of the great vision of the eighteenth century—the vision of Lessing, Herder, Condorcet. We have referred to it again and again as the answer to the problem of education: the education of mankind through teaching the pageant of the human spirit across time, the record of man's struggle against the forces that shackle his freedom, the story of man's development of his unique humanity. The question is, how do we best do this? How do we most effectively give a truly liberating self-appraisal? In Ward's day, he must have had to settle for what the Enlightenment itself settled for: a broad view of the development of society from ancient times, progressing through the famous stages of Vico's, Saint-Simon's and Comte's reading of history: from mythology and religion to metaphysics and philosophy; from metaphysics and philosophy to science. This was the best the Enlightenment could do, try to convince man that he was on the road to freedom. The program has been criticized again and again, ever since the nineteenth century; it was not convincing. In the twentieth century, with its great wars and world crises, it is less than convincing: It seems like a downright lie. We seem to have gone from mythology, to philosophy, to science, back to the most inane myth of all: the myth of progress. At least, this is what the critics have been saying.

But suppose that we go back and reanimate the Enlightenment vision of science, the one that was proposed by Diderot and Rousseau. Suppose that we understand the science of man as an ideal type of science: a science that postulates an ideal toward which men might strive, and then seeks to help realize that ideal. And suppose that we put the idea of progress at the basis of this ideal, and that we understand progress as the progressive liberation of human energies, of free subjectivity on the part of the greater masses of citizens. If we do reorient our science around this ideal, then we have to say that the Enlightenment vision was the correct one, even if history did not turn out that way. We can agree that man has not yet shown that he has made progress; that progress since the nineteenth century is a myth. But we have to add very quickly that the reason we have made no progress is that we have not consciously tried to realize a rational ideal of man in society. We have not put forth a design of man, nor have we tried to shape man in its image. No wonder the idea of progress dropped dead: We left it to evolution, and not to our own energies! We violated the whole Enlightenment mandate for the science of man. It is as though the whales all decided that things would get better automatically for the whales, simply because the oceans seemed to work in their favor; and meanwhile, the Nantucket whalers were putting out to sea in small boats. Nineteenth century man, in a word, was a school of whales deciding on their balmy progress in the vast ocean of the new industrial world; the Nantucket whalers were the social forces which they blissfully left unexamined and uncontrolled. Little wonder, then, that modern man has been harpooned by his own myth of progress: He did nothing actively to take possession of the disintegrative forces of his world.

Once we realize that progress is an ideal that we have to help shape and achieve, we can restate the Enlightenment vision of the panorama of history. It is not that man *has* progressed, but that he *could* progress. And he could progress only if he understood the forces that hold him in bondage. So that, our *tableau de l'esprit humain,* our panoramic view of the development of the human spirit, is actually a picture of the present constraints on that spirit. And this, as we have seen, is precisely what our New Moral View of the World tells us, and why it permits us to fulfill the Enlightenment program for the liberation of man.

What, then, is the basic orientation for our curriculum; the single point from which everything derives; the standard which serves as a guide for all of our probes; the unique vision that informs our whole course of study; the most suggestive truth of all; the truth that is the most important for man to know; the one that awakens his most intense curiosity; the one that bathes his mind and electrifies it at the same time; the one that relates knowledge in all its comprehensiveness and historical breadth to the single inquiring mind—*What is this truth?*

It is the great Rousseau's truth; the one that caused him to fall swooning to the ground; the one over which he cried with hot tears of torment, joy, and discovery, soaking the whole front of his coat; the truth that he sobbingly flung out as a challenge to modern man; the truth that has been haunting us for two hundred years, and that is now ours to take up and use as a measure for all education—"Man is *good.*"

Man is good; but society renders him evil. This was Rousseau's world-historical message. What is more suggestive as an orientation for education; what is more proper for men everywhere and at all times to know; what is a better focus for everyone to get agreement on; what takes root more deeply and intimately in the personal life, as a lifelong perplexity, than this question of man's basic nature? What more exciting intellectual adventure than an education animated by this basic quest, that man is good, but that society renders him evil?

Furthermore, this proposition is at the same time the *single unifying principle* for our whole curriculum. It is the natural principle of our whole general theory of alienation, the one that marks it as a genuine synthesis of knowledge. As we saw in chapters Three and Four, it was this genuine synthesis which education needed; and a genuine synthesis is not possible unless it is united by a natural principle springing from within itself. This is the principle that man is good, or more narrowly, the principle of "self-esteem maintenance" as I have elsewhere called it. (1962; 1964 a; 1965) It declares that man's behavior is neutral, not motivated by drives of hate or aggression; but rather, by the desire to "feel maximally good" about himself. It unites all the various kinds of behavior we described in Part II of our study: all the various types of aesthetic striving, of the striving for meaning on both individual and total social levels. In this way, our general theory of alienation explains the full field of evil that is caused by man to man, but it explains it on the principle that man is basically good. It is this great paradox that has taken us over a century and a half to solve; and as we have seen, we needed a whole New Moral View of the World as an explanation for it. Nothing less could do it.

But isn't this proposal itself a visionary dream? Isn't it farfetched to imagine that we could get compelling agreement on this thesis as a basic orientation for education?* It seems like the myth to end all myths. Yes, it is just that: *the* myth to end all myths. Not a myth in the false use of the term, in the derogatory sense of "science versus myth." But a myth in the true meaning of the word: myth as creative and generative; myth as providing a new and unmistakable guide for a whole world view; myth as an adumbration of a new reality that marshals our feeling and strivings; myth as an image with endless facets, ramifications, richness—yet, an image that is simple and clear; an image that

* I recently requested a large class of almost a hundred students to find out from other professors and respected persons whether man was good or evil, and whether if one changed society, one could thereby change human nature. Needless to say the answers reflected anything but agreement; only a few answers seemed to be animated by hard thought and long study; fewer still were without personal prejudice and bias. Strangest of all for our democracy, most of the answers were Hobbesian: man is nasty, and needs to be controlled by authority! All in all, then, they reflect the very confusion of our society today: What is man, and what shall we do with him? The most basic question about our world is thus the one we have least agreement over. Is this an argument against us—does it mean that we cannot use Rousseau's thesis as a basis for education? On the contrary, I think it supports glaringly the need for a clear answer to this basic question; otherwise, we will never get started on the problem of social consensus for social reconstruction; and this is the problem that is behind all the others. Even worse, we may "progress" back to a Hobbesian view of the State.

calls up our highest yearnings, yet that gives the most immediate and deep-seated satisfaction. This definition fits the eighteenth-century myth of man's basic goodness; it may well be the one we need to rise up out of the fragments of our failing world; it may lead us to the new birth.

It should not be difficult to get compelling agreement on this myth. It was in Rousseau's time, but it is no longer so today; we now have the compelling body of knowledge on just how society causes human evil; and we could teach it in the three different dimensions which explain it.

1. The history of alienation in one's own life. How evil arises as a result of the law of individual development.

2. The history of alienation in society. How evil arises as a result of the workings of society, and of the evolution of society in history.

3. The total problem of alienation under the conditions of existence. How evil arises as a result of the conditions of life itself.

This third dimension is, of course, the theological one; and as I hope we have fully seen, it is the indispensable crown to any education. Without it, the science of society is foredoomed to failure. Thus, the eighteenth-century thesis that man is good is no longer an argument *against* the theological view of man: It is perfectly compatible with this view. Only, the theological view has to be nondogmatic; it has to understand "sin" as springing naturalistically from the conditions of existence. In this way, the theological view of man's condition should be compelling to any rational man of good will. It answers the question with which Bayle opened the eighteenth century, and it answers it on its own rational terms: A society of atheists is *possible,* but it is not *desirable* for the fullest development of the human spirit.

Let us then review these three dimensions of our New Moral View of the World, specifically as they would form a curriculum for the university.

CHAPTER TWELVE

The General Body of Knowledge

"... what will characterize a university—a *studium generale*, a *universitas*, a *collegium*—is the sense of a common devotion, the sense that all the understandings of its different disciplines are the understandings of a mystery common to them all. . . ."

—Ian T. Ramsey (1964, p. 70)

What greater mystery than "What is Man?"—the question that has tormented man ever since he achieved the capacity to reflect on himself and on his life, way back in the dim recesses of primate evolution. It is the best mystery of all, because it is unanswerable. What greater challenge for the university curriculum, then, than to become intimate with this mystery; to become as knowledgeable as possible about the fate of something we cannot understand? The more we learn, the more it will contribute to our wonder; the more competent we become, the more humble and respectful; the more we uncover to exchange with our fellows, the more we will marvel at the exchange, the more we will marvel at *those who* exchange; the more we try to discover man, the more we will discover men; the more we learn about ourselves, the greater the willingness to trust and serve that which we cannot understand, that fathomless abyss from which we have sprung, and which unites us with all things. When we gradually discover that we are united with all things, we may learn our closeness with one another; when we find out all there is to know about how we came to be as we are, we will value above all that which we are *not yet;* when we begin to value this, we will have prepared the openness that alone could bring a new world into being. *This* is what a *university* must mean, and what it must try to do. Today our universities breed competition, separateness, hate, war; we may call them whatever we will—"hatcheries," "uni-nurseries"—but not universities. That institution has not yet dawned in any land on this planet.

1. The Individual Dimension of Alienation

The first thing that would have to be taught, in order for the new university to dawn, is the law of the individual's unfolding.

This means several things, many of which are now covered in our college curricula. We would learn how man is basically an animal, and how he developed from the other animals; we would study the growth of perception and language; the development of the self—those things, in sum, which are now roughly included under courses on "Human Development," "Developmental Psychology," "Personality," "Social Psychology," "Culture and Personality." They would show how every human being is born into his cultural world, and is molded by it into a social actor. They would show how man forfeits his place in the animal kingdom, in order to become a self-conscious human being whose life is directed by values and meanings. They would show that there is nothing absolute about these values or meanings, that they are relative to the society in which one grows up—what the anthropoligists call "cultural relativity."

But we have called this particular nucleus of the curriculum "the individual dimension of alienation." It is supposed to show the individual the history of his estrangement from himself, from reliance on his own powers. But as our curriculum stands today, it does not show this. We teach all about human development, all about growing up in society, in the variety of courses that we just noted. But now we may ask: Why does each specialty have to have "its own" distinctive say, when they are all saying pretty much the same thing—psychology, sociology, anthropology, social psychology? Why this needless overlap and luxuriant redundance, why so many offerings on the same subject? The reason, we know, is largely the fantastic specialization in our time: the urge of each department to its own area of power, the cloak of special competence, the greedy hoarding of the label of scientific respectability for one's own discipline. But within each department of this Tower of Babel, the same ineluctable disease of modern science is at work. We do not have any clear agreement on what is important for man to know about the child's early training period. Consequently, each discipline bloats itself on its own esoterics and special problems, on the elaboration of details, the examination of empirical studies, of models, and so on, and on, and on. The student is buried under science, and instead of finding out about himself, he finds out how vastly knowledgeable scientists are, and how difficult the study of man is.

There is only one way to cut through this miasma, one way to bring order into the fantastic redundancy and trifling, one way to place the student above the flood of facts. And that is, to make the whole thing meaningful to him in his individual life. And the only way to do this is to make the knowledge self-critical. For this, we need our ideal model, the standard against which to measure the knowledge, a standard that infuses it with life and relevance, a standard that leads the individual to apply the knowledge to his own life and fate. The standard is, of course, the Socratic and Emersonian one: "Know thyself," know what prevents you from being "self-reliant." Know how you were deprived of the ability to make your own judgments; know how the world view of your society was built into your perceptions; know how those who trained you to see and think, literally placed themselves into your mind; know how they became the self upon your self, the "superego" upon your "ego," the voice of conscience whispering behind your voice.

This means that courses on human development will have to be oriented around its fundamental law—the law of the Oedipus Complex, or, as I prefer to call it, the Oedipal Transition. It will highlight above all how the individual becomes human by forfeiting the aegis over his powers. It will show how conscience is built into each child on the basis of his need for affection, and his anxiety over object-loss. It will teach him how his own animal sensitivities and need for survival cause him to shape himself to the design of his parents. It will show him how the social fiction is built into his primate body, and how he comes to strive for meanings that he never knew he had chosen. It will show, in sum, those things we outlined in Chapter Seven, and it will show them with the same orientation: how man is born into a world that he has not made, and that he is not permitted to remake. It will show how his lifelong habit was laid down, for the most part, during his early years, and how it has prevented him from making new and independent choices, from meeting new challenges and opportunities—in a word, from exercising and developing his own unique meanings.

In this way, courses on human development will be courses in the brainwashing that takes place in each society; they will give the person the knowledge and the impetus he needs to take his own life into his own hands—if this is what he wants. They will help him "see through" his own Oedipus Complex, the accidents of his birth and place, the relativity of the meanings that infuse his life. The insights of psychoanalysis will thus become the basic property of a free science of man, taught in the university to all students. No more esotericism of the medical profession; no more unaired dogma; no more exorbitant fees charged for sessions in closed rooms. No more "psychoanalysis" so-called—but instead, a free development of all our knowledge about what makes people act the way they do. Students would learn how different life styles are developed, and they would learn the full range of social and historical influences that shape these styles. No more futile reductionist research into brain cells and chemistry—no more alchemy to learn the "secrets" of human behavior. The students would study man in his social world, and would come to understand easily how the mental illnesses develop; how they too are life styles that the person resorts to, in order to try to keep his world convincing and meaningful.

They would learn, again, how truly Rousseau spoke when he said that man is not born evil, but neutral and potentially good; that evil is a result of weakness, of narrow, inflexible, frightened, clumsy, ineffective life styles; that only the strong person can perform the ethical act. Why only the strong? Because it takes strength to take the responsibility for one's own unique meanings; it takes strength to allow the world to be peopled with others whose meanings are unique and unexpected, who introduce in their very person an element of danger into the social encounter. The student would learn that man needs self-esteem, and that he seeks it in the manifold performances of his social roles; and hence he would learn that the constrictions on the life force, the constrictions on the free development of human energies, stem from the way we bring children up, and the kind of social roles we provide for them.

As the students learn what blunts and twists the free expression of life energies, they would also know how the life force itself is frustrated by society, by the codes for behavior prescribed by man, the unexamined conventions of our social world. They would be encouraged to think about themselves in terms of all these insights and knowledge, to help each other with their problems, if that is what they wanted to do, in free exchange. A new generation taught in the arts of self-criticism and self-discovery would unfold, while the university would truly be a seat of knowledge. It would seek to unfold the universal man, the man free from the automatic constraints of his own culture and times. The university would thus be the handmaiden of life itself, entrusted with the care of the most sublime mystery, entrusted with breaking the cultural mold that constricts evolution.

2. The Social and Historical Dimension of Alienation

The individual level blends, of course, very naturally into the social level. As the student learns how he is trained to function in a social role, he understands the social fiction. He sees how he earns his feeling of value by filling the status available to him in each society; in a word, he sees through himself as a performer on the grander social scene. His early child training shapes him to be a cultural performer, and from here it is but a step to analyzing the whole social system as a dramatic social fiction. The individual life history becomes an inexorable part of the social plot, and the individual destiny becomes the fate of man in society, in a particular society in history.

Now this part of the curriculum, as we know, is the domain of social psychology, sociology, anthropology, and history. And just as in our courses on human development, here too there is tremendous luxuriance and overlap: how social groups function, what a society is, how societies came to be historically, how civilizations succeeded each other, how classes function and are formed, how social change takes place, what happened in prehistory, what is happening now in small social groups and large ones—and so on, and on. Political science and economics also move in here, to stake out areas of special study, as do departments of Romance languages and English, and Germanic studies, and Literature. But here there is not only overlap and duplication; there is actually a truly great amount of diverse and important knowledge that one discipline alone cannot handle. What are we to do with this crushing mountain of knowledge, of fact and more fact, of a world that defeats the student before he can even begin to get under way? How are we to extricate him from all this, give him a firm footing in the face of the library stacks, rows and rows of books which mock his best efforts, choke his budding initiative, attack his very existence and personhood with their silent integrity and aloofness? We have the problem of giving the student a bearing in the face of all this, making it meaningful in his life, in the most forceful way possible. We must bring the human person up front, put him back in the center, establish him as a locus of control; he must have reverence for books, but for more than their volume of ink and paper; he must be beholden to mankind's accumulated wisdom, but an independent and rightful heir to that wisdom—someone who can take command of it, and shape it to his life.

Again, just as with the knowledge on human development, there is only one way to handle this problem, and that is to make the knowledge self-critical. Only here, in order to make it self-critical, it has to be made frankly social-critical, historical-critical: This is the social and historical dimension of alienation. The mountain of knowledge here is so great, what standard could we possibly apply that would make it directly personally relevant, that would organize it in some coherent and meaningful way? What standard could we apply without losing the breadth and richness of the data, without sacrificing the probings of experts, without slighting what is good in all the branches of knowledge about man in society? What standard would allow the student to make sense out of the whole panorama of history, out of the whole social system in time and space, without losing the breath-taking vista, and without sacrificing the rich detail? What standard would allow each student to learn that society is a joint human adaptation to the hard facts of material survival, in all its dimensions; what standard would allow at the same time the understanding that the social system is a vast social fiction, a dream staged by man for man, a splendid creation of life meaning on the level of the total society? What standard would allow man to understand the growth of knowledge and ideas, the development of the human spirit, as well as the foibles, weaknesses, and impermanence of the symbolic structures elaborated by man?

The standard is the one we sketched in Chapter Six: it can be nothing else than the ideal of communal equilitarianism under God, the ideal of the Stoics, and of the Biblical Hebrew and Christian community. It is the ideal that shows every social system to be a social fiction, and that shows civilization to be the uncritical style of social life across the face of recorded history. It is the standard that passes judgment on the default of two to five thousand years of Western history: the default of community, the failure to create a social system worthy of free and equal men. It is the standard that was passed on to us by the ancients, as well as by Augustine, who accused the "robber-state" of enslaving man; it is especially the standard left us directly by the eighteenth and nineteenth centuries, with their new visions of reconstructed societies. But it is a standard which only today do we have enough knowledge to begin to build with.

A. *The history and sociology of the State*

The student would have to understand two major things: what happened in history that led to the great unequal scramble that we call the "civilized State"; and how the social system functions as an interrelated dramatic fiction. He will thus have a basic general framework with which to understand how evil arises in society; specifically, how man has been prevented from achieving self-reliance in a community of men. He will see history as the development of inequality, exactly as the ancients had already seen it, and as the nineteenth century scholars thunderously reminded us: the saga of war, greed, acquisition, social classes, fragmentation, the exploitation of man by man. He will see the social system as we sketched it in Chapter Six: as a great dramatic fictional staging of life, on the level of the total society. In this way, he will learn that the failure to reconstruct society is itself the source of social evil; he will learn that man's failure to take hold rationally of his social institutions is a type of stupidity. And that this social stupidity is the abrogation by man of the responsible power over his own destiny; it is merely an extension, then, of the automatic early learning that we call the Oepidus Complex—an extension of the unexamined life into the whole social arena.

The curriculum would be composed of courses that show human society on its most basic, simple, and "primitive" levels: the life of a community of equals, celebrating their social meanings with a maximum of dramatic intensity. It would study the rise of the State as the breakup of traditional community, the full development of classes and their struggles, of the pursuit of money and private gain, and so on. For the Western world, the Greek experience is the best and most direct one, and can be read very clearly: the great breakup and the individualism that began with the reforms of Cleisthenes. He would learn how Roman law sanctioned the new merchant economy, and thus legalized the disruption of the older community, right down to the present day. He would see the Middle Ages as a half-hearted attempt to make men responsible to each other in a network of shared obligations, an attempt to transcend personal life with a higher perspective, a consecrating of earthly life with divine meanings. It was the closest that Western man has come to reinstituting the older sacred primitive community. The student would learn how it, too, failed to contain and further the human spirit, and developed into the new, flowering, individualistic Renaissance and Enlightenment. He would see that the modern

State arose by breaking the old bonds of loyalty to small intimate groups and associations; that society gradually became rootless and monolithic. But he would understand too how necessary this was for the freedom of the individual from social constraints, the constraints of the primitive tribe, of the extended family, of the guild, the clan, the religious sect, the Church. He would learn how individualism flowered in Athens with the breakup of the old bonds; how it again flowered in the Renaissance with the breakup of the medieval life; how it once again developed in the nineteenth century, in the new industrial society, when feudalism was finally laid to rest in the Western world. He would study the French Revolution as the great symbolic event of modern times: the attempt to reconstruct society anew along equalitarian models; the attempt to raise man to a dignity and brotherhood he has never yet enjoyed. But the student would learn that this great attempt also failed, because it resulted merely in new social classes, a new division of the spoils. He would see that the abolition of private ownership in land was not carried through, and so the new society was not born. The great Roman potlatch was simply continued into the twentieth century. He would study the utopian socialism of the nineteenth century, and the revolutionary communism of the twentieth, as attempts to carry through the French Revolution, efforts to make once and for all a free society of equals, devoted to higher ideals than merely private gain. He would learn how these revolutions also crush the human spirit, because they subordinate man to the rule of men, instead of freely educating everyone, and liberating men to their own full flowering, and ultimately to the service of transcendant divine meanings. All in all, the student would learn to analyze the panaroma of history as the history of alienation from community; he would learn to analyze the various ideologies of the modern world as failures to establish the most liberating type of community; he would learn how the human spirit has been trapped in history, and how it is kept bottled in the modern ideological State. All this would be his education as a future shaper of his own society, as a mature hand in the process of experimental democracy and continued social reconstruction.

Those who have been wrestling with the problem of the decline of classical education can now see what a splendid thing the "alienation curriculum" is. We can replace the old classical education, and yet give all the advantages it gave; we can go beyond it to make our knowledge truly modern and meaningful for contemporary man. After all, what was the great strength of the old classical education that we have not been able to replace? Nietzsche said it: it was "Greek and Roman antiquity as the incarnate categorical imperatives of all culture" (1924, Vol. 3, p. 128). In other words, antiquity as a critical ideal model, a standard by which to judge the shallowness of contemporary life. This is what the humanistic studies of the Renaissance had earlier said, when they revived the classical learning: "These are *our models.*" This was a truly aristocratic education for the many, as Douglas Bush has recently reminded us (1959, p. 50). The classical education had the great advantage of teaching the student what we now call "cultural relativity": He learned a foreign language, learned intimately the ways of thought and life of a wholly strange culture. This is the benefit that Toynbee recently urged that we retain—the insight into the relativity of cultural values (*A Study of History,* Vol. 12, pp. 586-87). In this way, and only in this way, can man get a commanding perspective on his own society. When the classical education declined, we looked around for a way to substitute what it had given, and anthropology seemed to be the natural and logical successor. (This was Douglas Gilbert Haring's proposal.) Rousseau was the prophet of this new turn in the curriculum when he urged in *Émile* that everyone have what we now call a "cross-cultural experience," so as better to judge their own society: "I take it as an incontestable maxim that whoever has seen only one people knows only the people with whom he has lived, he does not know man" (1762, p. 575).

But what happened to anthropology? Why has it never succeeded in replacing the classical education? It gave us relativity; it even gave us anguished glimpses into the starkly fictional nature of human meanings. But this was just the trouble: It gave us only glimpses; for the most part, the anthropologist has always been just a disquieting anecdotalist, titillating us, or upsetting our social gatherings, with his inevitable exceptions to human customs: ". . . but among the Yoruba they . . ." The trouble with anthropology, like all the disciplines of the human sciences, has been the common modern disease, the disease of objective science, of value neutrality. Anthropology did not follow the program the Enlightenment laid out for it, in Rousseau's vision of an ideal type of science. Only today are a few anthropologists again trying to make contact with this original tradition, by using the primitive as an ideal type. When we understand this, we can understand that anthropology, while it taught cultural relativity, failed to give the major strength that the old classical curriculum had given. It failed to provide a specific critical model by which to judge contemporary society. And with this failure, the best insights degenerate into anecdotalism.

Now our task is clear. The weakness of the classical curriculum was that Greece and Rome were not the best models. Before the reforms of Cleisthenes, Greek individualism was still dormant, the person was still submerged in his traditional group loyalties. After the reforms, individualism developed, but the new society disintegrated along with it. The great historical potlatch was on. When the Athenians annihilated the Melians, because they would not take their side in war, they became the model of modern imperialism and colonialism, but not of the humanism we are still searching for. And when the Athenians sentenced Socrates—who is our true model—to death, they struck out against the reason we still seek. When Plato, finally, designed his *Republic,* he left us a utopia that we shudder to imagine. No, no models these, except for rich imaginations, and except for a great deal of our own anxious correction and extrapolation. The Athenian model will not do, unless we limit it to Socrates alone; and the primitive model will not do, because it does not hold up the kind of freedom we value, the freedom of the individual from the constraints of his social group, from the slavery to social opinion. Instead, we need a constructed, scientific ideal-type that is subject to continued modification and change—just like historical society itself is. It has the disadvantage of being abstract, whereas Greek and Roman models are very concrete; but it has the advantage of being truly ideal, and fully modifiable with our own experience and findings. It is the proper model for an experimental democracy; and it can only be given by a curriculum centered on the idea of alienation. This is the truly aristocratic model for the masses: It gives us continuing self-criticism, and leaves our future wholly open. It points the direction of our liberation by showing us exactly how freedom is limited in society; it urges us on by showing us that all the forms that history has so far designed still shackle the human spirit.

This, then, would be the core of the *second* or social dimension of our alienation curriculum—the history and sociology of the State, against an ideal model of self-reliant man in a free community of equals. The student would learn the forms, variations, and elements that make up all historic communities; he would learn what differentiates collectives from true communities, by studying the interrelationships of social structure as that structure underwent historical change. This is exactly what the great Max Scheler called for, when he asked us to give antiquity its real historical character: He understood that it was not our ideal model. Scheler did not want the ancient values, nor the idiosyncratic nationalism of antiquity; he wanted a really Christian civic education, and he understood that in order to have this, we needed to develop in the student a fully critical "sense of State." His thoughts on how best to do this are well worth quoting at length (1921, p. 426, his emphasis):

> . . . a continual indication, pervading *all* relevant instruction, of how this or that literature, art, science, philosophy *fitted* into the State of the time . . . why certain groups of values—late-stoic philosophy for example—stood outside, which features were conditioned by the nature of the social groups exhibiting them, and which *could* have arisen—given cultural potentialities latent in existing forces—but were frustrated by political conditions. To my mind, this indirect cultivation of the sense of State and community, constantly drawing attention to the fact that even the highest fruits of the spirit are *inter*dependent with political and social conditions (thus the intellectualism of Greek thought was dependent on the institution of slavery and slave-trading —and vice versa)—this method should renew the whole of thinking, in the direction of a deepened sense of State, much more intimately and permanently than any direct "civic instruction" geared to the State of the day. But the most important consideration is that the sense of State . . . should be

> attained, if at all, only as a particular formulation of an intensified sense of community. If the pupil is to see and grasp *clearly* the actual ensemble and historical interplay of existing communities, the teacher must put before him a network of basic sociological concepts which is applicable irrespective of the particular variety of human group; the network must comprehend all *essential* forms of community, presenting the State as only *one* among many such forms—family, clan, race, people, . . . and so on.

Scheler, in other words, clearly understood the problem of educating for *community* as an ideal by which to control the education; and of using the history and sociology of the State as the basic core of that education. But I quote Scheler at length also in order to introduce a dimension into our curriculum that is only now becoming possible, but which crowns all other dimensions. Scheler asks us to study why groups of values stand outside of a society, at a given point in history; how values are conditioned by the nature of the social groups that exhibit them; and even, what kind of values *might have* arisen at a particular time, values that were latent in the existing cultural potential, but which were frustrated by political conditions.

Now, we can understand that if we could do this, it would give us the fullest possible critical perspective on the interrelationships of the social structure throughout history; it would give us the most compelling evidence to support, revise, and fill out our ideal model; in a word, it would give a most complete empirical scientific guide for our contemporary problems of living in community. It would give us a grasp on history that allowed us to learn as much as possible about the full range of human potential in society. And what, then, is the dimension of our curriculum that now allows us to complete this kind of study?

B. Historical psychology

It is the maturing dimension of historical psychology; and it is now maturing because we have a very rich and sophisticated understanding of the *individual* dimension of alienation. It was only when we could truly understand what hindered self-reliance on the level of the individual personality that we could begin a mature historical psychology; it was only when we advanced beyond the narrow Freudian formulations on human behavior that we could see man in the full dimensions of society and history. We stopped seeing him as a creature of narrow instinctual drives and biological satisfactions, and could understand him as a groper after meanings; and when we speak of meanings, we speak of the whole range of social and historical possibilities open to human action. It allows us to talk about meanings realized and realizable, about meanings latent in the potential of man's social world; it allows us, in a word, to talk about what Scheler wanted—about the full relationship of human values to the state of a society in which man is born. It is the final crown on the Enlightenment scrutiny of history and society, and it is the latest gift of post-Freudian psychology. Instead of talking about how *nature* baffles man, we can carry Rousseau's beginnings to their furthest reach, and can talk about how society, in all its interrelationships, causes human "stupidity," causes a constriction on available meanings and values.

This is not the place to expand on the possibilities of historical psychology; it is better saved for a separate work. But we have already had several glimpses, in chapters Seven and Eight. We know how social groups seek for unity, intensity of meaning, highest conviction for those meanings; and we know that this seeking for maximum meaning is intimately linked with what society allows at a given point of history and with a given type of social organization. Thus, we can talk about historical opportunity, and "social stupidity"; but not "social stupidity" in the sense that the eighteenth century liked to talk about it: as superstition, outmoded beliefs, rudimentary stages of human awareness; rather, we can talk about it in terms of the physical organization and of the social fiction of each society—even the most supposedly "advanced." This allows us to understand not only the fetishism of commodities, but any fetishization of the human world, sex fetishization, self-fetishization, and so on. Fetishization is a word that shows us how man narrows down his meanings when his society does not educate for, nor make possible, broader ranges of self-rewarding experiences. It is not an absolute concept—none of our concepts are—but it is the perfect "ideal-typical" concept; it helps us to focus on what is broader and richer in comparison to the way things actually are.

We can understand other types of social stupidity with a richness that has not before been possible: Scapegoating, for example, is, as we saw, a clumsy and easy way to achieve the unity of one's own group, to reaffirm one's own values and meanings, to exercise firm control over one's social world by offering up the sacrifice of the evil stranger. We can also understand why it takes an even heavier toll in the modern world perhaps than it ever did; today man has been fully emptied of the quality of his individuality; he has become finally a fully quantified thing, to be tallied like any commodity. At a time when we thought we were becoming "civilized" and outgrowing "irrational" conduct, we can understand that man never outgrows his need for intense and unified meanings; if anything, then, he is bound to become more vicious, as his ability to satisfy this need is more and more restricted under the shallow conditions of modern life. Potlatch for potlatch, we are more dangerous than the Assyrians and the Romans.

But most of all, we are coming to understand mental illness itself as a general problem of social stupidity, as a problem of constricted action and meaning, for which education and social structure are directly responsible. This means that we understand the significance of the great manias that seize social groups, and we can relate these manias and hysterias to the state of their society in its historical period. The "dancing manias" of the Middle Ages, for example, tarantism, and similar hysterical types of expression of a constricted human spirit (as the great Russian sociologist Nikolai Mikhailovski already understood in the nineteenth century). We are coming to understand individual failure as a problem of education and opportunity, in a word, exactly as the Enlightenment hoped we would. We are coming to understand human destiny as a problem of social role, and of education and flexibility in the face of social roles.

Our curriculum, then, will offer all this rich knowledge in its study of the sociology of the State. And specialized or interested students will be able to go deeply into the problem of how a particular society elicits mental illness—just as we now understand how our own society fosters menopausal depression by limiting the roles available to women after menopause. In this way, they will have the fullest possible view of the dynamics of alienation in society and history.

3. The Theological Dimension of Alienation

Finally, our alienation curriculum would be crowned by the theological dimension. Just as our individual, social, and historical dimensions teach us how alienation comes about in the individual life and in society, so our theological dimension naturally completes the picture by teaching the law of the limitations of human satisfaction under the conditions of existence.

There was a time when the proposal that a theological dimension be required in a core college curriculum would have met strong protest. Unhappily, that time is not yet past: secularists, scientists, sectarian religionists—all might find reasons for keeping a theological dimension out of a required course program. Their protest is a natural and justified one, if it means that we should not introduce a particular theological point of view as a required belief; or, if it means that we should not require any body of knowledge that is not subject to the critical requirements of all universal knowledge: empirical control, examination and discussion, full and free debate aiming at potential refutation.

What can we answer? If we required of students that they study a body of knowledge that did not meet these universal criteria, we would indeed be subverting the aims of the university in a democracy. But there is no longer any problem; we need no longer make a dogmatic defense of theology. For the first time in history, we seem able to introduce a fully mature theological dimension into our education that meets the most rigorous critical criteria. This is truly an event of great historical importance. Not only are we *able* to do so, but we *must* do so, if we are to carry what we know to its fullest point of analysis and synthesis.

We saw the reasons for this in chapters Eight and Nine, and there is no point in repeating here the argument for theology. It is the natural complement and continuation of our best knowledge about man. We saw that we cannot talk meaningfully about human striving, unless we introduce descriptive ontology; and we saw further that if we talk about descriptive ontology, then we must proceed to its logical conclusion, which is the perspective of theonomy, as Tillich calls it. This means that the insights from Tillich's great *Systematic Theology* would form an integral part of our naturalistic study of man. The empirical study of man would be continued into descriptive ontology, or the full study of "being" in the dimensions of existence. Only in this way could our neutral Rousseau-ian view of human nature be carried to its furthest point of analysis. Only by studying all the ambiguities of existence would the student come to understand fully how evil is inevitable in life. He would then see that man can achieve sporadic and fragmentary healing of the ruptures of life only by a perspective of theonomy on all the dualisms that characterize human striving. He would learn how to give life the dimension of ultimate meaning, the dimension which alone pulls our world together in an unconditional way. This would show him the one thing man needs above all to know: the direction in which he can experience the maximum exercise of his freedom. And as we saw in Chapter Nine, this is the freedom to contribute our own energies to the eternal meaning of the cosmos, the freedom to bathe our daily life in the highest possible intensity and scope of meanings; and these must be divine, self-transcendent meanings.

Thus, we see how theology is the logical complement to a science of man based on an ideal vision of man. The secularist and the scientist need no longer protest, if they are willing to accept the version of Enlightenment science put forth by Diderot and Rousseau. If they are not, then there is of course no point in talking about the solution of the problem of education on any level, or in any meaningful way. There will never be any way naturally to unify the curriculum, except by drawing it together from a perspective of human need and use. If we allow society as it stands to tell us what man needs to use, then we can continue with our present fragmented curriculum, which holds together only because it turns out people who fit into their society as it stands. It is a professionally and vocationally oriented curriculum—and that is a "kind" of unity. But if we want a unity that is aimed at the release of unknown human energies, then only an alienation curriculum can give it; and an alienation curriculum is not complete without required courses in the limitations of human satisfaction under the conditions of existence itself. If the secularist and the scientist accept this, then they need have no qualms about Tillich's theology. It is firmly based, like the science of man itself, on the *"Protestant* Principle," on the principle of an uncompromising critical attitude toward all dogma. This means that it allows a relentless criticism of any social fiction that constricts human energies, no matter what institutions are empowered under that social fiction—be they even the Church itself, in any of its forms.

Finally, we must understand that the science of man must be crowned by theology, in order fully to design a standard that transcends pragmatic relativism. And that standard, as we saw, is the standard of the life forces themselves, as they develop in the individual person. Our theology, like our science, opts squarely for the human person, against any social fictions which constrain the free development of his personhood. And these constraints cannot be fully understood without a theonomous perspective on human ambiguities, as Tillich has so forcefully shown in Volume III of his *Systematic Theology*. In this way, the theological part of our curriculum gives the fullest support to the communitarian ideal, by showing further how a true *community* differs from a mere *collective* of empty individuals. The student would understand that the theonomous perspective can only be realized in a free community of equal men, devoted to the self-transcendent creation of meaning. The Biblical ideal of religious socialism is thus the natural complement to the science of man, as the great Walter Rauschenbusch and Harry F. Ward knew; it is an objective measure of the inadequacies of any social fiction. In Rauschenbusch's and Ward's day, this was a hopeful vision that slowly and tragically ebbed because it was still premature. Now that sociology itself has discovered the social fiction, there can be little compelling argument against their vision. The science of man and theology are ready to join forces.

Why did it take so long to bring theology naturally into science? We saw one reason: We had to wait until the science of man itself matured; we had to wait for it to rejoin its own neglected Enlightenment vision, and we had to wait for it truly to crown the Enlightenment beginnings on the problem of human nature. And this was not achieved until very recently. We had to understand man fully as an animal who strived after meanings; we had to see history as the problem of the decline of community; and we had to understand personal failure and social failure as both due to the constrictions on responsible action. When we understood this, we could naturally merge the scientific and the theological perspectives because both of them gave us the ideal of fully developed personhood in equalitarian community; the Biblical model and the Socratic model were natural partners. This is nowhere better understood than in the historical problem of "sin." "Sin," as we saw in Chapter Nine, can only be understood in relation to the problem of autonomy. It is almost impossibly difficult for the individual to assume the responsibility for his own meanings; he must, by his very nature as a creature immersed in the infinite, try to ground his acts in superordinate authority, in self-transcendence of some kind. The weight of sin, then, is the weight of meanings that are not related to a broad and self-transcending framework; they are meanings that do not justify the individual in the light of the eternal significance of the universe. With sin, man is cut off, he stands *alone with meaning,* separate from the ground of things, uprooted in his own finitude. This is what gives sin its deep anxiety. As Pascal and Kierkegaard so well knew, sin is existential anxiety, because it is man standing alone with the full burden for the meaning of life. Few men can stand this; and if even these men would stand truly erect, they could not stand it. Man can only stand sin by limiting his perspective, by narrowing his questions, by bending his gaze. Even those who would be strong—say, a Sartre or a Camus—take refuge from the burden of private meanings by claiming that life is "absurd." It is only absurd because it is absurd for them to be alone with their trivial meanings. This is the logical outcome of the revolt against the theological dimension of life. When men said that the idea of sin was absurd, they were right: sin *is* absurd because it means that man is alone responsible for the meaning of life. And it is this absurdity which must drive modern man back to a theonomous perspective on his existence.

When we understand this, we can also understand "sin" as an historical and social problem, as we also said in Chapter Nine. We know that it arose as a cumulative problem in the ancient world; it arose when the integral primitive communities began their inevitable breakup. It was then that daily life became more and more separated from the cover of divine meanings, from an integral pattern of myth and ritual that consecrated most of the important acts of the individual in community. With this breakup, man lost his firm rooting in the divine ground, his daily life became increasingly secular—which means increasingly narrow and shallow, increasingly pragmatic, increasingly autonomous. And it was here that the cumulative "terror of history" began to make itself felt. Man had lost his contact with continual natural cosmic rhythms; he ceased to be nourished in the feeling that his life was transcendentally significant; the anxious burden of "sin" thus pervaded more and more of his daily cares.

Finally, as we saw, when we understand this historical dimension on the problem of sin, we can understand too that it was not "nerve" that "failed" in the Greek world, as Gilbert Murray thought. Rather, it was something much more fateful, much more beyond the control of individual decision and energy; it was community in transcendent divine meanings that "failed." It was the Greek world itself that failed, that failed to sustain man among men. The terror of history yielded one great fruit: the development of individualism, out of the decline of community. Today we accept history without the old terror, and we want even more individualism than the Greeks imagined. But their problem is still ours, and it is still not a problem of failure of nerve; we must find a way to reunite history and individualism with the transcendent meaning in community. Only in this way can we deprive them of their inner destructiveness. This is the great lesson we have learned after twenty-five hundred years of wandering across the face of "civilized" history: We need to combine Socratic self-reliance with a new life-giving myth in a new community.

So we now see fully how our naturalistic understanding of man's problems makes the theological perspective the perfect complement of our curriculum. It pulls together the individual, social, and historical perspectives, and makes alienation a problem that ideally can be solved. Without the theological dimension, we could not understand how man could ever experience a true resolution of his anxieties, how he would ever discover a proper direction for his full freedom. We know that he needs nothing less than a true community of free men living a theonomous life. We have a fully sketched ideal of what experimental democracy must mean. Only with this ideal can man design the highest vision of the good; only in this way can he see the good as the evolution of the unknown forces that take root in his being; only in this way can the entire college experience be forged into a unity for the highest development of life itself.

4. Conclusion

So much, then, for the general content of the three dimensions of our alienation curriculum. There is one great problem that remains, but it seems premature to attempt to solve it at this time, even though we must raise it. If we are truly to pull our curriculum together with a theonomous dimension, then we must assign a meaning *to* history; we must agree on a "central historical event" that gives significance to the whole panorama of history. And as we know, we can only assign such a meaning by taking a perspective from beyond and outside history. What I am saying is that the life of free men in community must be united by a myth of the meaning of life itself, a truly dynamic and creative myth. This would unite our whole perspective by giving our education its ultimate and agreed ethical grounding in the most forceful and creative way possible. For Christianity, of course, the center of history is the center that overcame the terror of history in the ancient world: the coming of Jesus as the Christ. It gave the world the ethical nourishment that has sustained it until very recently; it told us that God cared about man; that man, even under the pitiable conditions of finitude, was supremely important for God; and the proof of that importance is that under the conditions of existence, even God Himself must suffer and die. Man's existence was thus given its highest mandate, its greatest dignity and nobility.

Does education in a democracy need *this particular* world-historical myth; is this the ideal that will permit us to develop the cosmic mystery from within our individual personhoods? Is it true, as Ian Ramsey says in the words which follow upon our epigraph to this chapter, that the mystery common to all the disciplines "in a Christian university will be talked of specifically in Christian terms"? But if this is true, what are we to do with those to whom Jesus is not acceptable as the Christ; what are we to do with those who follow other religions and creeds? How can we get them together "on the fighting edge of the cosmos," as Munson stated it, without some central historical myth of the Judeo-Christian type? Or perhaps all creeds permit us to get the essence and tragedy of the human condition, give us a conception of the immensity of transcendence, the infinite abyss of the unknown, the terrible awesomeness of the idea of God, the power of otherwordliness? Can we go in a direction such as that suggested, say, in Dewey's *A Common Faith,* or by William Ernest Hocking's "World Faith"?

These are questions of great magnitude that, as we said, we cannot begin to answer here. Our answer would only have a false finality, for a curriculum that is only itself a theoretical beginning. Too many discussions have already been raised on the problem, too many informed voices have recorded their views and suggestions, for us to attempt any simple and premature statements here. Let us then leave the question open, as an ultimate problem that a curriculum of alienation will have to solve. But if our efforts are sincere, and if our curriculum gets under way, it may give us what we need in the best and most natural way possible. If we give the mass of men an education truly worthy of their highest strivings, the problem may solve itself in the one way that we have most fervently been hoping: by creating from within new, free, human energies, a new and vital religious myth that brings our society together and allows it to move forward into the unknown with an unprecedented creative, historic thrust.

CHAPTER THIRTEEN

The Place of the Curriculum in the University

"The same education and the same habits will be found to make a good man and a good statesman and king."

—Aristotle

Mankind has always paid homage to its great thinkers; and its greatest have always been the theoreticians, those who by force of abstract thought have reordered the world of knowledge. It holds true on any level: In the primitive hunting band, the one who is most valued is he who can conceptualize the whole territory of the tribe, and imagine what route the wounded animal will take, out of all possible routes; in the Western world, it is a Plato, an Augustine, an Aquinas—he who reorders thought into a new synthesis that buoys men up for another little while. No wonder the thinking public fell at the feet of the great Newton; it was he who reconceptualized the world at the anguished decline of the medieval cosmology. It was truly as the great poet wrote: "God said, 'Let Newton be . . .' " and all was well again.

In our time we can point to no one man who solved our moral crisis; instead we have a whole tradition of thinkers who presented us with a New Moral View of the World. If we adopt it and use it, we can find our way again, we can rise up to a height in a clearing, we can breathe and stand erect; light has broken into our world. For man, this new vision has the radicalness of revolution. How many archaic giants are laid low; how many tortured problems solved; how many thick knots cut with a single clean blow! Look here! The "knowledge explosion" is a myth, a demonic myth fashioned by the alchemy of experts to plague us. But no longer. Now we have a core curriculum with a single orientation that cuts through the mountain of disjointed facts. It is as Howard Lee Nostrand so well reminded us: "The fragmenting of the culture and the curriculum is not rightly attributed to the expansion of knowledge, nor to the attendant specialization . . . the amassing of knowledge beyond an individual's capacity had been going on in companies of scholars since before the Moslem center Al Azhar, without necessarily disrupting the unity of a culture" (1963, p. 147). All we needed was a new theoretical ordering of knowledge, with man as center; all we needed to do was to refer *our* knowledge to *our* situation. This is what imagination does. Those terrible stacks in our libraries, those forbidding rows of attractive books in our paperback bookstores—this maze of anxious temptation and quiet power: Suddenly our relationship to it changes; no longer is the balance of power on the side of the shelf, it has swung back to the seeker; no longer is the subject overwhelmed by the object, it is now he who picks and chooses; the living finger lands firmly on the dusty book. And look again! No longer are fact and theory hopelessly separate, no longer is there a gulf between what we imagine, and what we need in order to check, control, and extend our imagination. Science, philosophy, life, action—each touches intimately the other.

We saw in Chapter Ten how we have achieved what our best thinkers have been calling for without success up to now; we have a single required core curriculum for our universities: an alienation curriculum, an anthropodicy of the human condition in our time, a New Moral View of the World that would be taught to all. This is the "compulsory curriculum" that Joseph Needham called for (1946, pp. 112-13); the single core curriculum that Mark Van Doren wanted (1943, pp. 112 ff.); the curriculum composed of relatively few subjects, based on a narrow formula and a simple classification, all interconnected with a common center. It meets H. G. Wells's vision of a World Encyclopedia, or "Super-university," Ortega's proposal for a Faculty of Culture, Hutchins' plan for the new university. It gives everything that Hutchins asked for: the subject matter that would be uniform for all; the "first principles" that would illuminate all dilemmas of fact and of current problems; the most "generalized understanding of the nature of the world and the nature of man" (1962, p. 108); it gives the world of thought comprehended as a whole.

All this, then, we reviewed in Chapter Ten; but now we can see further where it all leads, what it permits: It gives us exactly the reorganization of the university that Hutchins wanted. It allows us to attack the departmental system, and the terrible fragmentation that it encourages. It plays down the emphasis on mere data gathering, and on research for the sake of research. It attacks what Hutchins called the two major disordering elements of the university: "unqualified empiricism," and "vocationalism" (1962, p. 117). Fundamental problems again assume their rightful and natural seniority at the center of the university, and at the center of its preoccupations. Those teachers who are concerned solely with data gathering, or with vocational training, will naturally be edged out of the lopsidedly important position they now hold—just as Hutchins foresaw. Perhaps even the "professional schools of the university would disappear as such" (p. 111). The conduct of the university becomes all important, the conduct of the university as a *university,* as a locus for the dissemination of self-liberating knowledge to greater and greater masses of students.

This is what Ortega, too, wanted when he called for a single Faculty of Culture that would be the heart of the university. As he saw it, this was the faculty which would teach the core body of knowledge, continually digest and synthesize it, continually feed it with the inquiry that the university conducted. In this way, synthesis takes its rightful place at the center, and even though it feeds on research, the researchers take their rightful place at the periphery of importance in the university, just like in Hutchins' scheme.

Do we need to fear such a reorganization of the university? Is it dangerous to propose a separate Faculty of Culture as a locus of synthesis, as Nostrand (1963, pp. 8-9) warns us? But we saw that the anthropodicy is not based on any rigid list of "Great Books," nor does it draw its "first principles" from any such list. It is composed of basic knowledge about human alienation, and its content varies with the validity of that knowledge: Is it relevant to new problems? Is it outmoded? The principle is flexible and open—it is the principle of man's basic goodness. The ideal is modifiable and perfectible—it is the ideal of human freedom in community. The body of knowledge draws from the present, as well as the past; it changes and grows. All vital knowledge, as Paul Weiss (1960) so well reminded us, is an organic growth process. It lops off, modifies, digests, and moves forward under its own changing imperatives. In other words, the Faculty of Culture, based on the core curriculum of alienation, is not imperial or authoritarian, and cannot be. The absolute *content* of our Faculty is revalidated daily by each inquiring mind. It is not an "absolute" content in the traditional sense. It is not biased toward rationalism, but is fully naturalistic; it does not favor religious knowledge over scientific or naturalistic knowledge; it does not lean to tradition or accumulation, unless they meet the rigorous test of new discoveries, and the perspective of present criticism. In these ways, the Faculty of Culture is prevented from exercising any kind of tyranny on the university; it is relativist and pragmatic; it is based on an anthropodicy of alienation that itself is a *theory,* in which values are not prejudged or assured. No values, that is, except one: the value that controls all others, the value that stands critically against the past, and vigilantly over the present—the value of the individual personhood and the fullest expression of responsible freedom.

As we saw, it is only with such a value that a separate university is possible *at all,* because this is the value that prevents the university from exercising the tyranny of science itself, the tyranny of any vested interest—even that of knowledge. This is the value, as we saw, which fulfills our Enlightenment mandate, without succumbing to the great danger of the Enlightenment proposal for a separate university: the danger of making a "State within a State." Only in this way can Ortega's, Wells's, and Hutchins' proposals for a complete reorganization of the university be naturally and safely accomplished.

This kind of control on authority is at the same time a control on what makes coercive authority possible, namely, irresponsible esotericism. We know that knowledge needs to become esoteric in order to develop, that all scientific debates move inevitably into esoteric knowledge. But as Diderot, Condorcet, Saint-Simon, and Comte saw, there never was any control on esotericism *from within science itself*. Science pushes relentlessly toward its own special problems, which means that it pushes toward specialization, trivialization, irresponsible esotericism. It pushes, in effect, toward authoritarianism and futility both. Condorcet, as we said, thought that the solution lay in full publicity of knowledge, and in full publicity of the doings of the scientific body. In this way, he thought that an informed public would serve as a control on science. Perhaps this would be true, from an ideal point of view; but we do not live in an ideal world. Science itself must help the control; the brake on authoritarianism and esotericism must come from within the unity of science itself. How can this be? It can only be, as we said, by uniting science on man, by making a science which has as its ideal the furthering of human subjectivity and freedom. In this way, we have a quietly insistent obligation on all scientific work, from within the imperatives of science itself. And the basis for this unprecedented achievement was the great discovery of the nineteenth century: that all our knowledge about man was knowledge about man as a free creator of meaning. Everything has to be brought back to what is humanly meaningful, even the most advanced and esoteric knowledge of science itself.

When we thus control esotericism with the principle of human freedom, we make our Great Conversation possible, right at the heart of the university. Each specialist is in some vital way a generalist, when what he knows is knowledge about the shackles on the self-reliant freedom of man. And each datum about the shackles on the freedom of man is in some vital way understandable by other men. No more sterility of knowledge, because it must be brought back to the problem of human freedom; no more outmoded knowledge because human freedom is a problem in the present world and controls our perspective on the past; no more endlessly inverted debate because human freedom cannot remain an inverted problem. When it becomes inverted, freedom is on its way to being lost—as we are learning today. Only in this way can education make sense because it gives us a basic body of knowledge that can be understood by all teachers, exactly as Hutchins and Van Doren wanted. It is a basic curriculum that encourages them to teach one another, even as they teach the students.

1. The Principle of the Economy of Knowledge

But it is especially the students who have the vital and controlling role to play in the whole process of education. As we saw in Chapter Ten, with the alienation curriculum we can make the university a locus of mass education, without the great danger of mass education. We do not need to dilute the elite nature of truly excellent knowledge. We allow naturally for the application of Ortega's "Principle of Economy." Each student undertakes to explore the dimensions of his alienation in his time. What task has such vital and personal importance? Each student will want the best knowledge about his own alienation, and he will take as much as he can digest. He will be on his own, but responsibly on his own: unawed by experts, yet not disdainful of the best they have to give. No longer will he have to read books that are read only by experts after a lifetime of preparation, unless these books make sense to him and to his needs. He can lop off and economize, as he tailors the curriculum to his needs and possibilities. Once he has digested the general core knowledge on alienation, he can go ahead on his own steam. Best of all, with the alienation perspective on all knowledge, even the most esoteric knowledge yields more easily: the student will already know, in a sense, what to look for, what he will find. The more capable and interested students, those who vitally want their own fullest liberation, will put together a richer and deeper picture of alienation. Those who are less capable, and less impelled toward freedom, will put together a sketchier and shallower picture. But all will put together *some kind* of integral picture. Thus, the best knowledge remains difficult and somewhat aloof, the general and lesser knowledge becomes the common property.

For example, all students could easily digest an overview of the history of the failure of community; the rough laws of early development and training of the child; the general functioning of the social system as a social fiction, and so on. Thus, they would get a picture of man's basic goodness, the problem of community, and the ideal of self-reliance. The better students would go into these same matters, but more deeply. They would study problems of critical social aesthetics—the problem of scapegoating, for example, and fetishization in all its aspects, and in its relationship to social structure and history. They would study not only the general problem of early child training, but also problems of critical individual aesthetics, such as sadism, masochism, fetishism, and the various "mental illnesses." They would go on to Historical Psychology in all its breadth and richness, and study the relationship of styles of life to styles of society, in the various epochs of history. The best students would go deeply into ontology and theology, and study the intricacies of human ambiguities under the conditions of existence. In this way, they would have the richest possible picture of the nature of man and the possibilities of human liberation. (And I am leaving out of my discussion literature, the arts, and the other sciences, since they are out of the range of my competence; but imagine how they will join to complete the richness of the picture the student will have available about the constraints on life, and the opportunities of the developing life force.)

This also allows us to solve once and for all the growing problem of adult education. What could be better than teaching to adults the basic alienation curriculum, and letting the principle of economy govern their own learning? They would relive all the intense emotional excitement of the young, as they threw these liberating perspectives on their even more mature lives; they would have more to contribute from their own experience, more leads to the facts of their working existence, a more creative use of their leisure time. They could go on to study any problem in the greatest degree of depth and richness that they are capable of; and they could devote their full time to it. In this way, we would add adults to the Great Conversation—even to the community of science itself.

This kind of mass-elitism allows us to combat student rebelliousness, destructiveness, and apathy, *in the entire society of learners*—young as well as old. We can now see that by placing the control over learning into the hands of the students, we achieve something truly great: We allow everyone a positive part in the knowledge process itself. It is a control not only over what one will learn, but also what there is to be learned; it is a control not only over the esotericism and the authoritarianism of science, but also over the professors themselves. And with the new responsibility of the students for their own development, this control would not be a capricious tyranny, but part of the Great Conversation of the university. How many benefits would accrue from this! Are we now hung up on the dilemma of teaching versus research? But it is a pseudo-problem; the Faculty of Culture, as we said, would be at the center of the university, and with its core curriculum of general knowledge, it would automatically force research to the periphery of the university. The student himself would have a critical part in this process, because by the natural pressures of his curiosity he would control the flow of knowledge: Central things would remain central; durable things would continue; modifiable things would be modified by new knowledge as it arises. Research controls, checks, feeds, but does not dominate the general principles and the core curriculum.

Contrast the situation today! The student has no control, and knowledge does not control itself. The result is a fiendish anarchy, viciously competitive, without standards to measure the value of the competition; the loudest voice wins; the grayest temples command the most respect; the simplest and most striking research gimmicks gain allegiance, whether they are intellectually meaningful or not. We know the sad situation, so there is no sense in dwelling on it. Each professor tries for student allegiance to his "discipline." Each discipline joins in the great scramble for converts; claims that it is a "true science," and contorts itself to prove it. Fad is king. Worst of all, everyone claims "equal time" for student attention. The result is incredible confusion, and violates the whole knowledge process, reverses the whole hierarchy of scientific importance. Methodologists claim equal time with theorists, model-builders claim even more time than those who teach fundamental, general principles! It is as though we were to give shoemakers equal time with shoe-designers, or practical nurses equal time in the medical curriculum with doctors. But method has never been primary in knowledge: Scientific method is merely the directions one follows *under a particular theory;* but the theory is the thing. And science is not *a* method, or methods, or even a body of knowledge. Science is an activity with a distinctive attitude. It differs from ideology and dogma, not by any special method, or even by any special knowledge, but, rather, by its willingness to revise any and all of its findings in the face of evidence.

Yes, we know these things very well, but yet we allow the practical nurses and the shoemakers of science "equal time" to win student allegiance. No wonder everything is in a whirl. Teachers who do not teach; researchers who command more respect than theorists; three-hour lecture periods that bear no relationship to the knowledge that is to be imparted in the three-hour time. Why do we hold so frantically to the three-hour lecture system? Simply because we still pretend that knowledge is being imparted, no matter who is teaching, or what is being taught. It is largely show and sham; and it is all because we have no core curriculum, no basic body of knowledge that is the "one best" body, that carries its own higher authority. And the three-hour measure, as we sadly know, is our only way of tallying up the value of knowledge, and permitting a proportional cash payment—both by the students, and to the professors. But now that we have such a body, the student can be liberated from this farce. The lecture can again become meaningful and central; it can last as long as a professor needs to exhaust his particular topic; it can take place as often as the students want to be refreshed or pushed beyond their readings and independent work. More time could be allowed for student-interchange on the basic anthropodicy, as well as on its finer points. The professors would step in to control and carry forward the process. Method need not even be taught in the core curriculum. As Ortega so well understood, method is not necessary for the understanding of a science: The results can be understood without knowing how they were arrived at. If, for example, someone gives us a map of buried treasure, we can get right to it without having to quibble on how the map was drawn. And the treasure is our anthropodicy of alienation; how we got it is a specialized and more peripheral problem. The good professor, then, is the one who has a comprehensive idea of the general body of knowledge which he must teach; he does not even need to be a scientific investigator himself, as Ortega has reminded us. The selection of the outstanding professors will depend on their talent for synthesis and gift for teaching, and not necessarily on their rank as investigators (*cf.* Ortega, 1944, pp. 92 ff.). As we are learning today, some of our best generalizers and synthesizers of ideas are coming from departments of English, and literary criticism, and romance languages, and American studies. The big ideas fall to the big minds, no matter where they are found, or what disciplinary label they carry.*

2. Conclusion

There we have it. All the benefits that would befall us, once we made The New Moral View of the World the central body of knowledge that would be taught to everyone in the university. We would have a Faculty of Culture that would not be authoritarian; a Great Conversation between teachers, between students, and between teachers and students; a union of fact and theory that relegates research to its proper position, that fights vocationalism and rampant empiricism; a synthetic body of knowledge

* With this orientation, many a false problem would also be solved: I am thinking specifically of the problem of "more intimate" contact with the professors, and the efforts made to break the university down into smaller classes. I believe that this problem is largely the outgrowth of the failure to present real content in the general lecture courses. For example, the student, who sees so many "renowned" professors, and is exposed to "so much" knowledge, has to have some way of explaining "why" he is not getting a good education. It must be, he concludes, that he is not getting "close enough" to the professor, that the "distance" in the classroom is preventing the transmission of knowledge. It is all so vast and impersonal, and the professor is so well meaning. The student could never suspect that the reason the professors fail to communicate, for all their specialized knowledge and reputation, is that they are failing to give a meaningful education; and, they would fail equally, even if the student got as close to them as their skin.

that commands student allegiance, and that fights apathy and disarms rebelliousness and destructiveness; that provides its own natural Principle of Economy, and allows the student to control what he will learn, without squandering a vital basic education. It allows him, too, to control the knowledge process, the lecture system, the whole conduct of the university.

And all this takes place *naturally,* positively, not negatively; purely and simply because the university is a locus for the unfolding of individual freedom and subjectivity. The university becomes *naturally* student-oriented, student-centered, student-run. And this is the way it must be, not only because of the imperative of self-liberating knowledge, but also because of the heavy responsibility that is placed on the students themselves. If they are liberated from the old constraints; if they no longer suffer the fads of science, the idiocy of specialization and fragmentation of knowledge, the blind competitiveness and careerism of the professors, the quantification of the knowledge process; if they are finally placed above all this, given a vantage point from which to examine their lives, their society, their world—if, as we say, all this falls to them, then the greatest task of all is also theirs: *They must do nothing less than build the newer and truer forms of social life.* They must create the new symbols, the new myths, the new institutions, the new world that has been so long trying to be born, so quietly pining in the womb of time.

No doubt many of them will look back nostalgically at the time when the university was merely a nursery; when one could be a Big Man on Campus, and yet be safe in the world. But this will no longer be possible; The student will have to pay the price of his new Prometheanism: the world too will be his, his responsibility, and he will have to step forth with the anxiety and humility that befall the true man.

Epilogue

"... in a dying world, creation is revolution."
—Waldo Frank

When the nineteenth century rose up against Hegel and German Idealism, it was because it was gasping for breath: The air was too thin with rarefied theory. So much theory, so little living in the real world. Now we have committed a similar sin. We have extolled the theorists all through these chapters, those minds who gathered for us the great gift of a New Moral View of the World. And even more than the nineteenth century, we live in a world that scorns theory, that fears it. So let us now add some balance to our story, and toll for the theorist.

A theoretical vision, no matter how true to fact it might turn out to be, no matter how painfully long it took to be shaped, is still little more than a dream, unless it is put into practice. James Russell Lowell lamented that "thoughts that great hearts once broke for, we breathe cheaply in the common air." But we can lament even more, and say that the best thoughts may never become part of our heritage; we may leave them in oblivion, and continue to play out our destiny blindly and violently. It seems that in our dying world to create is too revolutionary. I do not believe that the ideas presented in this book can possibly speak to our time. They do not fit into the *actual conditions* of life in any country. Democracy is an ideal, and as Plato taught us, the real world does not welcome interference on the part of philosophy.

It is some eight centuries since the Calabrian monk Gioacchino da Fiore gave the world his vision. It was a vision that foresaw the development of the Spirit out of the womb of time. This would be the third great age of evolution: The first was the age of the Father; the second, that of the Son; and the third, that of the Holy Spirit. Gioacchino's vision was a great and radical one, for it meant that the destiny of Christianity would be played out here on earth, would be realized here, and not in some Heavenly City. Scholars tell us that this vision influenced many of the radical Franciscans during the Middle Ages; and that later it was carried over into German Idealism, especially in the work of Schelling and Hegel. It also probably contributed to the idea of the progressive realization of God-manhood, in the work of the Russian philosopher Vladimir Soloviëv. Man himself is the open vessel through which the Spirit speaks from the depths of nature; and with the beginning of history, man has stepped forth out of the womb of eternal time. The latest thinker to give powerful voice to this idea is the great Paul Tillich, in his profound discussions on the New Being.

In the eight centuries since Gioacchino wrote, we have gradually learned what was needed to release the fullest powers of the life force as they are contained in man. We learned that man was not an open vessel, but that he could become one, if he could throw off fully the shackles of alienation; and we learned where to look for those shackles. But in these eight centuries we learned something else too. We heard the great psychologist Luther speak of the bondage of the will, but this did not trouble scientists until the twentieth century. It was then that we saw what bondage of the will truly means: that try as he may, man cannot seem to order his world according to his visions. Again and again it crumbles, yawns open, and swallows him up; and always in greater and more terrible numbers, or so it seems. We have learned, in effect, that it has never been up to man to make the New Being. And now we see that our best ideas still do not speak to our time; which means that it is not even up to us to *prepare* the New Being, at least not on an intellectual level.

Yet we must give what we can, even though we know that we do not give what is really needed: The best comes from the abyss, and returns to the abyss. Our lives are like the traditional ending for Georgian tales:

> From heaven there fell three apples: one for the person who told the tale, another for the person who listened, and the most beautiful fell into the abyss.

And our tales, too, are no exception. Let us borrow this lovely image for our own imperfect vision, for the thinness of our theories in the face of what the world needs and wants. What was the story we *should have* told?

References

Adams, G. P. and Montague, W. P. (eds.) (1930), *Contemporary American Philosophy: Personal Statements* (New York: Macmillan) (2 vols.).

Altschule, Mark D. (1957), *Roots of Modern Psychiatry: Essays in the History of Psychiatry* (New York: Grune and Stratton).

Baldwin, James Mark (1915), *Genetic Theory of Reality* (New York: Putnam's).

Barzun, Jacques (1945), *Teacher in America* (Boston: Little, Brown).

Becker, E. (1962), *The Birth and Death of Meaning: A Perspective in Psychiatry and Anthropology* (New York: Free Press).

——— (1964a), *The Revolution in Psychiatry: The New Understanding of Man* (New York: Free Press).

——— (1964b), "Mills' Social Psychology and the Great Historical Convergence on the Problem of Alienation," in *The New Sociology,* I. L. Horowitz (ed.) (New York: Oxford University Press), pp. 108-133.

——— (1965), "The New Unified Science of Man: A History and Theory" (forthcoming).

Beesley, Patricia (1940), *The Revival of the Humanities in American Education* (New York: Columbia University Press).

Bell, Bernard Iddings (1949), *Crisis in Education; A Challenge to American Complacency* (New York: McGraw-Hill).

Brownell, Baker (1950), *The Human Community: Its Philosophy and Practice for a Time of Crisis* (New York: Harper & Row).

Bruner, Jerome S. (1962), *On Knowing* (Cambridge: Harvard University Press).

Burke, Kenneth (1955), "Linguistic Approach to Education," in *Modern Philosophies and Education,* Nelson B. Henry (ed.), 54th Yearbook of the National Society for the Study of Education (Chicago: University of Chicago Press), Chap. 8.

Bush, Douglas (1959), "Education and the Humanities," *Daedalus,* Winter, pp. 40-55.

Chalmers, Gordon K. (1944), "A New View of the World," in *The Humanities after the War,* Norman Foerster (ed.) (Princeton: Princeton University Press).

Chugerman, Samuel (1939), *Lester F. Ward: The American Aristotle* (Durham: Duke University Press).

Comte, Auguste (1848), *A General View of Positivism,* translated by J. H. Bridges (Stanford: Academic Reprints).

Dewey, John (1931), *The Way Out of Educational Confusion,* 1931 Inglis Lecture (Cambridge: Harvard University Press).

——— (1937a), "President Hutchins' Proposals to Remake Higher Education," *The Social Frontier,* Vol. III, pp. 103-104.

——— (1937b), "Education and Social Change," *The Social Frontier,* Vol. III, pp. 235-238.

——— (1946), *The Problems of Men* (New York: Philosophical Library).

Dilthey, Wilhelm (1962), *Pattern and Meaning in History: Thoughts on History and Society,* edited with an Introduction by H. P. Rickman (New York: Harper Torchbooks).

Duncan, Hugh D. (1962), *Communication and Social Order* (New York: Bedminster).

Erasmus-Luther (1524-1525), *Discourse on Free Will,* translated and edited by Ernst F. Winter (New York: Ungar, 1961, combined edition).

Feuer, Lewis (1963), "What is Alienation? The Career of a Concept," in *Sociology on Trial,* M. Stein and A. Vidich (eds.) (Englewood Cliffs: Prentice-Hall), pp. 127-147.

Frank, Philipp (1950), *Modern Science and Its Philosophy* (Cambridge: Harvard University Press).

Gascoyne, David (1952), *Thomas Carlyle* (London: Longmans, Green).

Gillispie, C. C. (1959), "The *Encyclopédie* and the Jacobin Philosophy of Science: a Study in Ideas and Consequences," in *Critical Problems in the History of Science,* M. Clagett (ed.) (Madison: University of Wisconsin Press), pp. 255-289.

Gorki, Maxim (1923), *My Universities,* translated by Helen Altschuler (Moscow: Foreign Languages Publishing House, third edition, n.d.).

Grattan, C. H. (ed.) (1930), *The Critique of Humanism* (New York: Brewer and Warren).

Greene, Theodore M. (1953), *Liberal Education Reconsidered,* 1952 Inglis Lecture (Cambridge: Harvard University Press).

Hazard, Paul (1963), *European Thought in the Eighteenth Century: From Montesquieu to Lessing,* translated by J. Lewis May (New York: Meridian).

Hegel, G. W. F. (1832), "Lectures on the Philosophy of Religion," in *Hegel on Tragedy,* edited with an Introduction by Anne and Henry Paolucci (New York: Anchor Books, 1962).

Henderson, A. D. (1944), *Vitalizing Liberal Education: A Study of the Liberal Arts Program* (New York: Harper & Row).

Hocking, William E. (1944), *Science and the Idea of God* (Chapel Hill: University of North Carolina Press).

Hook, Sidney (1946), *Education for Modern Man* (New York: Dial Press).

Hubert, Henri and Mauss, Marcel (1898), *Sacrifice: Its Nature and Function,* translated by W. D. Halls with a Foreword by E. E. Evans-Pritchard (Chicago: University of Chicago Press, 1964).

Huizinga, Johan (1955), *Homo ludens, a Study of the Play Element in Culture* (Boston: Beacon).

Hutchins, Robert M. (1954), *Great Books, The Foundation of a Liberal Education* (New York: Simon and Schuster).

——— (1962), *The Higher Learning in America* (New Haven: Yale University Press).

Jacks, M. L. (1946), *Total Education: A Plea for Synthesis* (London: Routledge).

Jacob, Peyton (1933), "A Reorientation of the Arts College: a Way of Quickening the Intellectual Life of Our Students," *Journal of Higher Education,* Vol. 4, pp. 407-412.

James, William (1902), *The Varieties of Religious Experience: A Study in Human Nature* (New York: Longmans Green).

Jaspers, Karl (1959), *The Idea of the University* (Boston: Beacon).

Jones, Ernest (1963), *The Life and Work of Sigmund Freud,* one volume edition, edited and abridged by Lionel Trilling and Steven Marcus (New York: Anchor Books).

Josephson, Eric and Mary (eds.) (1962), *Man Alone: Alienation in Modern Society* (New York: Dell).

Kallen, Horace M. (1949), *The Education of Free Men, An Essay Towards a Philosophy of Education for America* (New York: Farrar, Straus & Giroux).

——— (1962), *Philosophical Issues in Adult Education* (Springfield, Illinois: C. C. Thomas).

Kazantzakis, Nikos (1958), *The Odyssey: A Modern Sequel,* translated by Kimon Friar (New York: Simon and Schuster).

Klapp, Orrin E. (1956), *Ritual and Cult: A Sociological Interpretation* (Washington, D.C.: Public Affairs Press).

Lévi-Strauss, Claude (1961), *A World on the Wane,* translated by John Russell (New York: Criterion Books).

Loewith, Karl (1949), *Meaning in History* (Chicago: University of Chicago Press).

Manuel, Frank K. (1956), *The New World of Henri Saint-Simon* (Cambridge: Harvard University Press).

——— (1962), *The Prophets of Paris* (Cambridge: Harvard University Press).

Marcel, Gabriel (1962), *Homo Viator, Introduction to a Metaphysic of Hope,* translated by Emma Craufurd (New York: Harper Torchbooks).

Martin, Everett Dean (1922), *The Meaning of a Liberal Education* (New York: Norton).

Marx, Karl (1865), "Letter to J. B. Schweitzer," in *The Poverty of Philosophy* (Moscow: Foreign Languages Publishing House, n.d.), appendix, pp. 194-202.

Matthiessen, F. O. (1941), *American Renaissance: Art and Expression in the Age of Emerson and Whitman* (New York: Oxford University Press).

Mauss, Marcel (1954), *The Gift; Forms and Functions of Exchange in Archaic Societies,* translated by Ian Cunnison, with an Introduction by E. E. Evans-Pritchard (New York: Free Press).

Merz, J. Theo. (1914), *A History of European Thought in the 19th Century* (Edinburgh: Wm. Blackwood and Sons), 3rd edition, 4 vols., 1907-1914.

Meyer, R. W. (1952), *Leibnitz and the 17th Century Revolution* (Cambridge: Bowes and Bowes).

Mills, C. Wright (1959), *The Power Elite* (New York: Oxford University Press).

Mizruchi, E. H. (1964), "Alienation and Anomie: Theoretical and Empirical Perspectives," in *The New Sociology, Essays in Social Science and Social Theory in Honor of C. Wright Mills,* I. L. Horowitz (ed.) (New York: Oxford University Press), pp. 253-267.

Munson, Gorham (1930), *The Dilemma of the Liberated* (New York: Coward-McCann).

Needham, Joseph (1946), *History Is on Our Side: A Contribution to Political Religion and Scientific Faith* (London: Allen and Unwin).

Newman, John Henry Cardinal (1852), *The Idea of a University* (Garden City: Image Books, 1959, with an Introduction by George N. Shuster).

Nietzsche, Friedrich (1924), *Complete Works,* Oscar Levy (ed.) (New York: Macmillan). "On the Future of Our Educational Institutions," Vol. 3; "The Use and Abuse of History," Vol. 5.

Nostrand, Howard Lee (1963), "The University and Human Understanding" (unpublished ms).

Nygren, Anders (1953), *Agape and Eros,* translated by P. S. Watson (Philadelphia: Westminster Press), one volume edition.

Ortega y Gasset, José (1944), *Mission of the University,* translated with an Introduction by Howard Lee Nostrand (Princeton: Princeton University Press).

Phenix, Philip H. (1964), *Realms of Meaning: A Philosophy of the Curriculum for General Education* (New York: McGraw-Hill).

Ramsey, Ian T. (1964), *Models and Mystery,* The Whidden Lectures for 1963 (London: Oxford University Press).
Reichenbach, Hans (1953), *The Rise of Scientific Philosophy* (Berkeley: University of California Press).
Rosenberg, Harold (1964), "It Can Happen to Anyone," review article, *New York Times Book Review,* Dec. 20.
Rousseau, Jean-Jacques (1762), *Émile, ou de l'education* (Paris: Garnier Frères edition, 1961) with Introduction, Bibliography, Notes, and Analytic Index by F. and P. Richard.
Royce, Josiah (1908), *Philosophy of Loyalty* (New York: Macmillan).
Rusk, Ralph L. (1949), *The Life of Ralph Waldo Emerson* (New York: Scribner's Sons).
Sargent, Porter (1945), *Between Two Wars: The Failure of Education, 1920-1940* (Boston: Sargent).
Scheler, Max (1921), *On the Eternal in Man,* translated by Bernard Noble (New York: Harper, 1960).
Simmel, Georg (1959), *Sociology of Religion,* translated by Curt Rosenthal (New York: Philosophical Library).
Small, Albion W. (1910), *The Meaning of Social Science* (Chicago: University of Chicago Press).
Stefansson, Vilhjalmur (1940), "Was Liberty Invented?" in *Freedom: Its Meaning,* R. N. Anshen (ed.) (New York: Harcourt, Brace & World), pp. 384-411.
Tillich, Paul (1957), *The Protestant Era* (Chicago: University of Chicago Press), abridged edition.
——— (1963), *Systematic Theology,* 3 vols. (Chicago: University of Chicago Press).
——— (1964), *Theology of Culture* (New York: Oxford University Press).
Trilling, Lionel (1949), *Matthew Arnold* (New York: Columbia University Press).
Van Doren, Mark (1943), *Liberal Education* (New York: Holt, Rinehart & Winston).
Voegelin, Eric (1948), "The Origins of Scientism," *Social Research,* Vol. 15, pp. 462-494.
Weiss, Paul (1960), "Knowledge: a Growth Process," *Science,* vol. 131, pp. 1716-1719.
Wells, H. G. (1938), *World Brain* (London: Methuen).
Whitehead, Alfred N. (1959), "The Aims of Education," in *Daedalus,* Winter, pp. 192-205.
Williams, L. Pearce (1959), "The Politics of Science in the French Revolution," in *Critical Problems in the History of Science,* Marshall Clagett (ed.) (Madison: University of Wisconsin Press), pp. 291-308.
Willkie, Wendell (1944), "Freedom and the Liberal Arts," in *The Humanities After the War,* N. Foerster (ed.) (Princeton: Princeton University Press).

Zilboorg, Gregory (1959), *Freud and Religion: A Restatement of an Old Controversy* (Westminster: The Newman Press).

Zinsser, Hans (1937), "What is Liberal Education?" *School and Society,* Vol. 45, pp. 801-807.

Index

Adams, G., 80
Adler, Alfred, 149
Alembert, J. d', 50, 58
Altschule, Mark D., 155
Anouilh, Jean, 203
Aquinas, Saint Thomas, 12, 26, 27, 66, 67, 222, 235
Arendt, Hannah, 144–145, 193
Aristotle, 26, 35, 220
Arnold, Matthew, 9, 17, 35, 183
Augustine, Saint, 10, 173, 174, 181, 183, 202–203, 212–213, 219

Babbitt, Irving, 10, 11, 22, 23, 99
Babeuf, F. N., 128, 187
Bacon, Francis, 63, 72, 78
Bain, Alexander, 151
Baldwin, James Mark, 15, 124, 150, 166, 170–178, 180, 188, 191, 222, 224
Barzun, Jacques, 24
Bayle, Pierre, 167, 256
Beard, Charles, 116
Becker, Carl, 44
Becker, Ernest, 110, 150, 157, 175, 177, 190
Beesley, Patricia, 29, 63
Bell, Bernard I., 1, 41, 50, 78–79, 166, 240
Bellamy, Edward, 72
Bentham, Jeremy, 27, 128, 129
Berger, Peter, 188
Bergson, Henri, 15, 80, 139, 167*n*
Berkeley, George, 28, 120, 125
Boas, Franz, 137
Brownell, Baker, 219*n*
Bruner, J. S., 238
Buber, Martin, 183, 219
Burckhardt, Jakob, 87, 266
Burke, Edmund, 17
Burke, Kenneth, 36, 50, 145, 236
Butler, Nicholas Murray, 41

Calvin, John, 88, 89, 90, 109, 185, 207, 208
Campanella, T., 72, 187
Camus, Albert, 275
Carlyle, Thomas, 3, 13, 42, 78, 135, 213, 249
Cassirer, Ernst, 92
Chalmers, Gordon, 30, 37
Chapman, John Jay, 50
Chesterton, G. K., 11
Chugerman, Samuel, 251, 252

Cleisthenes, 264, 267
Comenius, J. A., 12
Comte, Auguste, 5, 69, 70, 76, 77, 87, 95, 101, 189, 193, 246–247, 252, 283
Condillac, E. B. de, 121
Condorcet, A. N. de, 16, 31, 46–48, 49, 50–51, 57, 58–59, 61, 63, 72, 76, 77, 94–95, 232, 241–249, 252, 283
Cooley, Charles H., 139, 150
Cornford, F. M., 137
Counts, George S., 238
Cousin, Victor, 246, 247

Dante, 8, 28
Darwin, Charles, 98, 124, 176, 178
Democritus, 121
Descartes, René, 119, 120
Dewey, John, 12, 14, 15, 19, 25–26, 32, 36, 79–84, 85, 98, 106, 115, 151, 158, 159, 171, 173, 174, 237–238, 278
Diderot, Denis, 22, 44, 57, 58, 61, 95–105, 112, 120, 121, 122, 123, 130, 151, 162–163, 171, 228, 245, 246, 247, 253, 273, 283
Dilthey, Wilhelm, 25, 125, 126
Dostoevski, F. M., 227
Duncan, Hugh, 145, 189

Eichmann, Adolf, 144–145, 193
Eliot, T. S., 11
Emerson, R. W., 3, 4, 5, 6, 25, 31–32, 38, 50, 51, 114–117, 158–159, 162, 226, 228, 229, 230, 236, 243, 248
Engels, Friedrich, 89, 97
Erasmus, 35, 162–164, 215
Erskine, John, 24

Ferguson, Adam, 117
Ferrero, Guglielmo, 135
Feuer, Lewis, 88, 89, 90, 228
Feuerbach, Ludwig, 7, 209
Fichte, J. G., 6, 97, 123, 124, 150
Fouillée, Alfred, 92
Fourier, Charles, 72, 87, 128, 131, 132, 134, 153, 169, 193, 219*n*
Francis of Assisi, Saint, 23, 187, 221
Frank, Philipp, 63, 64
Frank, Waldo, 83, 291
Franklin, Benjamin, 5, 116
Freud, Sigmund, 149–157, 166, 167*n*, 168, 178–179
Fromm, Erich, 88

Gibbon, Edward, 24, 117
Giddings, Frank, 193–194
Gillispie, Charles C., 96
Gioacchino da Fiore, 221, 292
Goethe, J. W. von, 6, 7, 22, 23, 97, 105
Goffman, Erving, 139
Goodman, Paul, 19
Gorky, Maxim, vii, 104
Grattan, C. H., 22, 231
Greene, Theodore M., 35–36, 50, 63, 236

Haring, Douglas G., 266
Harper, William R., 78
Hayek, F. A., 197, 246
Hazard, Paul, 43, 45, 55, 91, 94, 121
Hegel, Georg W. F., 66–67, 69, 70, 73, 75, 77, 103, 110, 123, 124, 126, 129, 150, 174, 176, 204, 208–209, 215–216, 292
Heidegger, Martin, 174
Heisenberg, Werner, 168
Helvetius, C. A., 44, 92, 121
Henderson, A. D., 35, 50, 236, 237
Herder, J. G. von, 6, 8, 16, 49, 208, 232, 252
Hinton, James, 213
Hitler, Adolf, 73, 144, 145–146, 197, 245
Hobbes, Thomas, 40, 127, 128, 171, 255

Hocart, A. M., 184
Hocking, William E., 203, 278
Holbach, P. H. T. d', 44, 92
Hook, Sidney, 24, 26, 27, 236
Hubert, Saint, 146, 190
Huizinga, Johan, 142–143, 169
Hume, David, 75, 94, 117, 125, 208
Husserl, Edmund, 124
Hutcheson, Francis, 75, 94
Hutchins, Robert M., 12–29, 66, 233, 234, 235, 236, 281, 282, 284
Huxley, Thomas, 35

Ideler, C. L., 169

Jacks, M. L., 211
Jacob, Peyton, 52, 53, 79
James, William, 15, 24, 28, 62, 98, 124, 125, 150, 166, 167*n*, 171, 212, 213, 224, 244
Jaspers, Karl, 64, 66
Jefferson, Thomas, 17, 31, 48, 158, 243
Jesus of Nazareth, 187
Jones, Ernest, 167*n*
Josephson, Eric and Mary, 228

Kallen, Horace, 36–37, 40, 41, 47, 48, 49, 50, 63, 234, 236, 240, 242
Kant, Immanuel, 16, 19, 28, 49, 75, 80, 81, 83, 84, 94, 123, 124, 171, 173, 232
Kazantzakis, Nikos, 213
Kierkegaard, S., 7, 216, 275
Klapp, Orrin E., 190
Kuhn, Thomas, 100

La Chalotais, 45
Lahotan, L. A. de, 91, 92, 131, 137
La Mettrie, J. O. de., 44, 71, 95, 119, 130, 246–247
Leibnitz, G. W. von, 7, 8, 9, 12, 25, 63, 87
Lenin, V. I., 43, 99
Lessing, G. E., 6, 8, 16, 46, 49, 53, 77, 97, 208, 210, 232, 252
Lévi-Strauss, Claude, 137
Lippman, Walter, 239
Locke, John, 75, 119, 121, 208, 248
Lowell, James Russell, 291
Löwith, Karl, 213
Luther, Martin, 27, 78, 162–164, 208, 215

Malthus, Thomas R., 28
Mandeville, Bernard de, 128, 152, 207–208
Manuel, Frank, 46, 47, 48, 59, 97
Marcel, Gabriel, 213, 219
Martin, Everett Dean, 35, 50, 230–231, 236
Marx, Karl, 7, 28, 42, 43, 73, 88, 89, 90, 98–99, 101, 102–104, 110–111, 112, 129–131, 134, 136, 139, 156, 157, 182, 208
Matthiessen, F. O., 4, 31, 32
Maudsley, Henry, 155, 157, 169
Mauss, Marcel, 146, 184, 186, 189, 190
Mead, George, 124, 150
Meiklejohn, Alexander, 237
Melville, Herman, 3, 116
Mikhailovski, Nikolai, 271
Mill, Stuart, 48, 76, 77, 247
Millar, John, 117
Mills, C. Wright, 36, 41, 42, 135, 139, 236
Mizruchi, Ephraim, 107
Montague, W. P., 80
Montaigne, M. E. de, 28, 35
Montesquieu, 117, 121, 162–163, 171
More, Paul Elmer, 10, 22, 23
More, Thomas, 72
Munson, Gorham, 167, 211, 231, 278
Münsterberg, Hugo, 15
Münzer, Thomas, 45, 187, 221
Murray, Gilbert, 220, 276

Needham, Joseph, 280
Newman, John Henry, 16, 78
Newton, Isaac, 95–122, 245, 247, 279
Nietzsche, Friedrich, 25, 29, 32, 35, 42, 53, 54, 63, 115, 135, 213–216, 230, 233, 241, 243, 248
Nostrand, Howard L., 4, 6, 81, 280, 282
Nygren, Anders, 181, 203

Ortega y Gasset, José, 17, 40, 53–56, 63–65, 233, 241–242, 281, 282, 284, 287, 288
Owen, Robert, 197

Pascal, Blaise, 44, 128, 275
Pavlov, I. P., 122
Phenix, Philip, 230
Pierce, Charles S., 98
Plato, 13, 26, 28, 35, 62, 66, 72, 89, 148, 168, 173, 267

Ramsey, Ian T., 257, 278
Rauschenbach, Walter, 166, 187, 209, 274
Reich, Wilhelm, 149–150
Reichenbach, Hans, 66
Rosenberg, Harold, 88, 90
Rousseau, Jean-Jacques, 11, 28, 42, 43, 44, 84, 92–105, 109, 111, 112, 117, 121, 122, 128, 131, 136, 137, 138, 146, 151, 152, 153, 158–162, 168, 169, 191, 193, 219, 228, 230, 243, 245, 246, 253–256, 260, 266, 267, 270, 273
Royce, Josiah, 15, 28, 124, 150, 166, 216
Rusk, Ralph L., 51
Russell, Bertrand, 125

Saint-Simon, Henri de, 76, 82, 87, 95, 97, 196, 246, 252, 283
Sallustius, 27, 214
Sanborn, F. B., 5
Sargent, Porter, 236
Sartre, Jean Paul, 174, 275
Scheler, Max, 183, 203, 204*n*, 219, 268–270
Schelling, F. W. J. von, 123, 124, 150, 171, 173, 176, 178, 208, 292
Schiller, Friedrich von, 6, 171, 172, 173, 178
Schleiermacher, F. D. E., 123, 150
Seeman, Melvin, 107
Sénancour, Étienne de, 131
Shakespeare, William, 16, 131
Shaler, Nathaniel S., 15
Simmel, Georg, 132, 139, 142, 169, 204*n*
Skinner, B. F., 243
Small, Albion, 5–6
Smith, Adam, 5, 75, 77, 94, 128, 129, 197, 208
Socrates, 13, 28, 35, 117, 121, 135, 138–139, 140, 147, 158, 160, 168, 218, 267
Soloviëv, Vladimir, 181, 292
Sorel, Georges, 28, 139, 147
Spencer, Herbert, 48, 70, 98, 126
Stefansson, Vilhjalmur, 137
Stierlin, Helm, 199

Thoreau, David, 243
Tillich, Paul, 66, 158, 183, 210–211, 222–224, 273, 274, 292
Tocqueville, Alexis de, 160
Tolstoi, Leo, 202, 213
Toynbee, Arnold, 266
Trilling, Lionel, 9

Van Doren, Mark, 16, 33, 34, 165, 225, 280, 284
Veblen, Thorstein, 18, 19, 41, 134–135, 136, 139, 142, 156, 157, 169, 184, 186
Vico, Giovanni B., 5, 16, 24, 27, 102, 117, 168, 232, 252
Virchow, Rudolf, 139
Virgil, 32
Voegelin, Eric, 122
Voltaire, 44, 92, 95, 102, 117

Ward, Harry F., 187, 209, 274
Ward, Lester, 158, 193, 251, 252
Watson, J. B., 122
Wayland, Francis, 4, 5, 6, 8, 115, 248
Weber, Max, 18–19, 41, 42, 133–134, 135, 139, 140, 169, 184, 186, 207
Weiss, Paul, 282
Wells, H. G., 56–61, 63, 65, 241–242, 280, 282
Whitehead, A. N., 62, 234
Wilde, Oscar, 217
Wilkie, Wendell, 114, 116
Williams, L. Pearce, 31, 47
Wundt, Wilhelm, 124

Zilboorg, Gregory, 167*n*
Zinsser, Hans, 63, 64
Zwingli, Ulrich, 207